This angry pen of mine

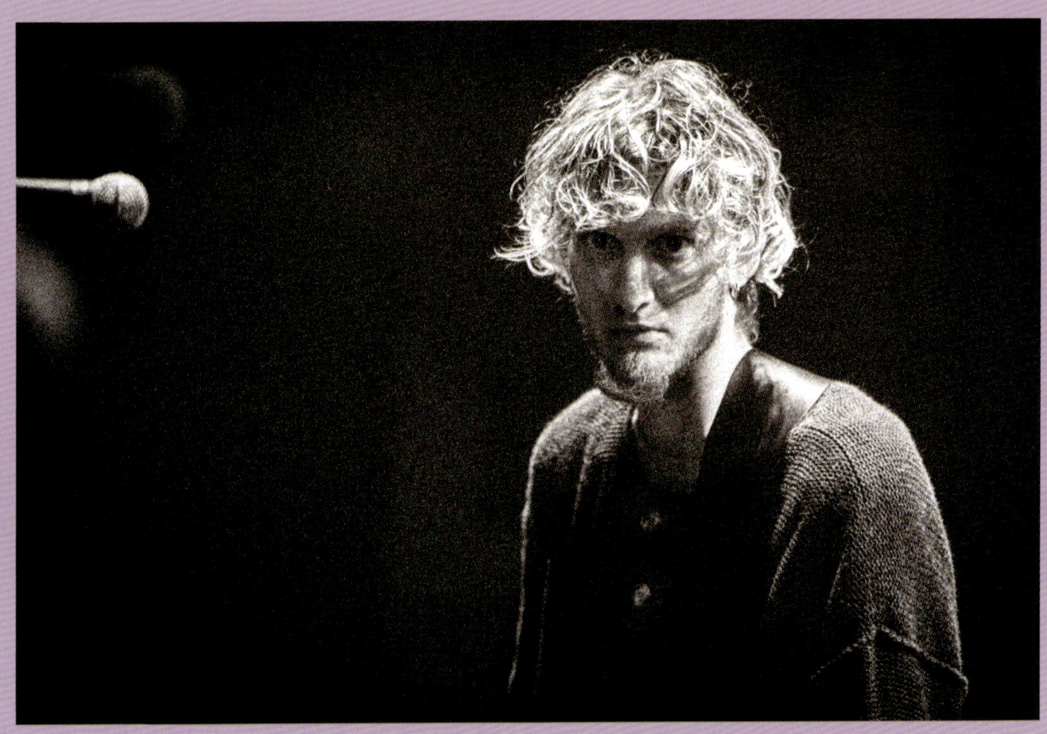

To Layne,

whose memories are imprinted

on my heart with the pen of an angel.

I can rest now,

Mom XO

This angry pen of mine

Recovering the Journals of Layne Staley

weldonowen

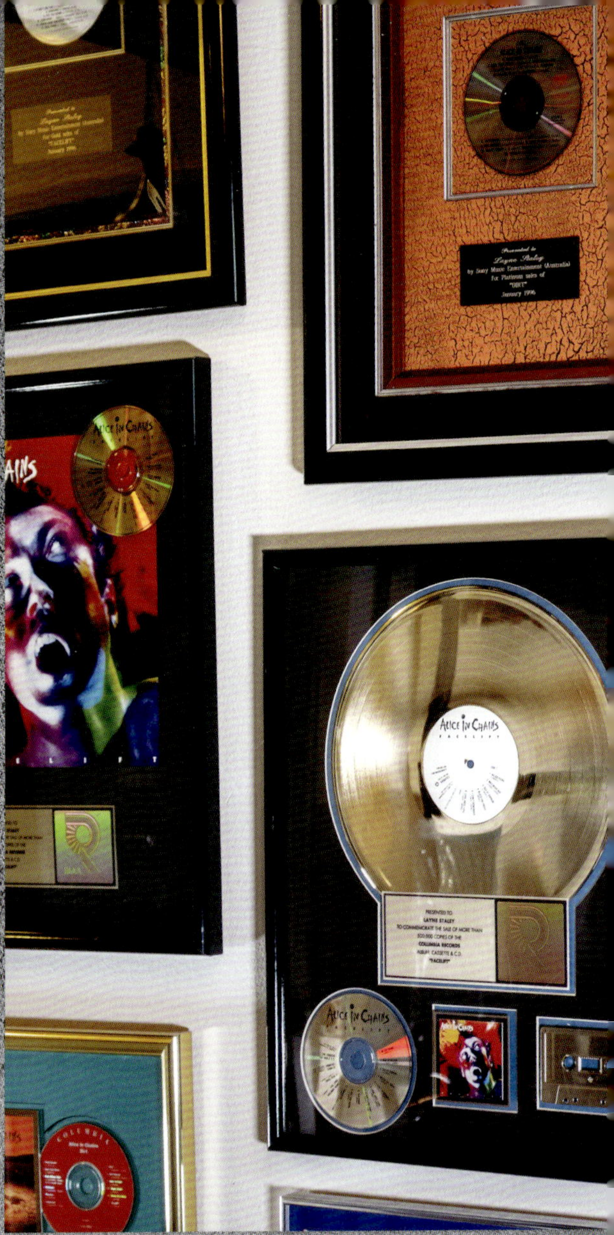

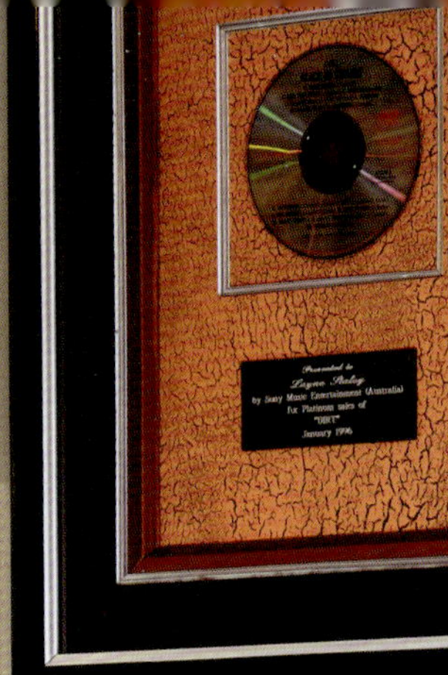

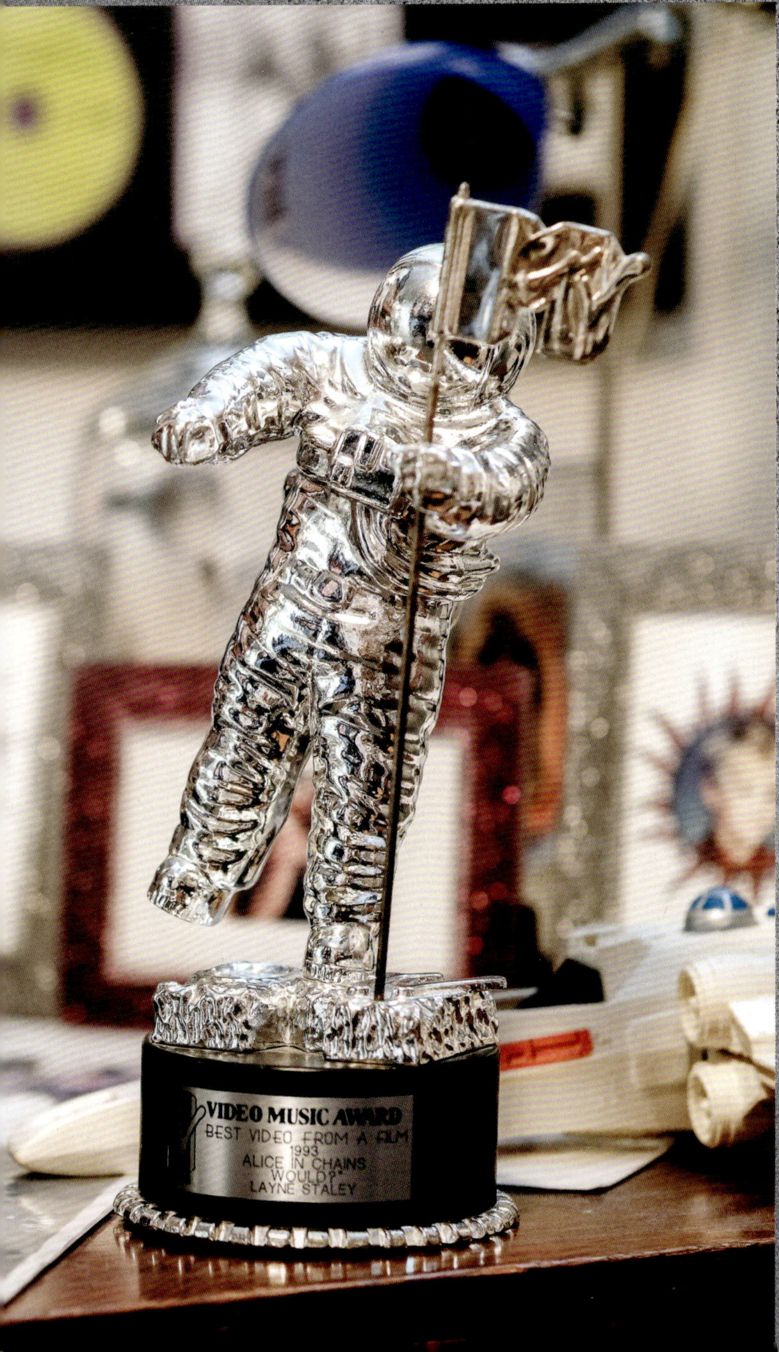

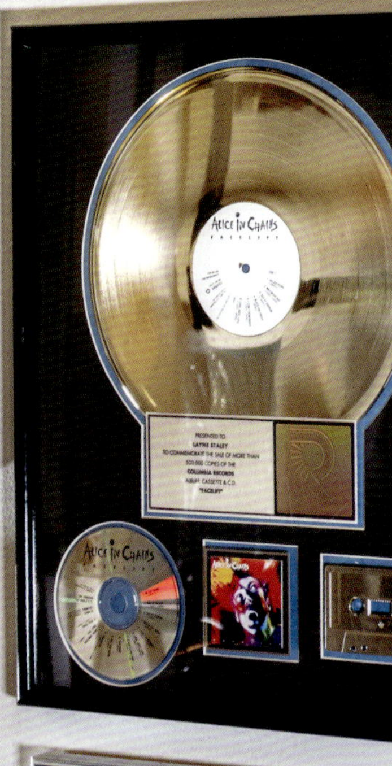

CONTENTS

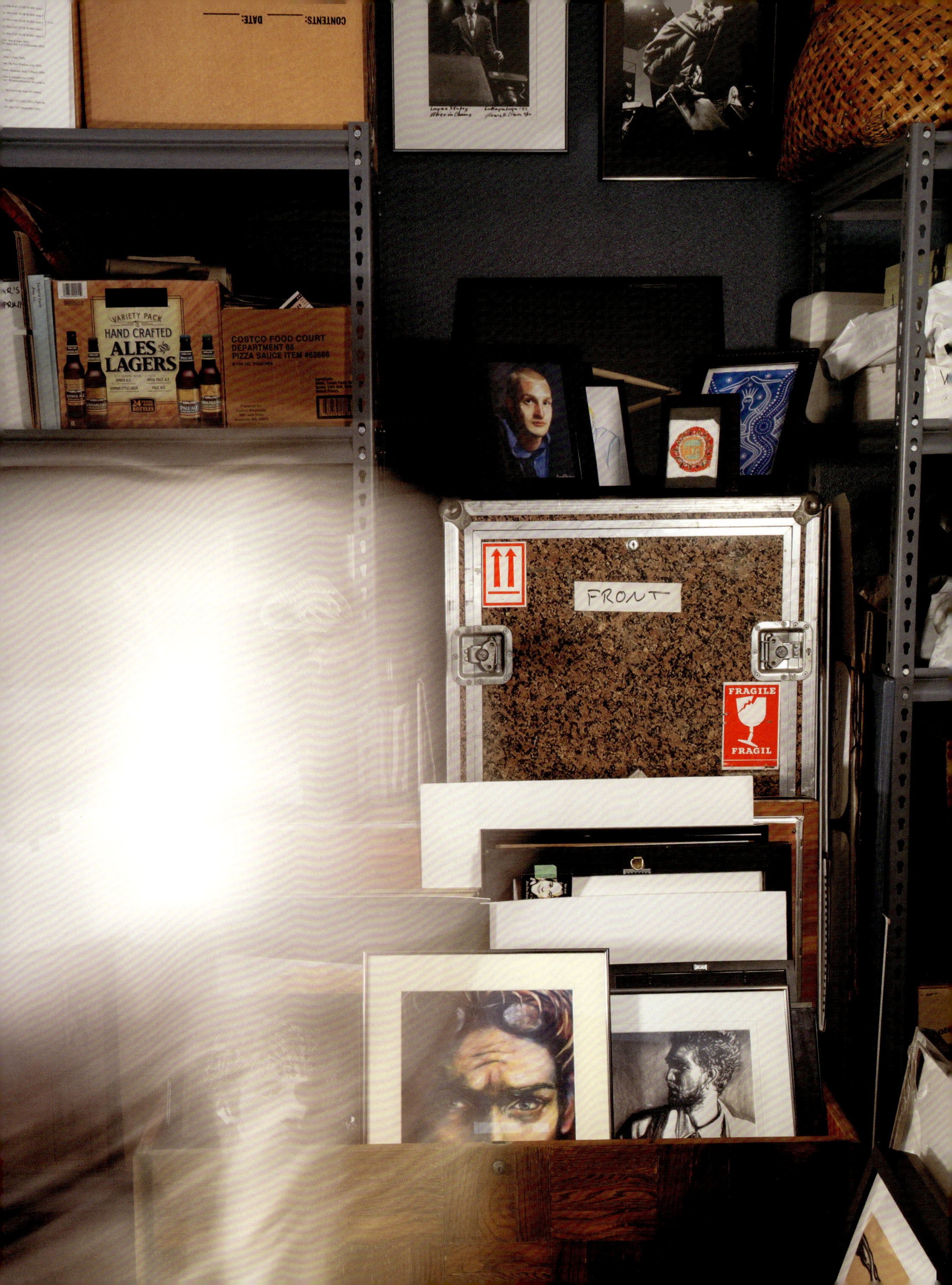

CONTENTS:
DATE:
VARIETY PACK
HAND CRAFTED
ALES
LAGERS
24
BOTTLES
COSTCO FOOD COURT
DEPARTMENT 88
PIZZA SAUCE ITEM #65666
FRONT
FRAGILE
FRAGIL

INTRODUCTION

My idea for a book about Layne was very different. I wanted to show the fun and funny, the witty, the smart, the nice, thoughtful person behind the stories; you know, to share the quirks and the moments that others could relate to. It took 23 years, but I think we've finally got a book that honors my memories of Layne.

I moved to Alaska in '93. The kids were living their independence; so, I thought that I'd try it for a change, too. I would fly home for holidays, and special occasions.

At one time, Layne flew me to Seattle to attend an underground gallery showing (located in Pioneer Square) featuring 3 of his self-portraits. He told me later that it was the proudest he'd ever been of any of his work. I was staying with Layne for several days at his apartment on Queen Anne when Sean Kinney came to the door one night. Sean told Layne that before going out on the band's next tour, Layne needed to get clean. So, arrangements were made for him to go to treatment, and I stayed at his place for a couple more days while he was away. Layne had to miss the showing, which was a great disappointment to us all.

While I was there, my daughter, Liz, called about the title to a little red Datsun wagon that Layne had given to his dad, Phil. I said I'd look for it. Layne wasn't the tidiest, bless his heart, so I started gathering up papers from under the coffee table, on the counters, shelves, everywhere. In the very last place, in a closet off the kitchen, I found the car title in a pile of unrelated paperwork that included photos, handwritten lyrics, phone numbers scribbled every which way, cards, letters, and more. Everything was a mess, but I thought, "I'm here until the gallery opening and beyond. I might as well put these in order." So, I went to Kinko's, bought a white hanging file crate, hanging files, and folders, and then I started organizing everything: photos, lyrics, contracts, documents, letters, awards, and what have you.

After the gallery opening, I went back to Alaska. Layne completed a short version of treatment and headed out on tour. Months without home, family, his girl, and his kitty. For a homebody, that must have been tough.

The other time that Layne flew me into town was for Demri's memorial service. She passed at age 27. Layne was 29. I came into town without much of a fitting wardrobe for the service for this sweet girl. Layne and I shopped for a nice outfit (which I still wear, in part, to his Tribute each year).

At the service, the minister cornered Layne, challenging him "to take Jesus into his heart." Layne told me about that encounter sometime later. He said that "I sure wish that you had been there, Mom." I had been standing right behind Layne, and I told him that "I had been right there, behind you, honey."

Layne was broken at Dem's passing; and, to add injury at this painful time, he was in the middle of moving. We slept on couch cushions on the floor, and during the day, a couple of guys moved Rubbermaid cans, full of stuff as we filled them, into vehicles, on their way to temporary storage. We don't know when; but, sometime after that, his storage units were broken into, and one of the items snatched was the crate with original lyrics and art. Luckily, it had come to me to make copies.

Soon after Layne passed (at 34, in 2002), a thief showed up on eBay with some of Layne's items for sale. The fans dissed him so hard that the auction site was removed. Another related incident follows. A Lynnwood police officer stopped a U-Haul truck with 3 occupants, which was at the end of a dead end, for being parked with wheels partway on the pavement. The girl slipped into the house, and the driver got out, greeting the officer. He enthusiastically offered to let the officer see the contents of the truck and proceeded to open up the back. The officer questioned what the shiny object was that was sticking out of a box. The driver explained that it belonged to Layne, a friend of his, and that Layne had given it to him as a friend, because Layne had several. The officer accepted the offer of the MTV video award, and it sat on a shelf in the Lynnwood Police Department until I learned of it several years later and retrieved it. I was given a redacted copy of the police report (which I can read through).

And now, after all these years, the copies that I made, along with some of Layne's journal entries and original art, are here. I hope this book gives you a glimpse of the Layne I knew, the one beyond the headlines, the one with a beautiful, creative, happy soul . . . my son.

—Nancy McCallum

My relationship with Layne was, well, complicated.

It wasn't like the one he had with his mom, Nancy. See, I was gone for a good number of years, and when I came back into his life, it was often about trying to get him clean, or him trying to get me clean. That's not something I want to dwell on in this book.

What I do want to share is the Layne I knew. He was creative, intelligent, sensitive, compassionate, and empathetic. You can hear that in his music. But because of his struggles with addiction, I think a lot of people got the wrong impression of him.

I was absent for much of his childhood, from when he was about six or seven until he was nineteen. I moved around, lived in California, Texas. At that time, I wasn't doing well myself and felt unworthy of being a part of his life. Those years were lost, and I regret that.

I came back into his life when he was starting his music career with Alice in Chains. He reached out, and we reconnected. But with him being involved in his music and me living out of state, we didn't get together often. There were lost years, and I didn't contribute much as a father.

Our relationship was . . . back and forth a bit. We were both dealing with our own addictions. But I kept in contact with Nancy and knew, secondhand, what he was doing. I didn't even know about the Alice in Chains deal until Nancy told me.

Layne's music, it resonated with people who were going through their own struggles, whether it was addiction or something else. His lyrics came from a place of pain, and I think people connected with that. He was definitely a force.

Nancy kept me somewhat in the loop, showing me fan letters and drawings. It was mostly her, though. 97% Nancy and 3% me, I'd say. But Layne and I had a great relationship, even if it was complicated.

I was a heavy metal guy from the '60s, and I think that influenced Layne's musical taste. His lyrics were an expression of his demons, his struggles. And people in similar situations, they understood. I'm a total fan of Layne's music. I know it backwards and forwards. I went to concerts when I could, hung out with the bands he was close to, like Mark Lanegan and Mike McCready. I was involved in his music as a fan and as a proud father.

It's hard to articulate our relationship, but I loved him, and I'm proud of the music he created.

Layne saved my life. He inspired me to share my recovery experience with others. My gratitude for this selfless act is to live the rest of my life based on the Twelve-Step principles and the unwavering love of God.

I hope that you enjoy this amazing book as it is truly a labor of love, a side of Layne that few have seen. This book, these lyrics and pieces of his life, it's a way to remember him, the real Layne.

Thank you to Layne's mom, who worked tirelessly to help make this book special. Also, thanks to Jim Elmer, Layne's stepdad, who played a huge part in Layne's life and is greatly missed.

Rest in Peace, Layne.

—Dad

Growing up, Layne and I were incredibly close.

Just a few years apart in age, many people thought we were twins because we looked so alike. Maybe it was the experiences we shared at our very young ages, but it often felt as if our brother-sister bond was unique and would withstand the test of time, get us through anything. We understood each other with few words necessary. I have vivid memories of us sitting cross-legged in the basement, facing each other, trying to communicate through ESP without saying words, just staring at each other, giggling at our success.

Long before the world knew his voice, I witnessed Layne's artistic journey unfold. While he always showed creativity through drawing, sewing, woodworking, and clay, it was music that ultimately captured his heart. At thirteen, he set up a microphone and drum set in our basement, inviting neighborhood kids over for what was essentially homemade karaoke—a simple beginning to what would become a profound passion. His early musical inspirations came from bands like Ronnie James Dio, Black Sabbath, and AC/DC. He once took a Bic pen, filled it with bleach, and drew band logos all over a pair of his jeans. His fashion sense was incredible; he could pull together any cool outfit at any moment, often with items he took from my closet and thrift stores. It was effortless and trendsetting.

Those teenage years weren't always kind to him. In high school, his artistic nature, slight build, and gentle spirit made him a target. He endured being shoved around, locked in lockers, and other cruelties. But Layne found his people—fellow artists and musicians who gathered at the back of the school, offering protection and understanding when he needed it most. By senior year, he had transformed those difficult experiences into determination: "I'm going to make a million bucks by the time I'm 21," he declared with the conviction only a teenager can muster.

Though he began as a drummer, Layne discovered his true gift when he auditioned as a singer for a band. Taking his talent seriously, he studied with vocal coach David Kyle—"the maestro"—who taught him to use his diaphragm and develop the voice that would eventually captivate millions. This was when his poetic sensibility truly emerged, revealing dimensions to his artistry that would define his career. Layne felt deeply that his voice was a gift he was obligated to share with the world. Even during his darkest struggles, he maintained that "if you have a gift, you can't not put it out there"—a philosophy he encouraged in others, including my husband, telling him, "You can't keep that talent to yourself."

Beyond his music, Layne possessed a warmth and humor that defined him just as much as his artistic abilities. He could leave you with stomach and cheek muscles aching from laughter, yet never at someone else's expense. I don't recall him ever uttering anything mean-spirited. When not touring or recording, he cherished simple pleasures with family and friends—making burritos, watching movies, listening to records.

His genuine kindness extended beyond his inner circle. After receiving his first tour paycheck, he and bandmate Jerry invited two homeless men they saw outside their hotel to come up, shower, eat, and watch television with them. That was Layne—success never changed his fundamental compassion for others.

Throughout his fame, he remained my big brother first. When we were together, our conversations rarely touched on Alice in Chains or his career—we talked about each other, about life's ordinary moments and deeper questions. Even when he was performing for audiences of 60,000, our relationship remained grounded in that sibling bond formed in childhood. He would return from touring to our family home seeking rest, where I believe he found genuine peace.

I witnessed his struggles with addiction firsthand for many years. He lived with me during several periods of his life, and I stayed close through twelve attempts at rehabilitation, always encouraging him and standing by his side. There were times I had to establish boundaries to protect myself and my own family—decisions that sometimes led to regrets about lost time together.

Continued on the next page . . .

When I was eight months pregnant with my son Oscar, I called Layne. We had just shared Thanksgiving, and I was concerned about his health. Through tears, I expressed my fear and my hope that my child would know his uncle. He reassured me, "Liz, this thing's not going to kill me. If it was, it would have long ago. I'm going to be there." I trusted him because he was my older brother, my protector since childhood. When Oscar was born, Layne arrived with his typical collection of bags, cameras, and gadgets. He carefully set up his movie camera on a tripod, positioned himself in a chair, and said, "OK, bring me the baby." That moment—captured in what would be the last known photograph of Layne—shows the pure joy he found in family, with my son looking up at him, tiny fingers grasping the clay beads around his uncle's neck.

When Layne died, we didn't learn of his passing for several days. During that time, I had vivid dreams of him each night—different visions that I later came to believe were his way of visiting me. In one dream, I saw him healthy and robust against yellow rolling sand hills, wearing an open Hawaiian shirt in a warm breeze. In another, he appeared so small beneath the covers of his childhood bed that I could barely see him. These experiences convinced me that he was with me then, and I still believe he remains with me now. As each year passes, it seems increasingly unreal that I continue to exist in a world without him.

I hope people remember Layne not just for his incredible voice and musical talent, but for who he truly was—a humble person genuinely interested in others, who never placed himself above or below anyone else, who simply did his best each day despite tremendous challenges. His example of remaining authentic in difficult circumstances inspires me to show up daily as the best version of myself. I share stories about "Uncle Layne" with my sons so they understand what an extraordinary brother I had, and I believe they feel that connection and take pride in who he was.

Layne's gift to the world extended far beyond his music—it was his humble, giving, loving, and caring nature. Things affected him deeply; he wasn't your typical rock star but remained accessible, without pretension, valuing human connections above all else. Even as he battled the disease that eventually took his life, he maintained a pure heart that touched everyone fortunate enough to know him.

The brother I knew, the one who sat cross-legged with me trying to communicate through ESP, who decorated his jeans with bleach-pen band logos, who cradled my newborn son with such tenderness—was so much more than his public persona or the tragedy of his struggles. He was Layne, my brother, a bright spirit whose light continues to shine through his music and in the hearts of those who love him.

—Liz Coats

The first memory that comes to mind when I think about Layne and how creative he was, was when I was 5 or 6 years old. He was about sixteen. He had a green Datsun, his first car. He reconfigured things so that instead of windshield wiper fluid going to clean the windshield, he had it coming inside to the dashboard. "Jamie, come in here," he called to me. I sat in the passenger seat while he set a glass down, pushed a button, and orange juice came out. He was so excited about it! Part of what made Layne endearing was when he was excited about something, he was so excited about it.

Music and art were areas of his life where he truly excelled. I remember him playing drums in the basement of our house. Once, he had me perform in a show, alongside the girlfriends of his bandmates. Layne didn't have a girlfriend, so I got to be part of this whole scene on stage to a song called "Fat Girls." I was just a little girl, psyched to be doing anything with my brother.

Before the show, we were at my dad's house in Bellevue getting ready, and Layne had me help him with his mohawk. We used the ironing board and a ton of Aqua Net hairspray to get it just right. Then, we headed out in his red Volkswagen Dasher across the bridge to Seattle . . . we hadn't thought about getting his mohawk into the car, so he kept his head out the window most of the time to make room for it. Absurd and funny to look back on! I was so excited to be a part of his show, and remember him being so full of energy and optimism for the night.

Layne was creative in many ways, not just with refitting green Datsuns into having orange juice dispensers (!), but he cooked, and drew, and did all sorts of art projects. His musical taste and creativity showed in a pair of jeans that he made with bleached-out names of bands like Ozzy Osbourne and Led Zeppelin on them. That says it all. He spent hours carefully bleaching these jeans with all the bands he was into at the time.

Years later, when I was in middle school, we'd go to all the Seattle concerts: Soundgarden, Pearl Jam, and seeing Alice in Chains, of course. Layne gave my sister Liz a demo tape of Pearl Jam with just three songs. I listened to that tape constantly in sixth grade, telling everyone my favorite band was Pearl Jam.

Seeing Layne perform on stage seemed normal at the time. If I'd been older, I might have thought, "Wow, this is really cool that you're making your dreams come true." But as a middle schooler, it was just what my older brother did.

The Christmas of '91, after Alice in Chains was signed, Layne and Demri came over to my mom's for the day. They brought Christmas presents for all of us that they had purchased, and it was a big deal. Layne was super excited that they could actually buy Christmas presents for people. It was a time of such pride for Layne.

Layne was sweet and kind. Even when I was a kid, I was aware of what he was going through, and I thought back then that Layne was a little too sensitive for this world. That's part of why people like Layne do what they do to cope.

He was one of the funniest people. He had this comedic relief about him. He was really good at mimicking people—not in a rude way, but doing actual impressions. He was entertaining without being egotistical. He didn't need to be the center of attention, but when he made a comment or offered some comedic relief, he was very good at it.

I hope people remember how he stepped up and had a voice, even when he felt insecure or scared to do so. For as long as he could, he got up, showed up, and spoke up, even though he was literally dying for a long time.

When I stayed with him last, we could talk about things I couldn't discuss with anyone else in my family. I was struggling with eating issues and bulimia in my teenage years and Layne was the one person I could talk to about it, and felt understood by. I hadn't gotten into drugs as a kid, but he could relate to the addictive part of me. I feel lucky I was able to talk to him about what I was going through. We got each other in that way. That was a bond we had.

Layne's naïveté is also what made Layne special. He was excited about life at one point, interested and curious. I think that this quality is what made the world a bit too harsh for him, too.

I'm proud of him and grateful that he shared with the world something that can live on. That also came with a lot of struggle and pain which I wish we could have taken away.

—Jamie Elmer

Growing up with Layne, I witnessed a creative soul trying to find his place in the world. While our three siblings—Liz, Layne, and myself—each experienced different facets of Layne's life, I shared what I call the "bro perspective"—doing donuts in his car, hanging with friends, and navigating the everyday adventures of youth.

Layne's artistic journey wasn't always clear-cut. He played trumpet "for like five minutes," then became a drummer for a long time before discovering his true calling as a vocalist. Music was the emotional river that he flowed down, opening something special inside him that other creative outlets couldn't quite reach.

When we were teenagers, Layne and I would sing together in the basement, writing lyrics whenever we could. I remember when he was about 17 or 18, and I was 16 or 17, he told me, "I really want to do this. I really want to sing." At the time, I honestly didn't think he was that great and told him so—something well-documented in our family history.

The turning point came when some friends of mine were forming a band called Sleze. They needed a singer, and I reluctantly suggested my brother. Layne auditioned, and they were blown away. I'll never forget walking down the high school hallway when James Bergstrom shouted from the other end, "Dude, your brother is fucking awesome!" They could see the frontman potential in him, the drive and talent behind that voice.

Sleze performed at our high school cafeteria, sometimes having to censor their material to avoid getting kicked out. I remember we made a flyer for one show where they were covering a song called "Bastard," which they had to change to "Flastered" to keep from getting in trouble. I even contributed with some other guys from marching band, adding a little instrumental horn segment to their demo tape.

What many people don't understand about Layne was just how gentle a soul he was. There's a dichotomy there—this shy person who didn't "do the whole school thing" but who, when passionate about something, could really drive himself and others. That's what he took on stage. Layne wasn't the tough exterior that many who never knew him might assume—he was a shy, gentle, funny artist who found where his creativity worked best.

I remember when Layne and I were around 10 and 12 years old, we were at the local park with a bow and arrow, shooting across the grass as sparrows flew by. By some one-in-a-million chance, Layne's arrow hit one of the birds. While I, as a typical 10-year-old boy, was impressed, Layne completely broke down. He started crying and was absolutely devastated that he had taken a life. I had to walk him home. That moment changed us both, and it showed me just how deeply he felt things. He had a caring heart at his core—it wasn't something he had to train himself to be.

Layne was committed when he found something he loved. I recall another childhood memory when we decided to run away from home on our Huffy bikes after being assigned weekend chores. A few miles and hours later, I was feeling panicky and suggested we call home. Layne looked at me and said, "Dude, you have no idea how this works. Why would we call when we ran away from home?" When Layne committed to something, he was all in.

This same dedication applied to his music. When we would go to the roller rink in Lynnwood to see local metal bands play, I'd put in a fake earring and wear some leather, while Layne would spend two hours perfectly spiking his hair, looking like the best rocker the world's ever seen. That attention to detail carried through to his professional career. Studio engineers tell stories about how Layne would want total privacy when recording vocals, learning to operate the equipment himself so he could do lyrics over and over until they were perfect.

Layne found joy when he could bring someone else along for the ride, when he did something that others could take significant joy in. I remember him picking me and my friends up in his infamous Datsun (I think it was a Datsun . . .). We wanted to do donuts on the grass but couldn't because the Datsun was front-wheel drive, so we learned to do them in reverse instead. After we'd been having fun for half an hour, Layne asked with genuine concern, "So the car is cool? Are we good with the car?" When we enthusiastically told him his car was "the fucking coolest car ever," the smile on his face was enormous. He truly got joy from seeing others having fun.

His humor wasn't the center-of-attention type. He was subtle, with a David Letterman–dry kind of wit, the kind of understated humor that comes out under his breath. This gentleness extended to his love for animals and all living things, consistent with his creative spirit and soft heart.

In his later years, as Layne struggled with addiction, I'd come back to town and try to connect, but often wouldn't hear back. My dad told me a lot about how excruciating the transitions were for Layne—coming on and off tour—and how he just wanted to be left alone sometimes. For the gods of '90s Seattle music, they couldn't simply go hang out in a park and write a poem; they couldn't leave their houses without being recognized. I think that weighed on him heavily.

The tragedy is that creatives need their space, but Layne eventually got none except when alone in his house. And there's no way an addict is going to recover by themselves—they need community. The only community around Layne was one that wanted to worship him, and that's not the kind of community that helps someone get sober.

What strikes me most about Layne's legacy is how his impact seems to grow stronger with time. I believe he and his work are more famous now than they ever were. We may never again see this level of emotional openness in songwriting—someone willing to let listeners into parts of themselves that most people don't talk about.

I don't think Layne ever sat down and thought, "I'm going to get a whole bunch of people sober by writing this music." But he was willing to take the first step by doing something different, writing some dark stuff that some people wouldn't understand. It was important to him to express those feelings authentically.

The stories I hear from fans are incredible—people from all over the world who credit Layne's music with saving their lives, not just once but every day. I can't think of many other artists who continue to have that kind of profound impact decades after their passing.

That's Layne's gift to the world. He's the voice that helped them survive their darkest moments . . . even more than twenty years later.

—Ken Elmer

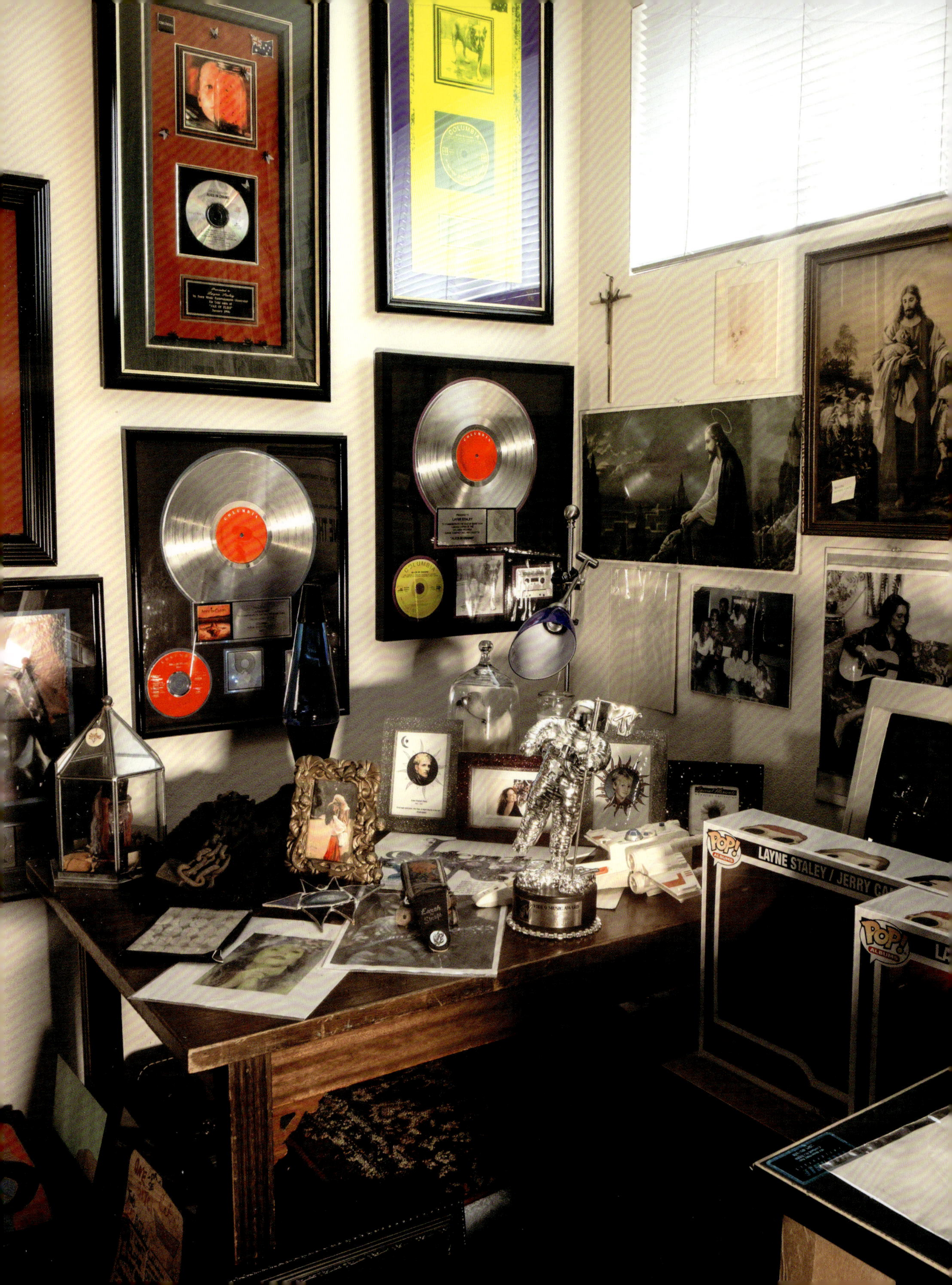

COLUMBIA
POP! ALBUMS
LAYNE STALEY / JERRY

A WORD ABOUT THE WORDS

Layne Staley's lyrics carved a unique space in rock music through their unflinching honesty and emotional depth. As the voice of Alice in Chains, Mad Season, and other projects, Layne transformed his personal struggles into universal expressions of pain, resilience, and self-reflection that resonated far beyond the grunge movement of the 1990s.

His writing was characterized by raw vulnerability: He confronted addiction, isolation, and mortality with a poetic gravity that never sought to glamorize suffering but instead illuminated the human experience in its darkest corners. What made Layne's work exceptional was his ability to balance unflinching darkness with surprising moments of clarity and even dark humor.

Unlike many of his contemporaries, Staley's lyrics avoided metaphorical obscurity, instead offering direct, visceral imagery that created an intimate connection with listeners. This authenticity gave his words a timeless quality that continues to speak to new generations of fans and musicians.

The harmonies he crafted created layers of emotional complexity, where beauty and dissonance coexisted, much like in Staley's own life. His journals and personal writings, glimpses of which appear in this collection, reveal a thoughtful, creative soul whose artistic expression extended beyond music into visual art and poetry.

In exploring Staley's writing, we discover not just the public persona portrayed in media headlines, but a multidimensional artist whose legacy transcends the tragedy of his struggles and early death, revealing instead the extraordinary gift of transformation, turning personal darkness into art that illuminates, comforts, and connects.

Tragically, much of Layne's written legacy will never see the light of day. As Nancy McCallum described in her introduction, thieves broke into his storage units, stealing crates containing original lyrics and artwork. This criminal act has robbed the world of fully understanding the true scope and depth of his creative output. We'll never know the complete breadth of his artistic vision or the full evolution of his writing over time.

What makes *This Angry Pen of Mine* so precious is that these surviving writings are like pieces of gold, unearthed by Nancy through her unrelenting prospecting over the years. Each fragment should be cherished as a rare window into Layne's soul, much like his music and visual art. These writings offer invaluable glimpses into the pain he experienced, expressions that complement and expand upon the emotions conveyed in his recorded music.

Layne wasn't organized in the conventional sense of keeping orderly notebooks or journals. Yet, remarkably, he seems to have preserved even the smallest bits of his writing. Some of what survived were mere scribblings on tiny scraps of paper: brief jottings that, despite their brevity, revealed profound depths. These scattered pieces suggest a mind constantly processing, creating, and expressing, capturing thoughts whenever inspiration struck, whether on proper stationery or whatever material happened to be at hand.

In these collected writings, we're granted access to unfiltered moments of Layne's interior life—sometimes raw, sometimes reflective, but always authentic. They stand as testament to an artist whose creative impulse extended well beyond the recording studio, offering us a more complete portrait of a complex and gifted individual whose legacy continues to resonate with listeners and readers alike.

—Edward Ash-Milby, Editor

Layne

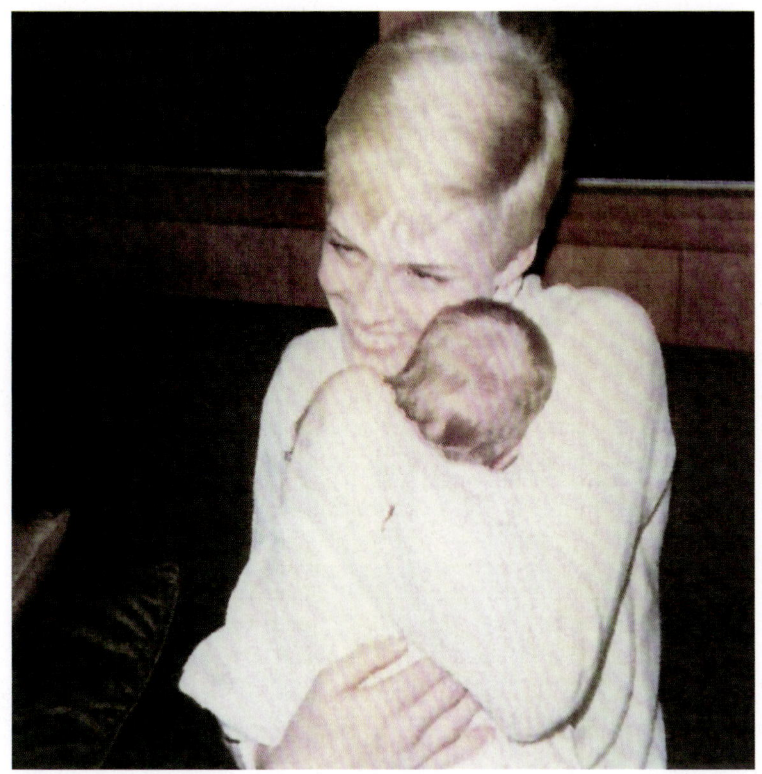

"Divine love isn't history. It's a current event." Nancy and baby Layne.

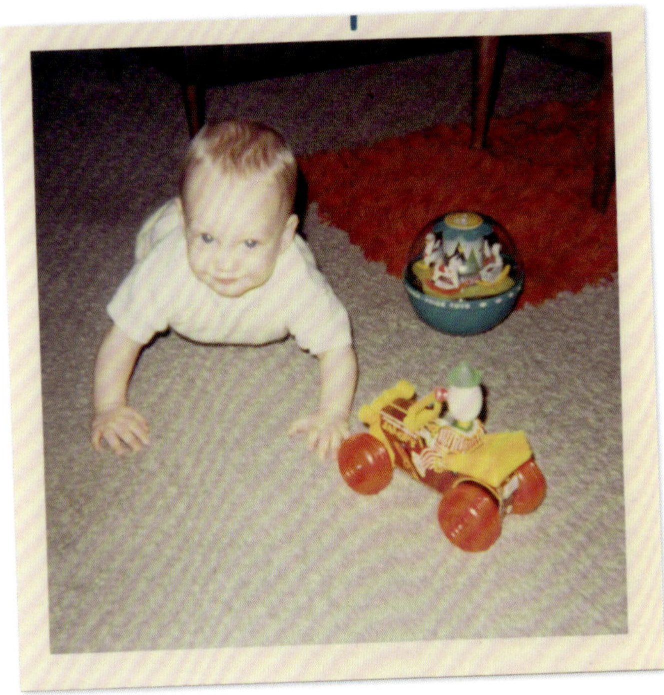

With a smirk amidst toys (and with that little glint in his eye), he headed straight for the nearest outlet!

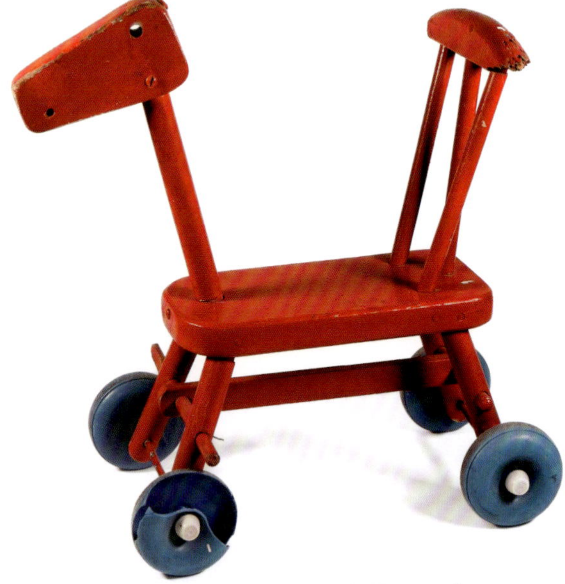

Layne's "Toot toot."

Liz (2) and Layne (5), often mistaken for twins due to their strong resemblance and Danish coloring. Although Liz was three years younger, she was a bit tallish. They had fun playing together. Downtown Bellevue, WA. Photograph by Nancy McCallum.

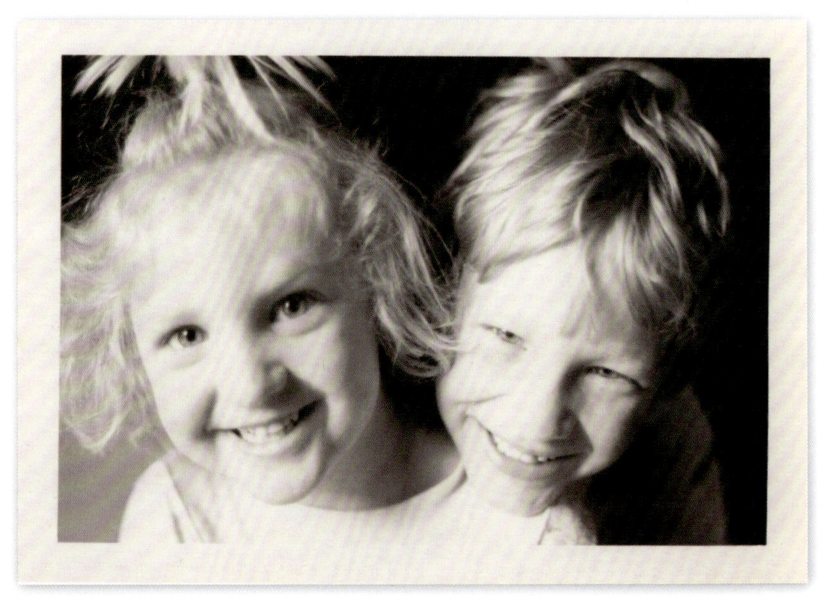

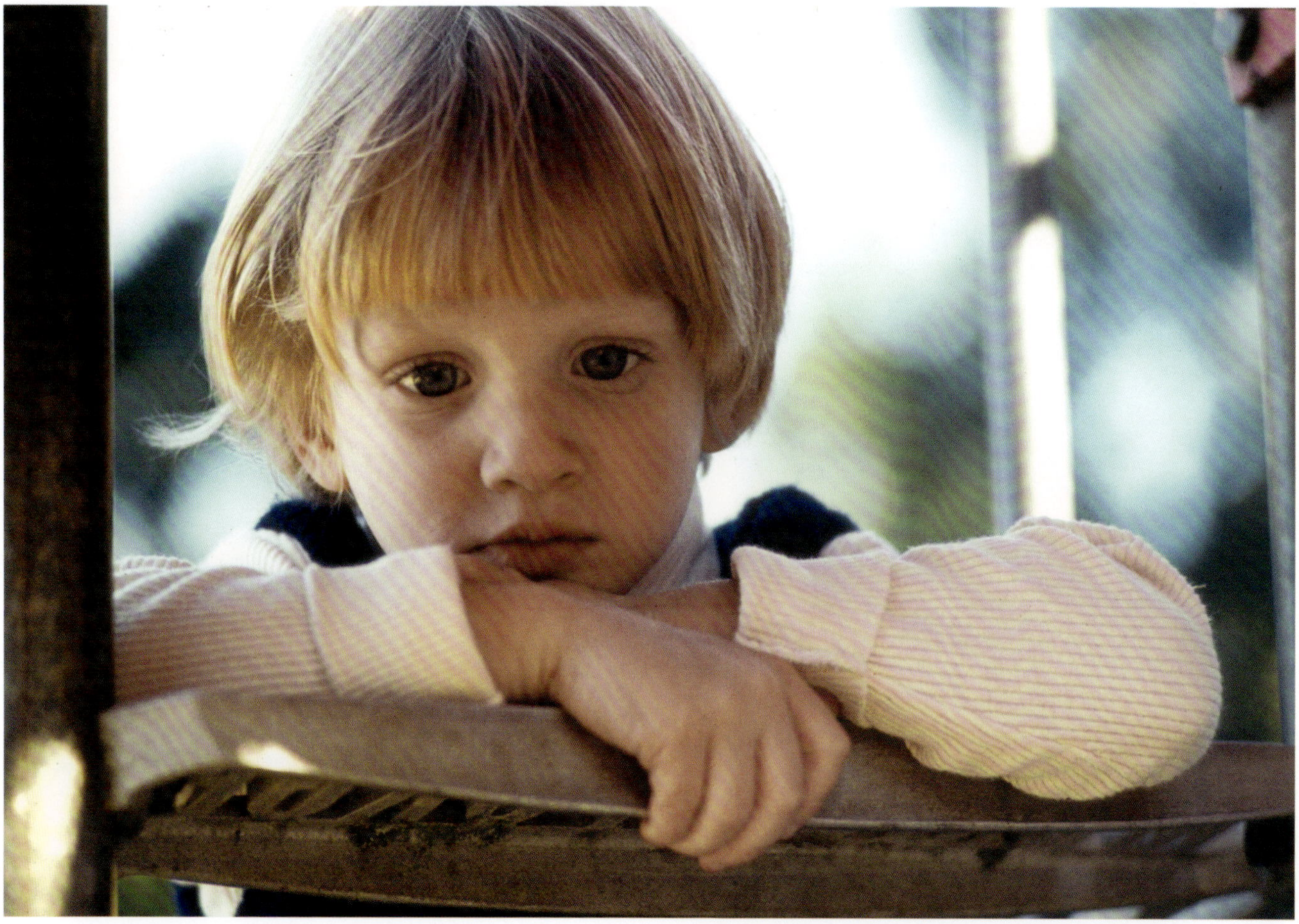

Layne, age four, with Liz and Nancy at Bovee Park in Bellevue, WA, fall 1971. Our outing included a friend from church, who kindly took this photograph. Photographer's name unknown.

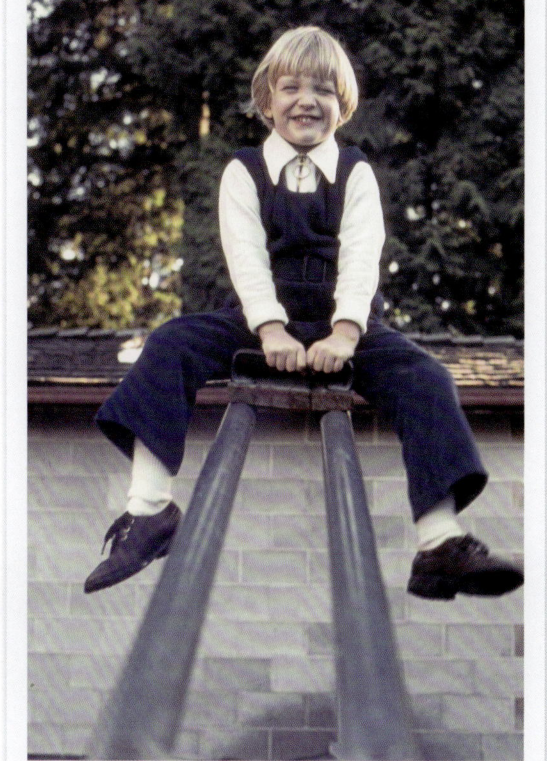

Teeter-totter at Bovee Park. A wide-wale corduroy suit, navy blue—chosen for his kindergarten school picture. He told me he had to get dressed up. The class was learning their colors. Some had brown hair, some had black, and some red . . . but Layne's hair was called "golden." Photographer's name unknown.

From the very beginning, Layne was special. When he was born, he didn't scream or cry like most babies. Instead, his little head popped out, and he just looked at the lights and cooed. They placed him in my arms, his dark newborn eyes looking up at me, and I said, "Hi Layne, I'm your mom." Those beginnings were quiet and sweet, setting the tone for the gentle soul he would become.

As he grew, Layne was noticeably quieter than his sisters who came along later. While Liz and Jamie were forthright, powerful, and "stompy-footed." Layne was thoughtful with a remarkably long attention span. Even at three years old, he would sit in his high chair, concentrating on his building sets. I'd just place half a sandwich near him, not wanting to interrupt his focus.

Music filled our home from the beginning—it was just part of growing up. My parents had beautiful singing voices and were wonderful dancers, so we naturally carried that tradition forward. One of my first memories of Layne with music is watching him as a toddler, standing at the edge of my father's stereo, holding on and watching the record go round and round. My dad would ask, "Layne, what's it doing?" and he would respond, "Dewey Dewey, Dewey Dewey." Such sweet moments.

Before he was three, Layne joined Mrs. Graham's rhythm band despite being younger than the required age. He loved music and sang all the time—one of his first songs was "Raindrops Keep Falling on my Head." He didn't participate in the recital, being shy and young, but he was already showing his musical interest. In fifth grade, he tried playing the trumpet for about three years, though he didn't have what his teacher called "very good embouchure."

Our family was musical in an everyday way—we would make up silly songs, mimic voices (Layne did a great Popeye), and dance around the house. It wasn't unusual to have music playing constantly. We were funny and loved to dramatize things—not Shakespeare drama, just fun parts of life.

As the oldest child, Layne enjoyed being the only one for his first three years. I adored him—there's something different about your first baby. When his sister, Liz, was born, I remember sitting him in a little velveteen rocker and placing her in his arms. I turned away briefly, and when I looked back, he had carefully slipped out from underneath her, leaving her safely in the chair. That was Layne—careful, considerate.

—Nancy McCallum

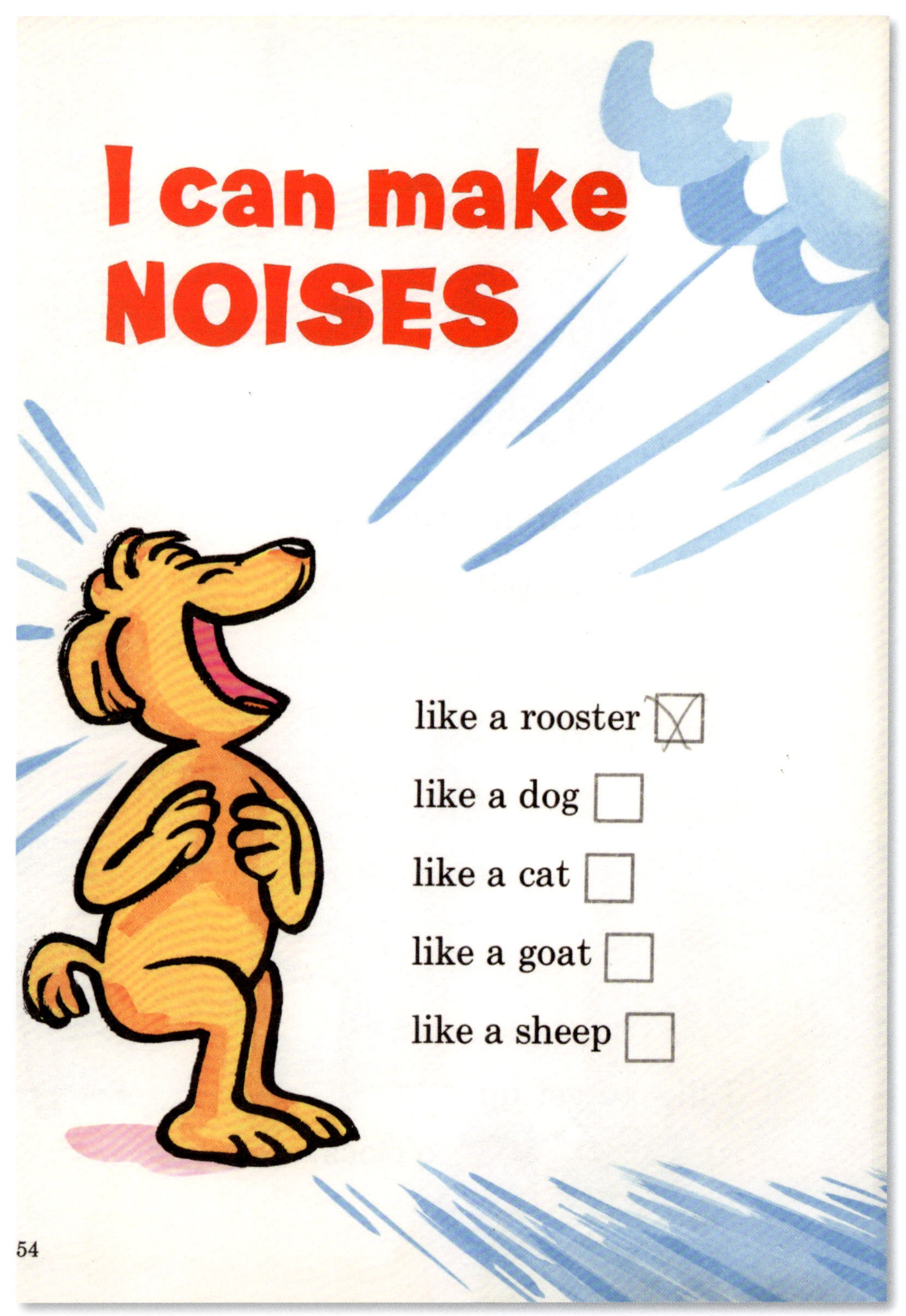

Layne checked the "rooster" box . . . a fun coincidence.

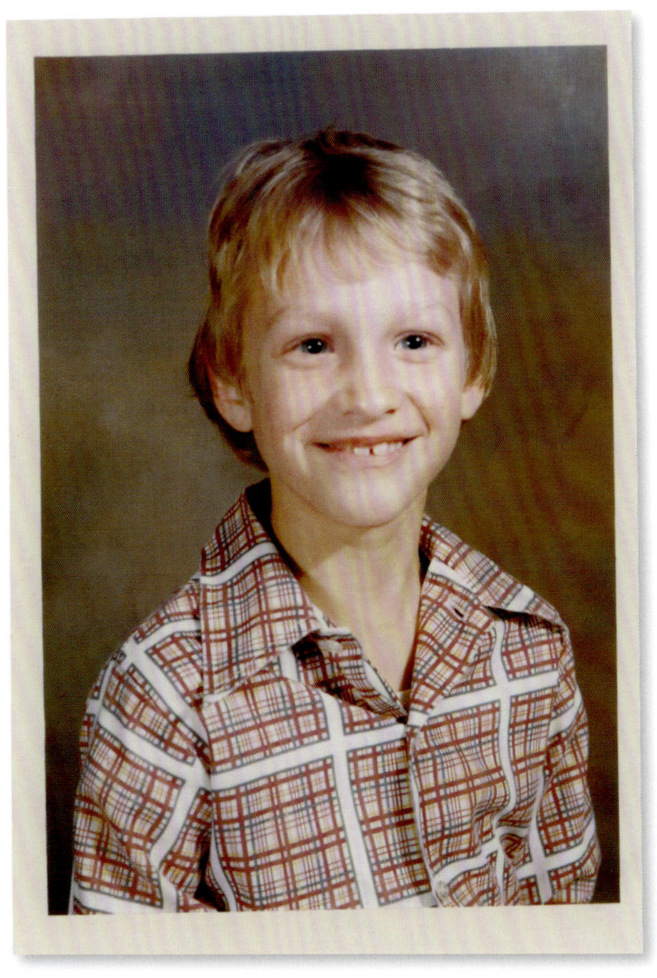

Age 7, Stevenson Elementary, Bellevue, WA. He inherited the split in his front teeth from Grandpa Layne.

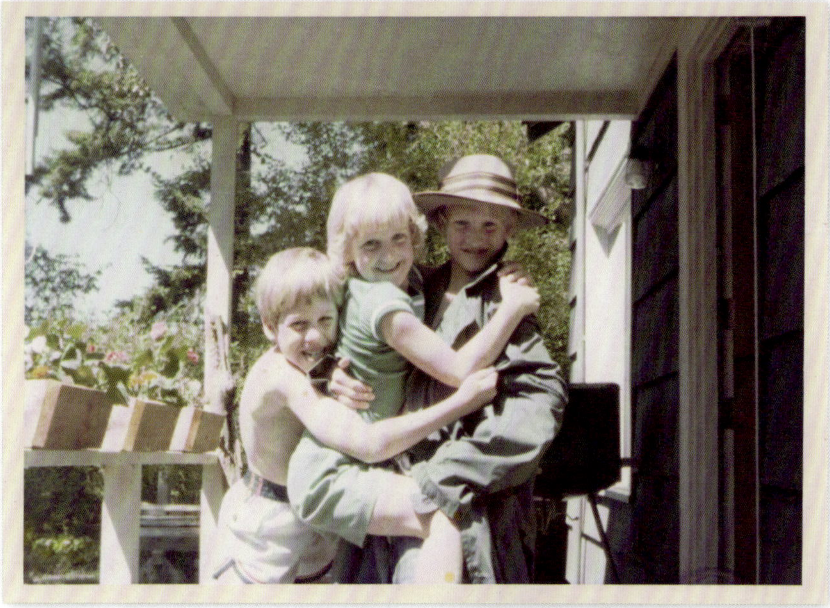

Layne (in costume), Liz, and Ken, ages 9, 7, and 8, respectively, enjoy a Fourth of July weekend in 1976 at their great-grandparents' house on Bainbridge Island, WA. This was the year of the American Bicentennial, and their great-great-grandfather, a skilled craftsman, built the original split-cedar fence and swinging gate visible in the background, intended to corral the family's pigs and chickens in the early 1900s. Photograph by Nancy McCallum.

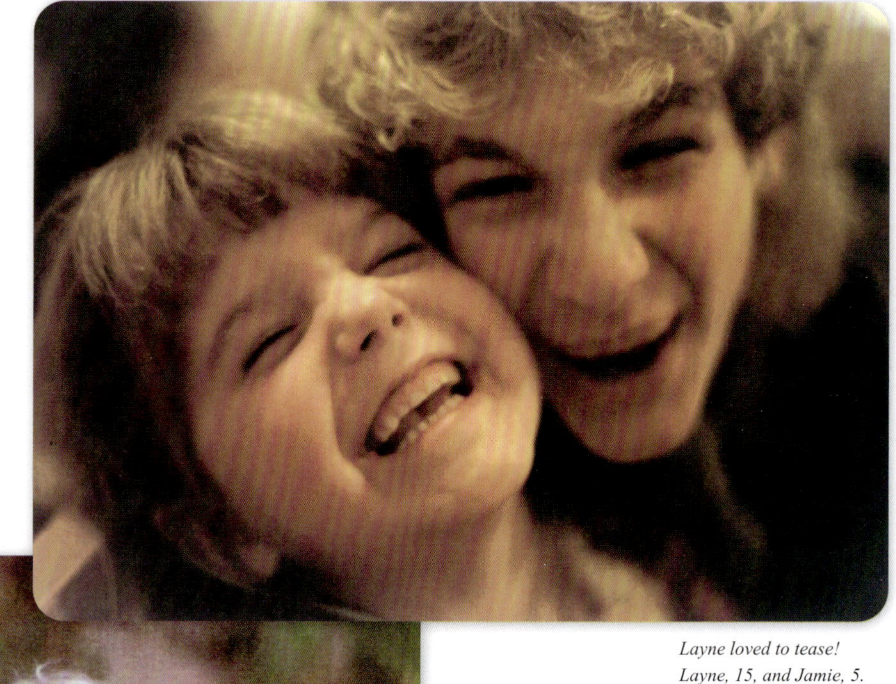

Layne loved to tease!
Layne, 15, and Jamie, 5.

An unscripted, unplanned surprise!
A beautiful, warm morning at our
new Lynnwood, WA, home. Layne is 8.

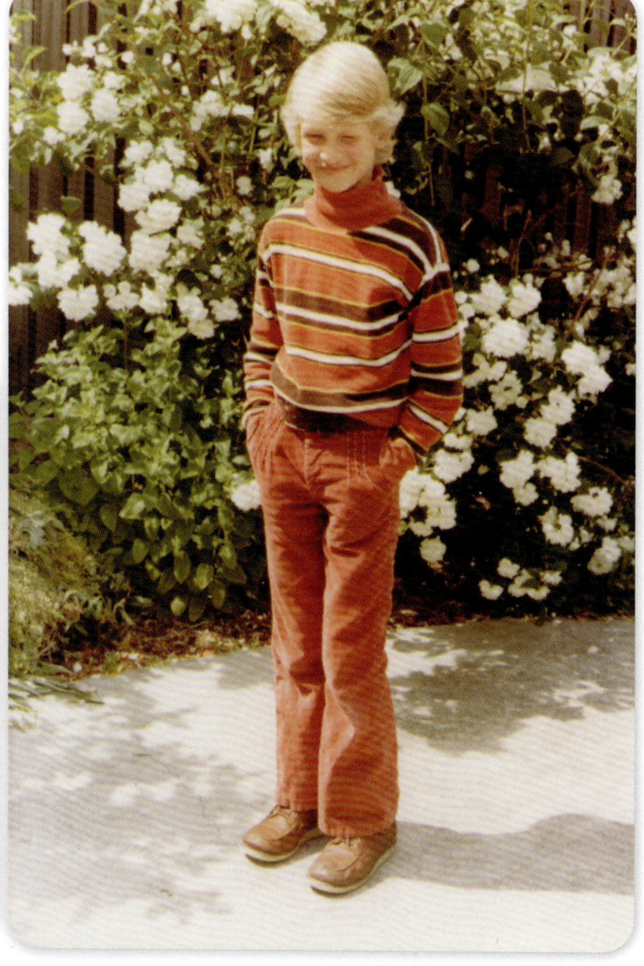

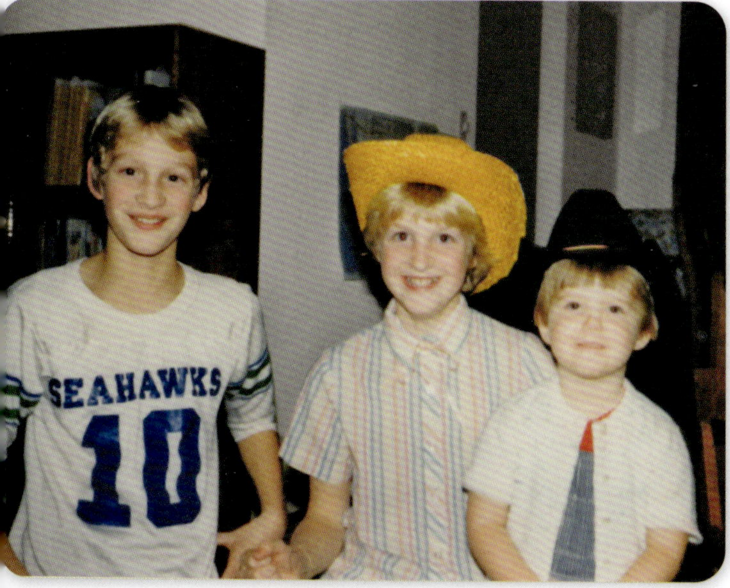

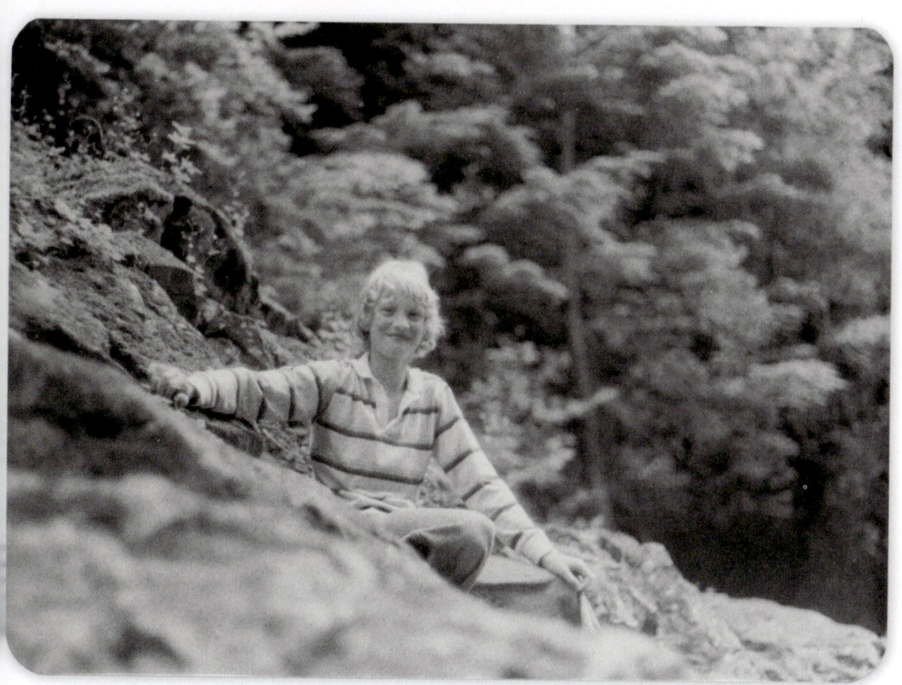

top left: Layne, 13; Liz, 10; and Jamie, 2. Jim Zorn was #10 for the Seahawks!

above: Layne in the garden at Grandma and Grandpa Elmer's. Spring 1975 or 1976. Easter dinner. Rust cords with velour shirt. Photograph by Nancy McCallum.

left: Layne, circa 1977–1978, likely enjoying a summer hike in the Pacific Northwest. Photograph by Jim Elmer.

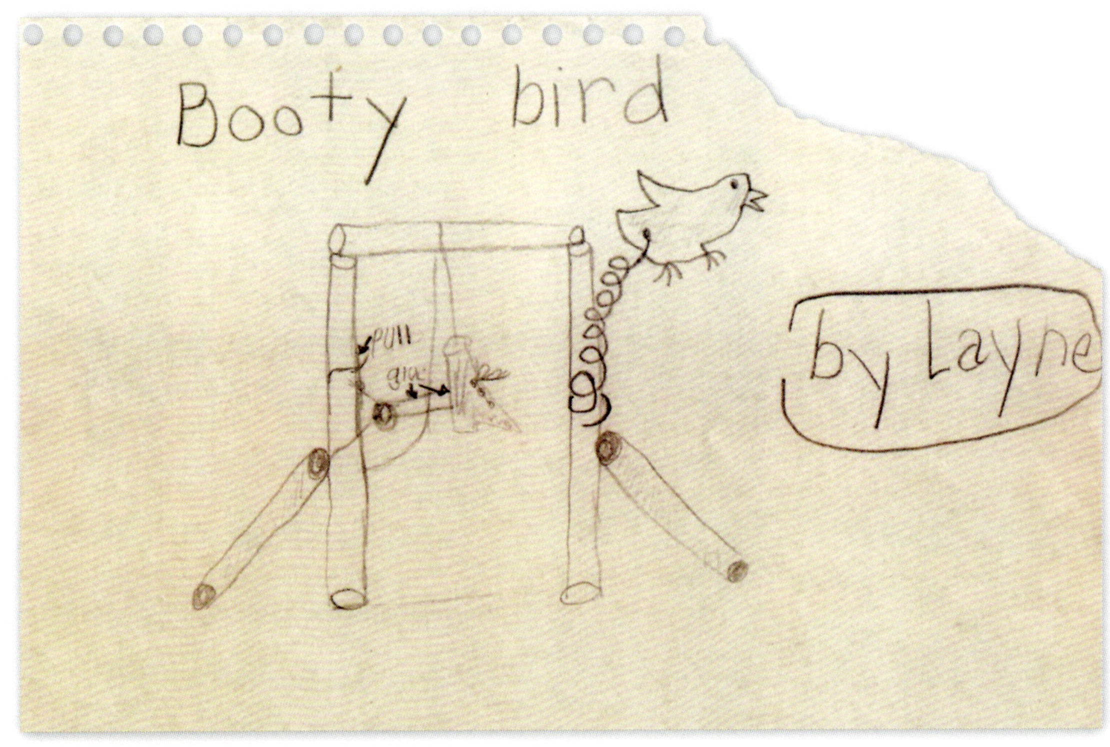

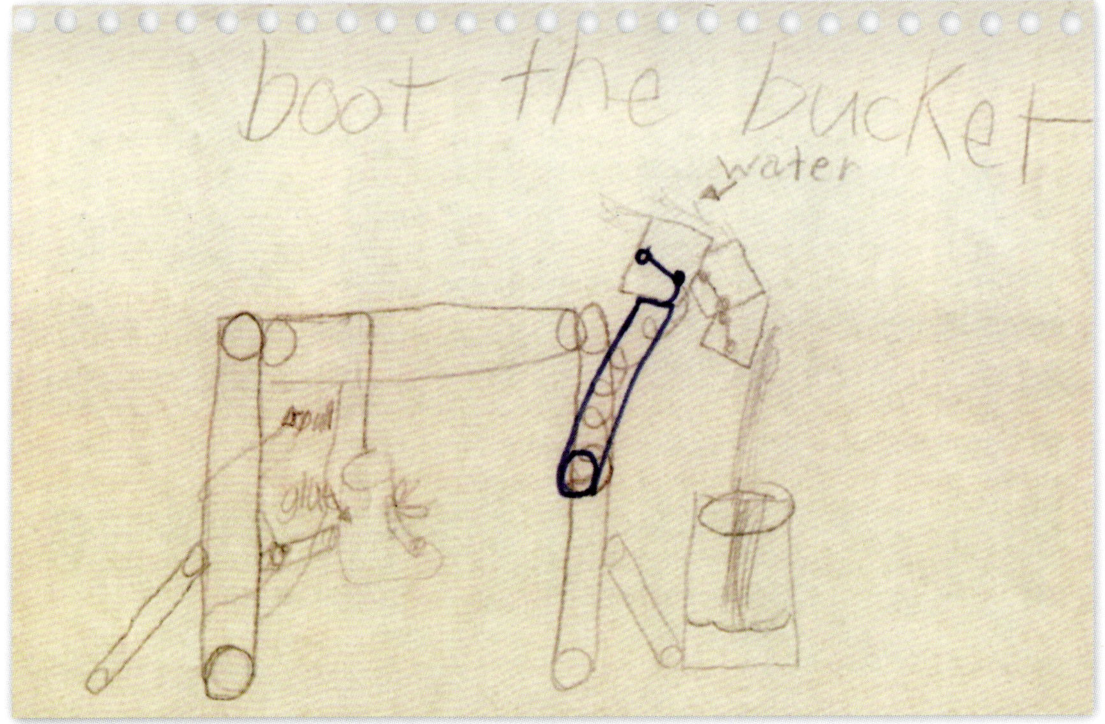

He made up a game similar to Mouse Trap.

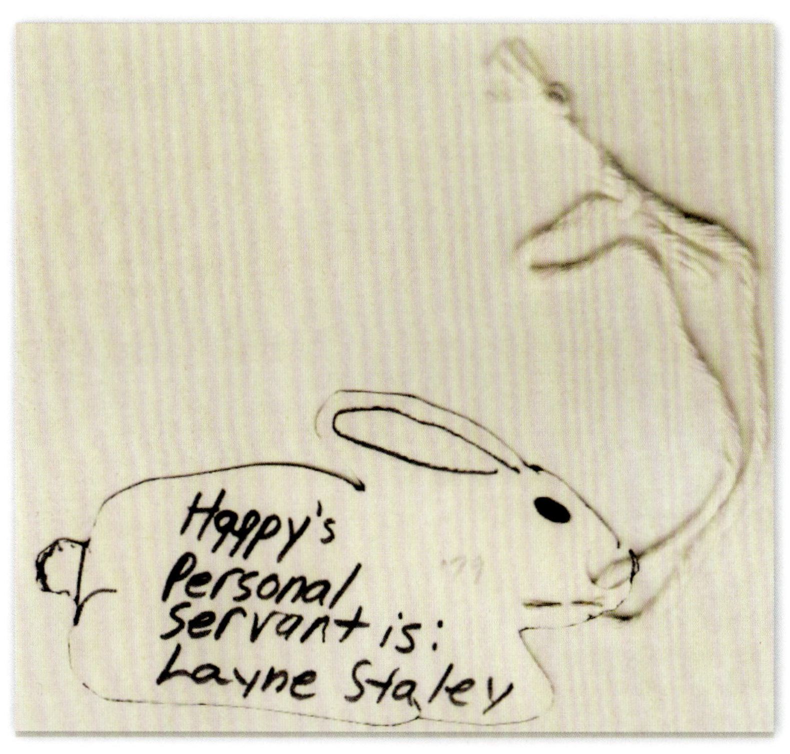

A testament to our family's tradition of creating gifts: Layne's handmade offering for Mom. This wasn't just a present; it represented his willingness to be there, whether for errands, projects, or simply playing with his baby sister. Fond memories of sourcing these plastic oven-bake kits from our trusty Fred Meyer.

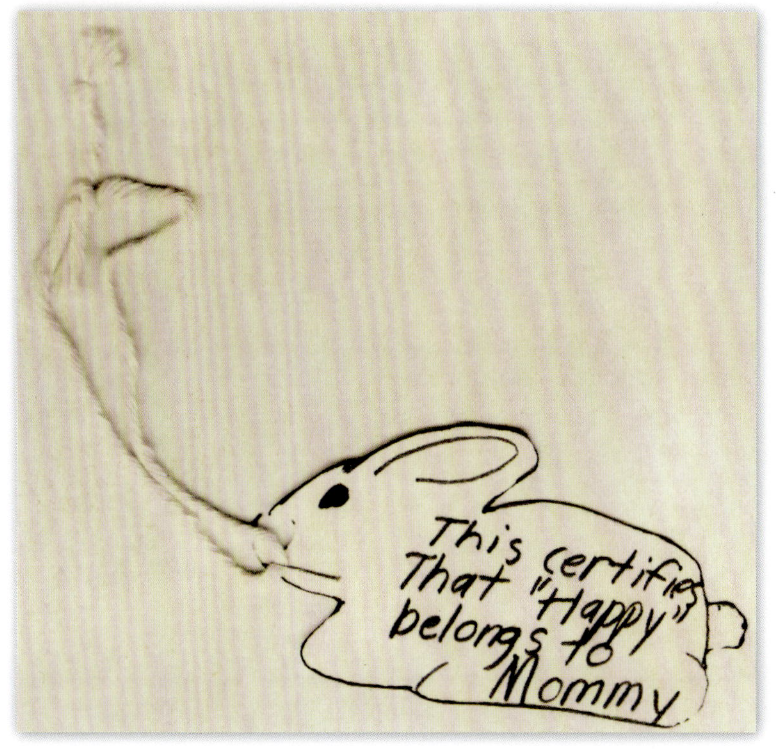

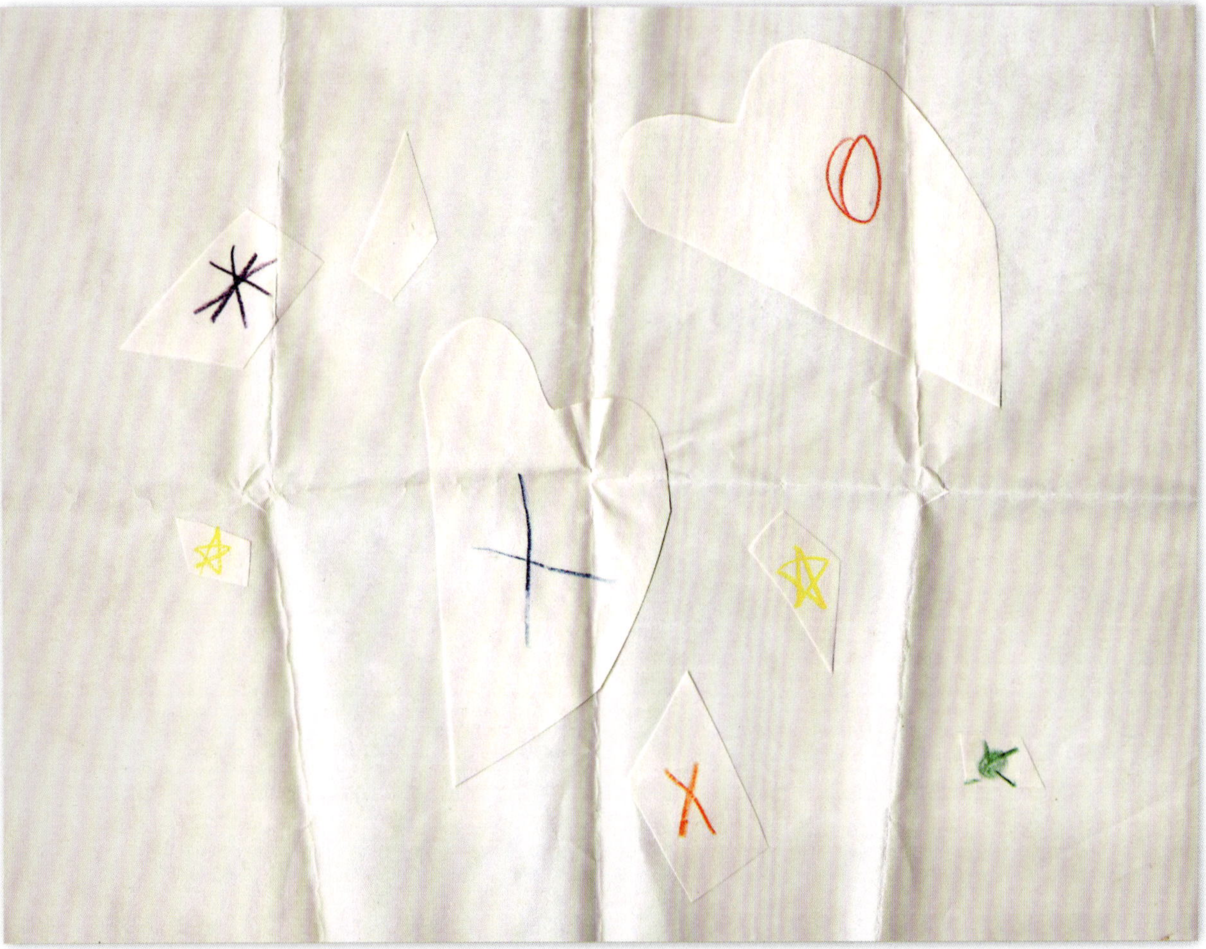

Jamie's note to Layne.

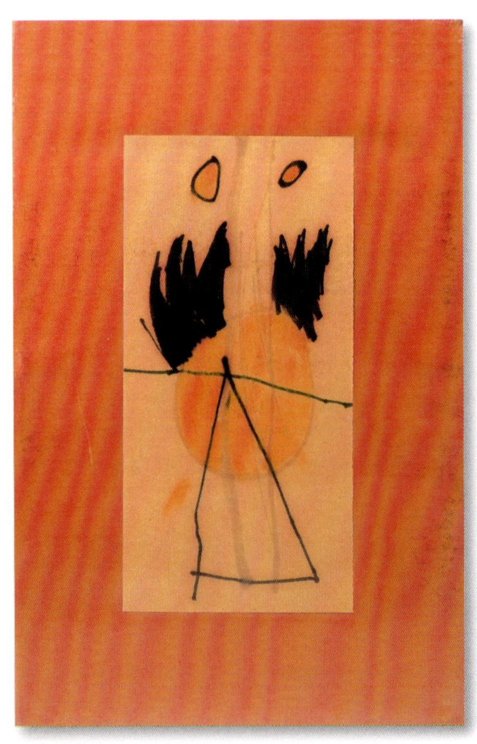

Layne's first painting from kindergarten, age 5.

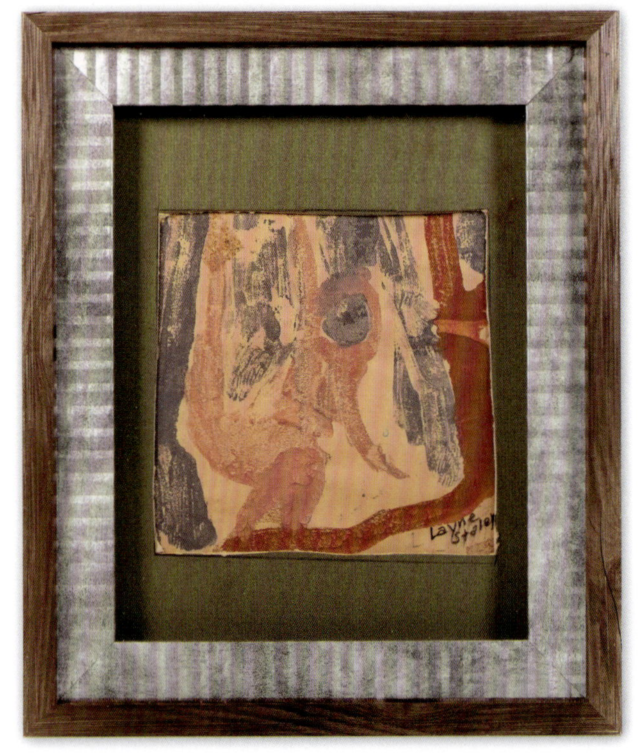

"Monkey in Branches" from Kalm Brae School, Redmond, WA, age 10.

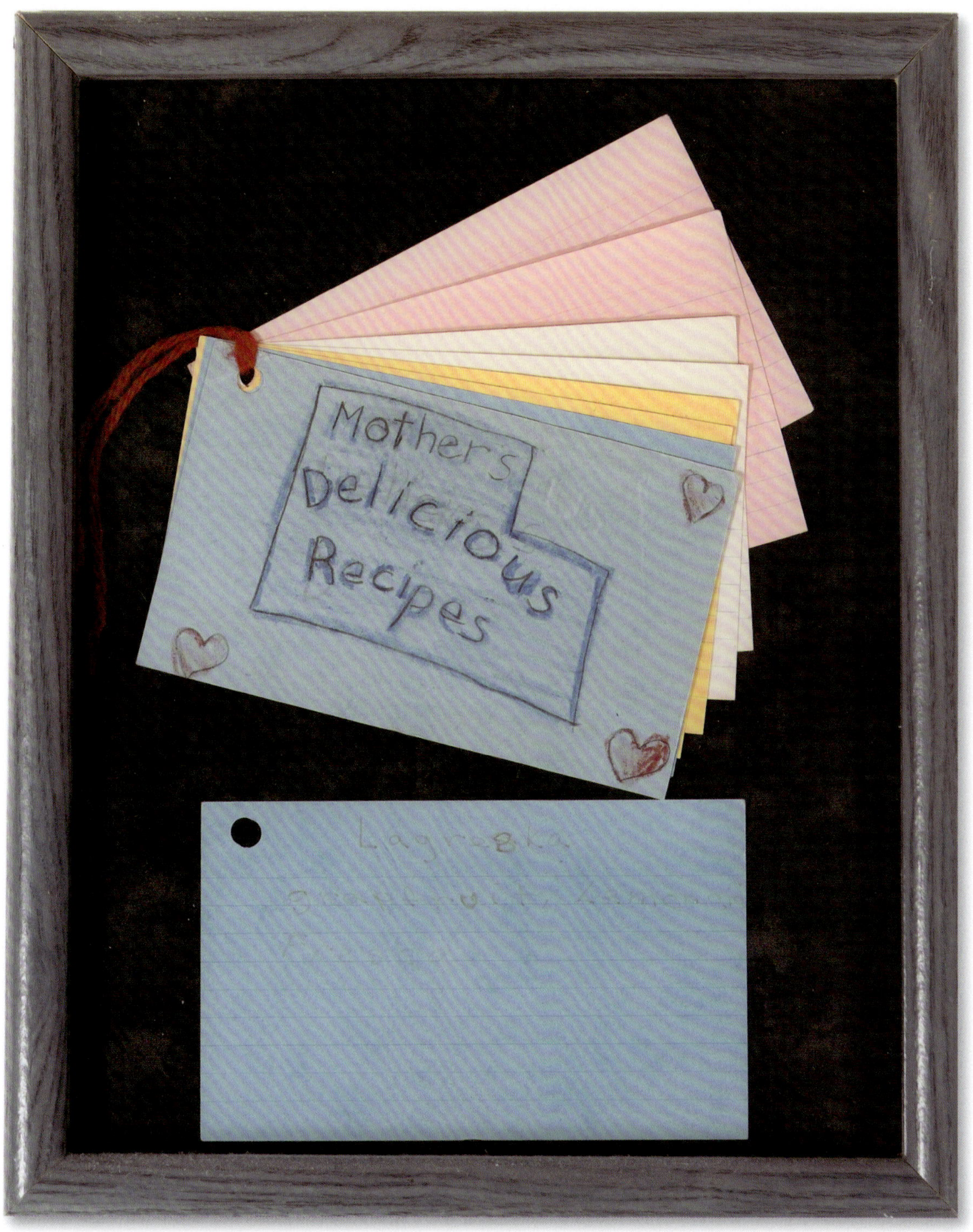

Mother's Day gift. Recipe for "Lagresca," lemonade and Fresca.
Made in the Boy Scouts.

PART ONE: WRITINGS

LYRICS, LISTS, AND LIFE

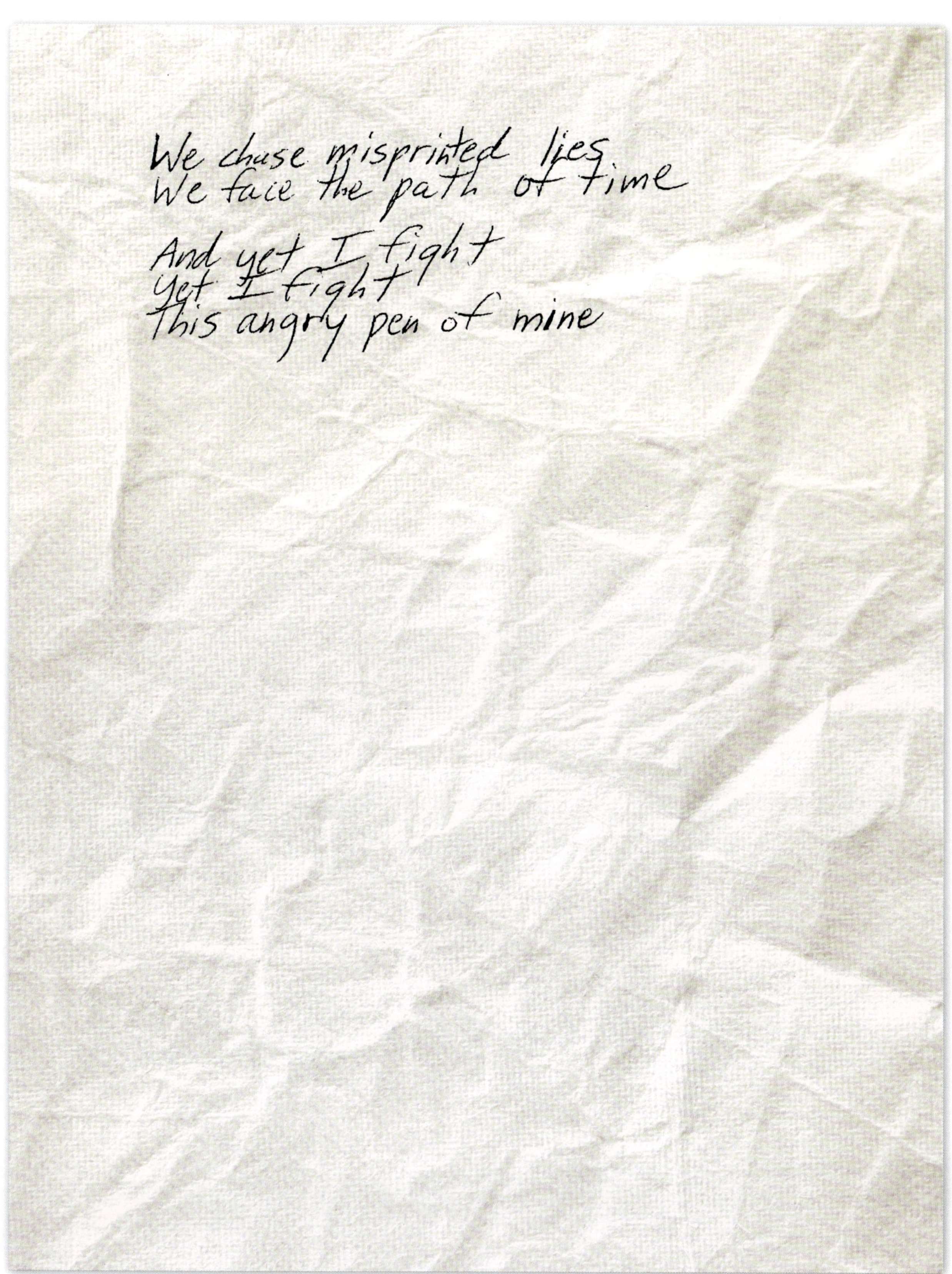

"Nutshell" by Alice in Chains. Released in 1994 from the EP Jar of Flies.

It happened 14 years ago
The transformation.
An innocent, lonely child
Abandoned himself
And for 14 years now
His borrowed mind Has taken on
Many new identities
Each with their own decided
List of rules, morals, and wicked habits

This was never an inconvenience
Until that boy of twelve,
Thought to have been left behind,
Began spying these atrocities
Fighting to regain the body
That was harboring these monsters,
And victory was always his,
But it was always given him with
the intention of a soon to be broken spirit

He has been witness to some awful things
He has mocked the dead
Then forced to walk among the dead
He could only watch
As the body he hoped to regain
Was sabotaged with poisons,
His blood once rich, now thinned and
Clogged with synthetic + chemical waste.

I want to travel, south of the
Medicine Wheel
Rediscovering innocence & humility →

Written at age 28.

An honest attempt to succeed
at something already lost to failed
attempts. Is greater than

A Failed attempt at
any one thing strongly
desired –
Is greater than a
~~brilliant~~ [illegible] explanation
as to why one cannot
succeed at many things,
that should be rightfully his/hers

A dishonest excuse to obtain
something already

hm... I never said I
wouldn't carry the weight

ahh

Black eyed girl
You brought the night
No matter bright of the
day

I have been used
And convinced I'm being saved
I have committed
Or rather enslaved
I have been ordered
To change in my ways
Not uncommon to have
Me contractually swayed
I'm reminded by one
In his well-beknownst way
While ordering dessert
And passing on the tray
I'm bound to

Wear the crown of fame
and I still feel like I'm
pretending

Wonder when I'll stop myself
from rules I'm still bending

Shouting (whispered)
Whispering (Shouted)
Laughing (wimpered)
Crying (laughed)

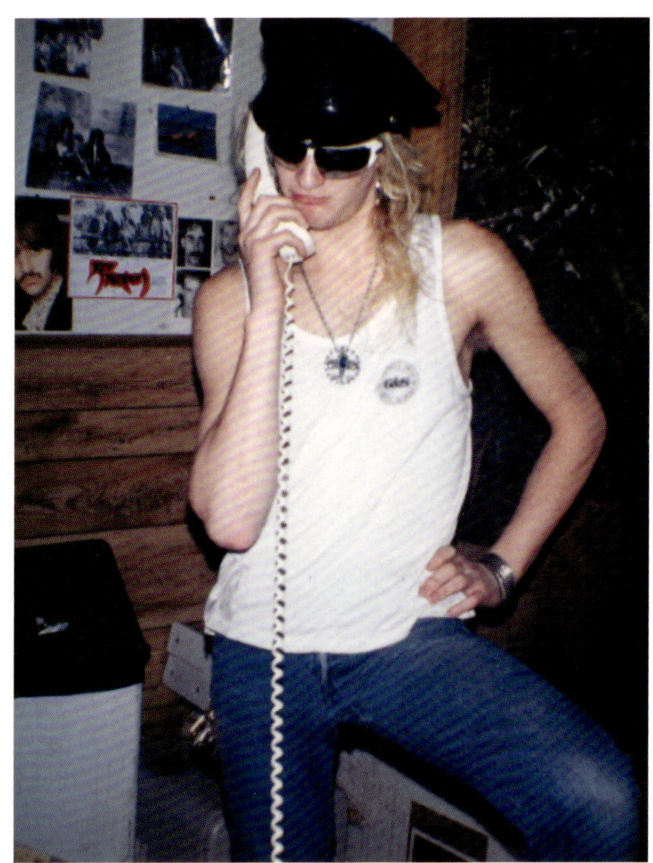

Cool . . . right? Layne during Sleze glam era, 1988.

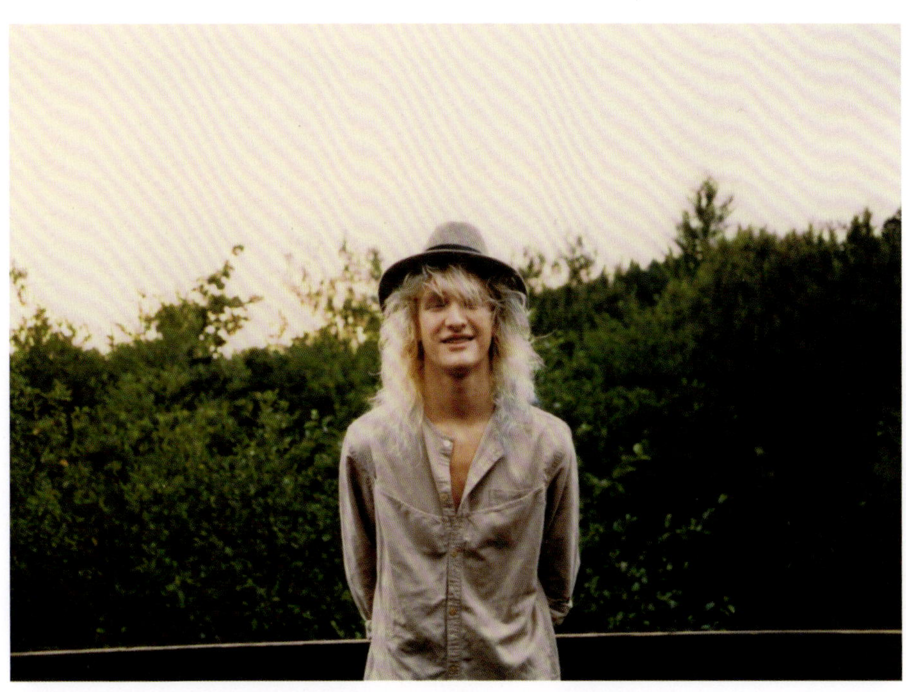

Layne poses on the deck of the SE 7th Street house in Bellevue, WA, around 1989. This photo was later creatively repurposed for the family Christmas card, much to the amusement of those who discovered the "missing" family member. Photo taken by Nancy McCallum.

Layne's growing (or drowning
ongoing nightmares, discrepencies:
awarenesses, hallucinations, or
possibly just a more realistic
quicker play on thought to
cheat mortality out of
a victim to wise to the
game (and the designers of, who are
never without ~~not with-~~
~~also apolligetically~~ self
~~out the adrenalin based~~
serving, false gratifying
shortcoming of a love for the
fall of others) who is well
familiar of the end of the
game, not taught to me

So...

I think that the length should be extended only if the hours are shortened. I know my attention span, and most other teens, cannot exceed 20 to 30 minutes on one subject. I think most people would enjoy, and get good grades if the school hours were to change from 6½ hours to 3½ with shortened holidays and vacations. School can be enjoyable only if the student is interested in his work. He or she cannot force him or herself to enjoy what they are learning therefore, the teachers job is not only to teach, but to teach in a way that will catch a child's attention and make him or her interested. Three and one half hours would be one half hour per subject. I think you would find that, even though it would take a longer length of time to teach a certain topic in a subject, the kids would pick it up much quicker if their attention did n't just drop. This is my opinion on Public Ed

This was written as a school assignment. Years later, his nephew, Oscar, wrote something very similar, also as a school assignment. Both are artists.

seen the brightest light
put up such a fight
hing all your life
urhing like a knife

now the reasons why
high or you will die

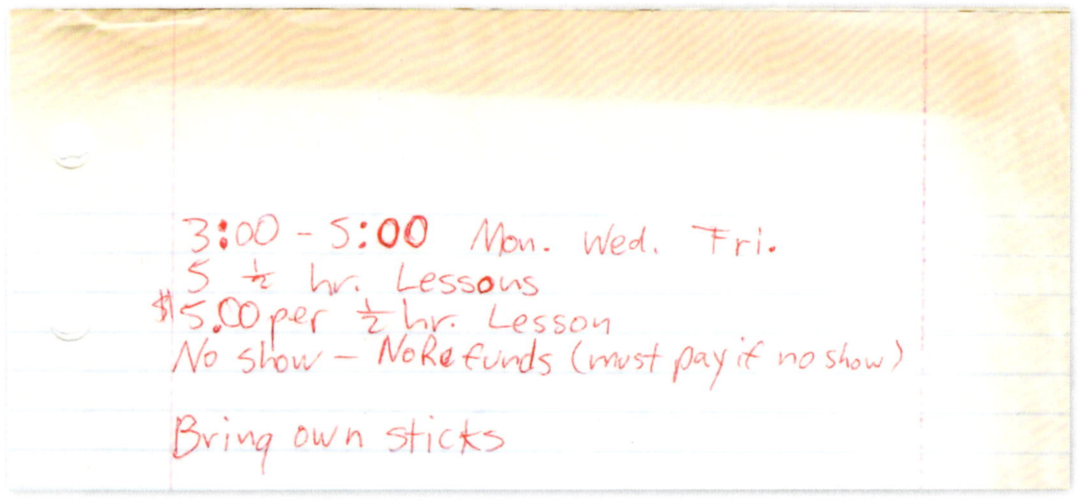
3:00 - 5:00 Mon. Wed. Fri.
5 ½ hr. Lessons
$5.00 per ½ hr. Lesson
No show - No Refunds (must pay if no show)

Bring own sticks

Planning his ad for drum lessons.

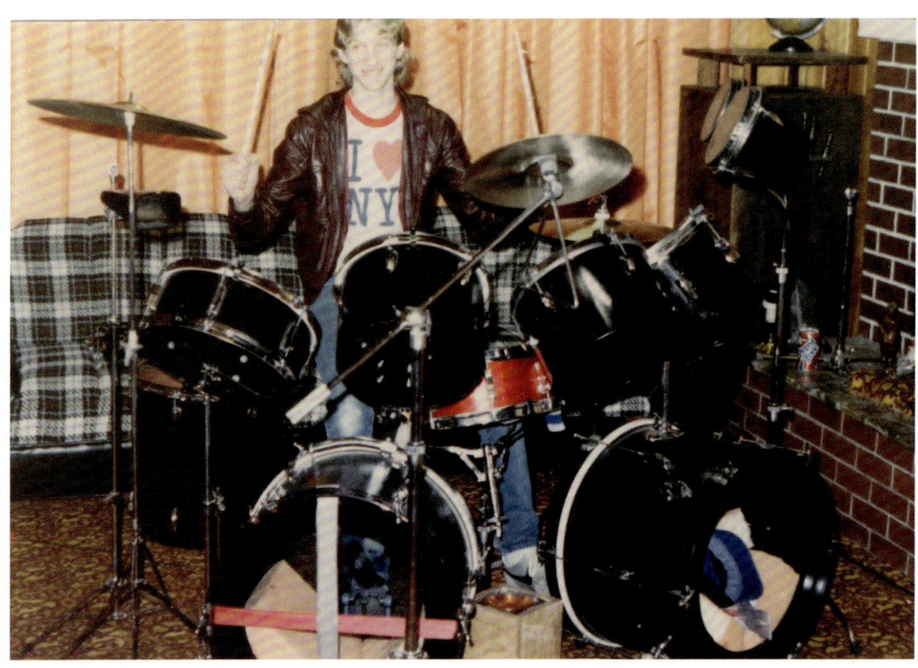

Layne, approximately 14 to 15 years old (circa 1981–1982), playing drums at the Meldahl residence. He later purchased these drums from Eric Meldahl. Photograph by Eric or Brett Meldahl.

Zildjian

1 - 13" top light hi hat cymbal
2 - 21" bass drums - black
3 - 12" tom toms - black
1 - 14½" tom tom - black
1 - 14½" floor tom - black
2 - 15" hi hats - quitars etc.
1 - ludwig hi-hat stand
1 - ludwig snare - red sparkle
1 - 8" small tom - black
1 - cymbal stand - adjustable
1 - 6½" small tom - black
1 - drumstool - red
1 - 8" cowbell - black
1 - 6½" cowbell - silver
1 - 4" cowbell - copper
1 - adjustable snare stand
1 - 16" zildjian turkish cymbal

Listing his drum set parts. This was Layne's very organized and business side.

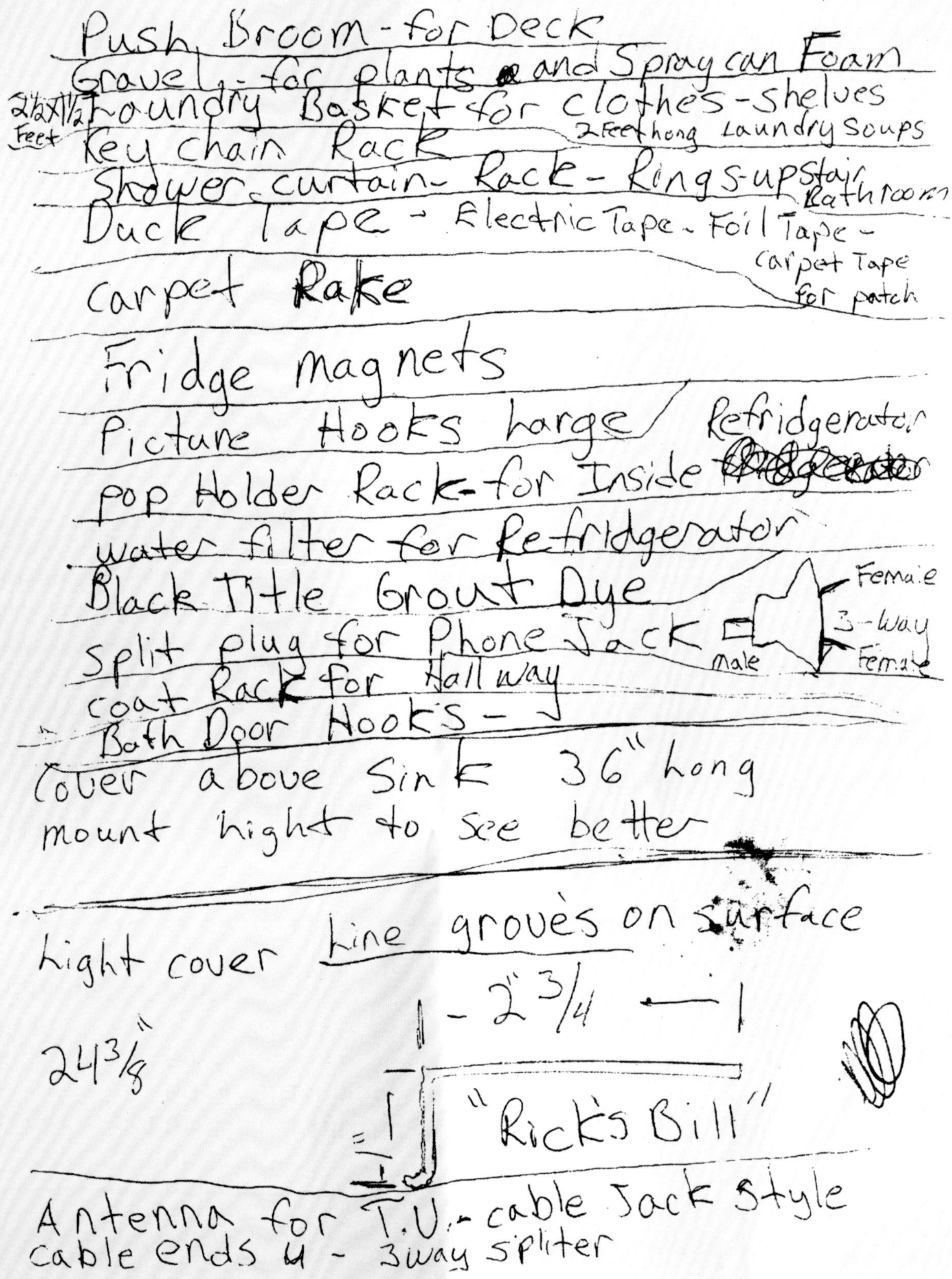

Push Broom - for Deck
Gravel - for plants and Spray can Foam
2½ x 1½ Feet Laundry Basket for clothes - shelves 2 Feet Long Laundry Soups
Key chain Rack
Shower curtain - Rack - Rings - upstair Bathroom
Duck Tape - Electric Tape - Foil Tape - Carpet Tape for patch
Carpet Rake
Fridge magnets
Picture Hooks Large / Refridgerator
pop Holder Rack - for Inside ~~Fridgerator~~
water filter for Refridgerator
Black Title Grout Dye
Split plug for Phone Jack
male
Female
3-Way
Female
coat Rack for Hallway
Bath Door Hooks -
Cover above Sink 36" Long
mount hight to see better
Light cover Line groves on surface
- 2 3/4 -
24 3/8
"Rick's Bill"
Antenna for T.V. - cable Jack Style
cable ends 4 - 3way spliter

Purchase and project list for his new home.

I been silver, I been blue
Been ugly and old
✝ Waitin 4 heaven - while in hell
I've done, it all for mother

I'm a one legged dog
Like a brand new baby boy

(Let my spirit free)
(Let it take control of me)

(In the morning glory days)
(I start driving it again)

Nuts of a Gerbil
Sreath of a Sturgeon
and various other fishes
We bid you farewell

I hate this paper with every
ounce of hate in me
And if this pen were a gun
I could much more easily
express how I feel

I know a girl who sits on the
lap of leprecy
She is infected but denies her
affliction
I know a girl

So your eyes are blind
~~Blind by~~ choice
Ears are deaf to reason

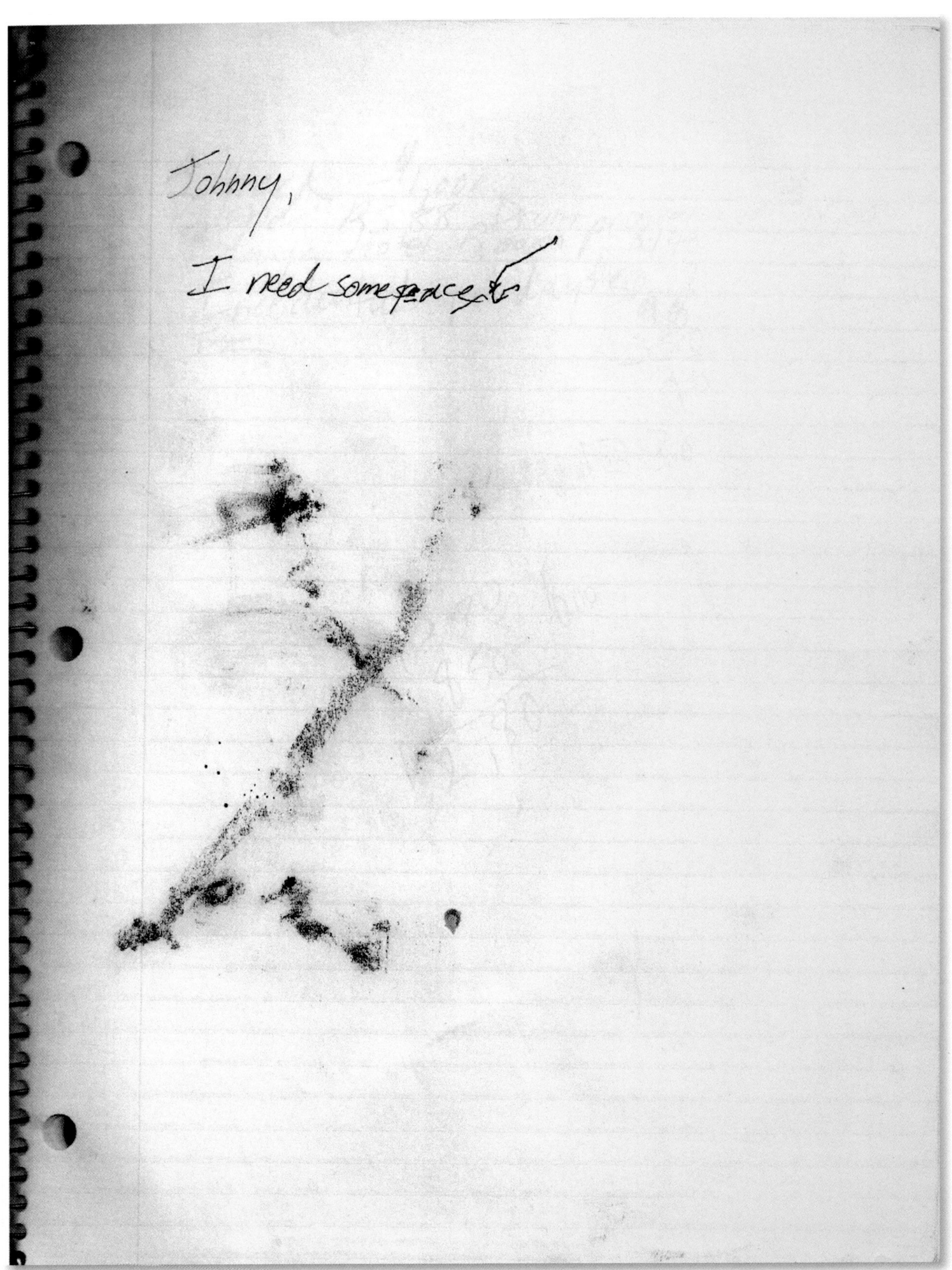

Desperate for solitude.

In the Park

see the crazy dopers in a line
burners, cooking as we stare in awe
To the left, fat lady in a shack
Gives away clean needles, in the park

Leopard vest holds rigs between his teeth
Against a tree, girl shoots between her legs
Business man rolls up suit jacket sleeve
Sunny, lovely day out in the park

Sunny day man I feel fine

Layne telling it like it is.

In the semifunctional
shell you randomly chose
On-line [illegible] in 1967.
Eeenie Meenie.. I know!
Well, it does for me
Because with my mind
preserved and heart
strong I will always
go against your ever
changing plan.

Congrats,

We Will meet
(And you laugh)

Until,

Layne

Those who are starved for
Salvation, need not be
Force-fed a savior
Proven millions will swallow
Jesus as easily as they would
A pill to numb pains...
Believe in me, you,
Hyppocritical faith does not
Wash the soul of that which
Causes guilt
For a clean conscience is not
Bought and sold
But rather, is achieved

August 28, '91

Layne rarely signed or dated his poetry unless he felt that the work was complete. He seems to be writing to himself, alluding to his birthday, August 22, 1967.

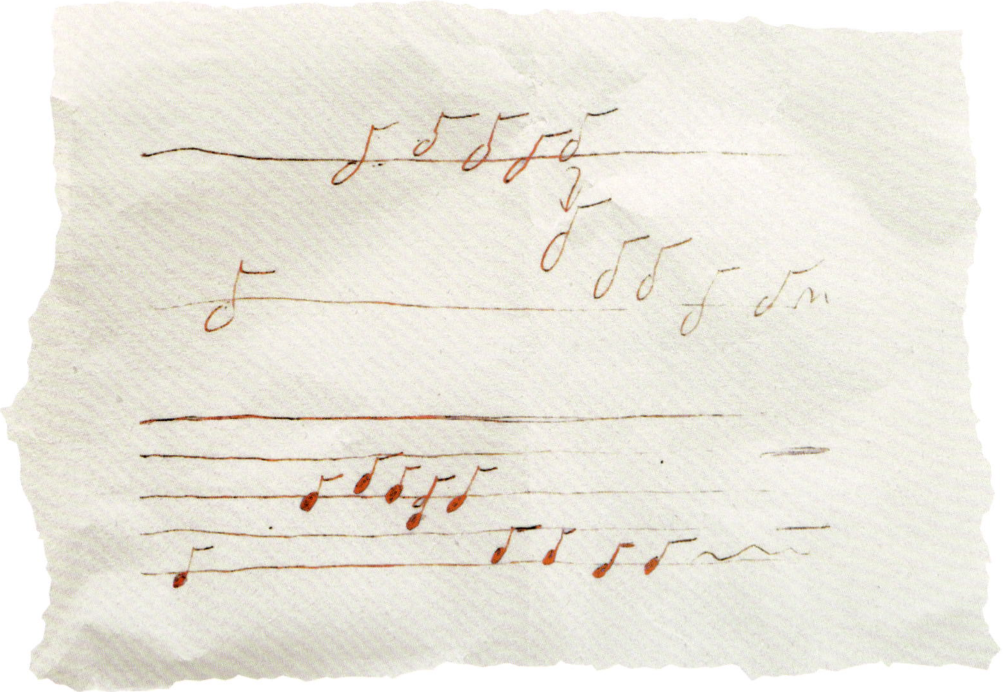

Feel the rythyme of the beat
And then you start to move and
get out of you're seats

You move to the floor you want
more, more, more
You never ever felt it before

intro & chorus

Hey Everybody - Clap your hands
We're gonna jump down, turn around
drink a few, rock out and dance

Yeah, Yeah, Yeah

Feel the rythym of the beat
& Now you start to move
& Get up off your seats

You run to the floor
You want more, more, more
You shake and spin till you fall

pre chorus

Baby, Baby, Baby I'm worth your time
If you know what I mean
Hey, Hey, Hey, come spend a dime
I'll turn you round, round, round

- chorus -

Drinking, Smoking, one night stands
It's the same routine
Forget those games, come see the band
Come on and have a ball

pre chorus

chorus

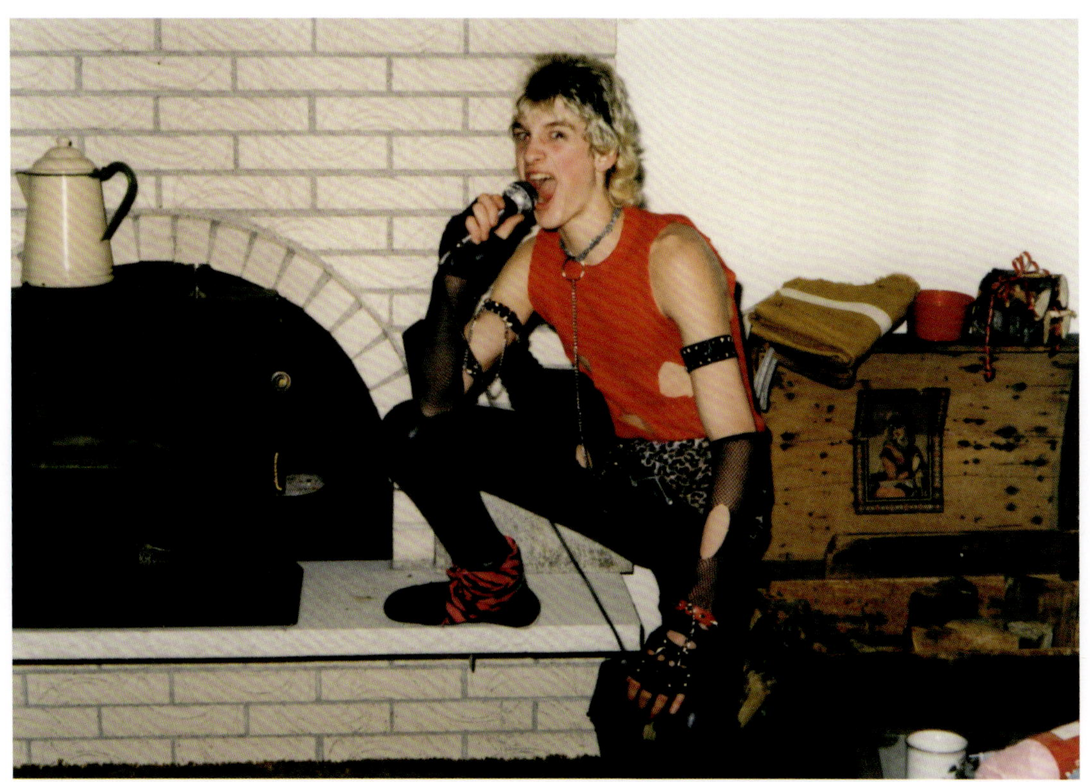

Halloween, probably 1982.

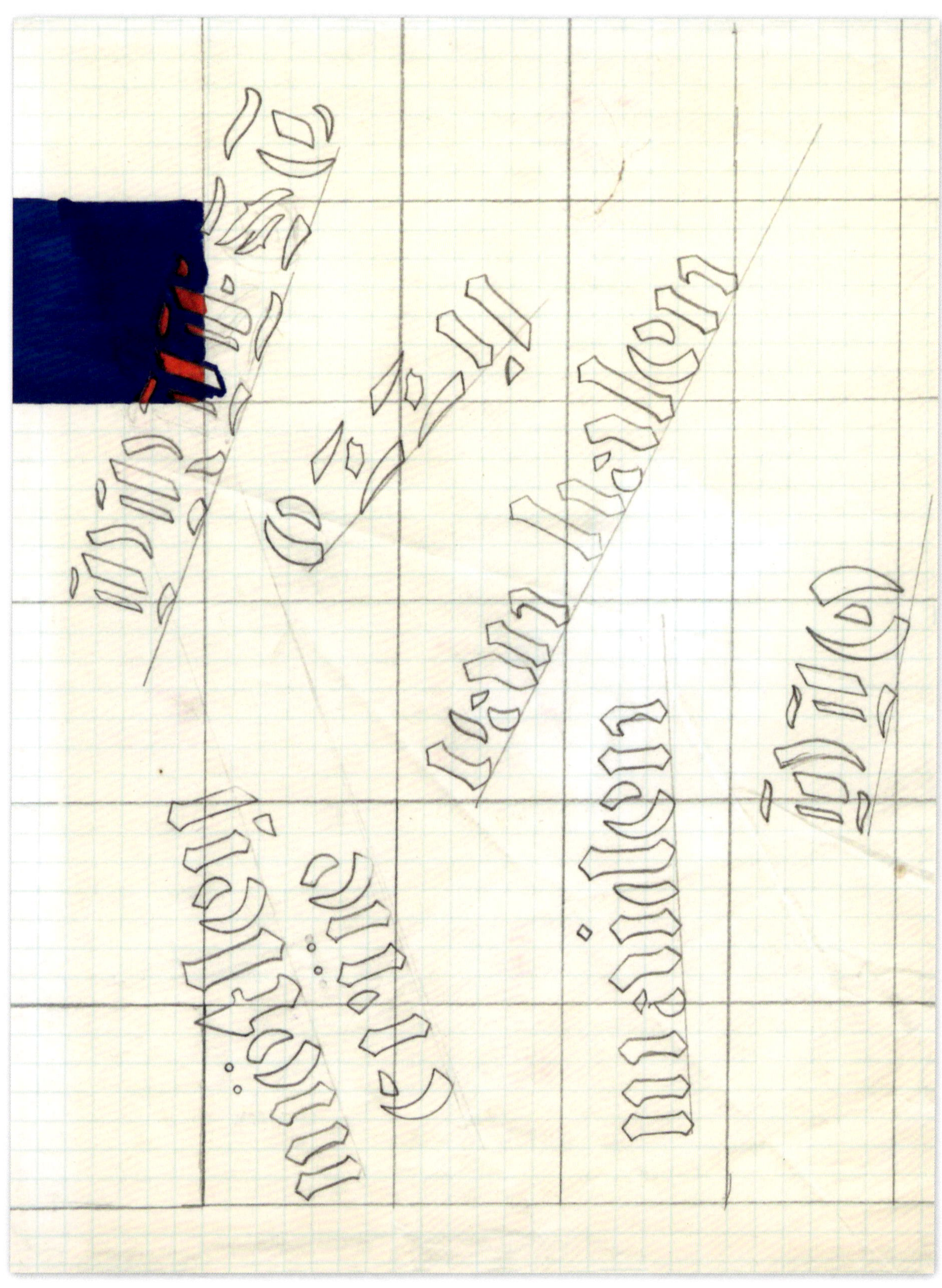

Layne's "homework."

Athletic Club - Wednesdays - 10:00 - 2:00

Drums at home - Mondays + Fridays 1-2:00

Woodshop - Saturdays in Afternoon tues + thurs 2-3:00

Job - ___?___

Band - Sundays 12:00 - 2:30

Computer - Mornings 9-10

Library - Every other Friday 10:00 - 11:00

Journey of a Tired old man

Sterile this is now
One good run may kill
So Stay weak gut now
9th day, rope frayed now

Why me? Why me? Why me? Why me?

You can see, oh
Got to say no
Let my hands go
Hang my head low
Cry in my lap
Need a good slap
Little more boy
Once again forever

Drop - Drink - Smoke - Choke
Drop Drink + Smoke it we'll try it together
Pale blue + chokin' this could be forever

Buy some time, grow now
Had good life, tired now
Brain pill quiets sow
Once love, ball + chain now

Inside my dream;

Hot winds blowing, whistling,
Nothing else in this dream,
Blowing, blowing, blowing, blowing...
No more.
A dream is my reality,
Wake up, wake up.

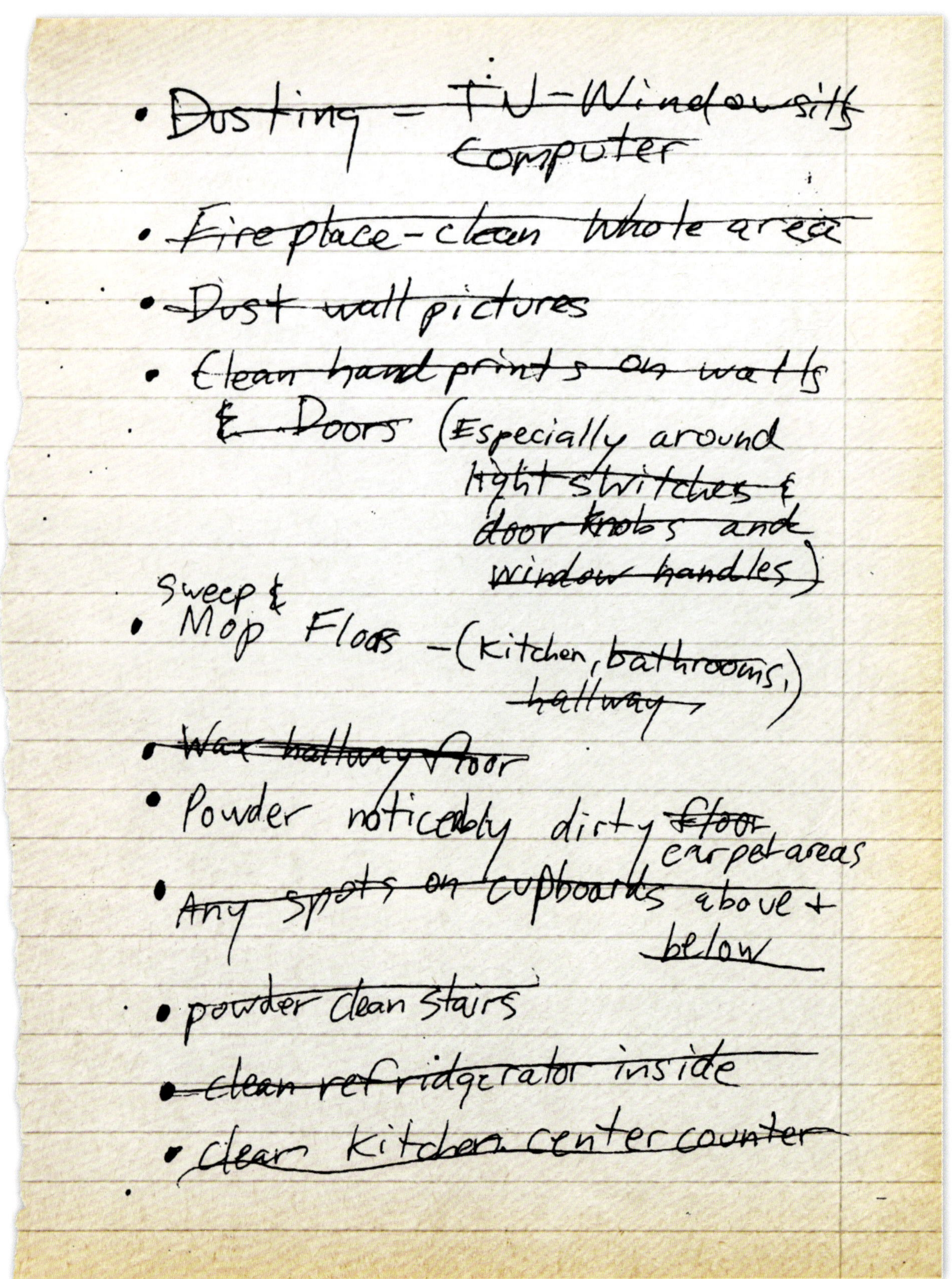

When he passed, Layne had every cleaning product known to man.

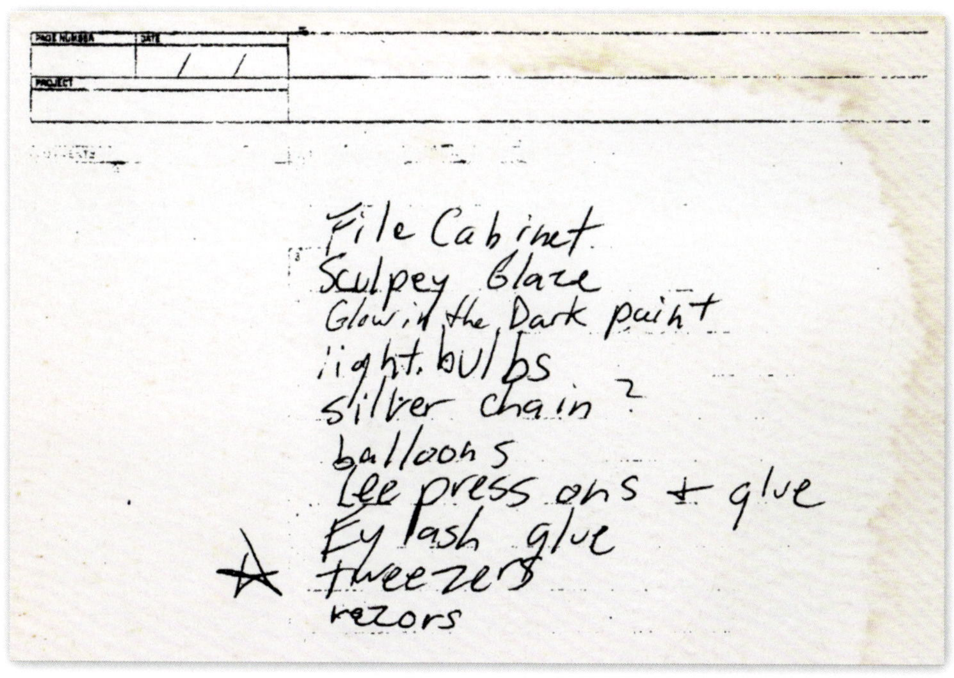

File Cabinet
Sculpey Glaze
Glow in the Dark paint
light bulbs
sillver chain ?
balloons
Lee press ons + glue
Eylash glue
☆ tweezers
rezors

Shrinky Dink paper
Glow in dark pen
Brass, copper pewter Aluminum
Paint brushes
feather boa
George Foreman Grill
Dremels
Com tower
GI JOE
Bartell's / Candy
QFC Apparel

Model Magic Homies?

* Cardboard backdrops
* GI Joe Cop
* Hand cuffs
* Dremels for Dad

large Plastic Storage bins

Sony Handy Cam

Greg
Jamie
Me

Bartells – Candy

More Freddies...

* Xerox Copies
* Magnetic backing
* H&L casters
* Extension for Play station

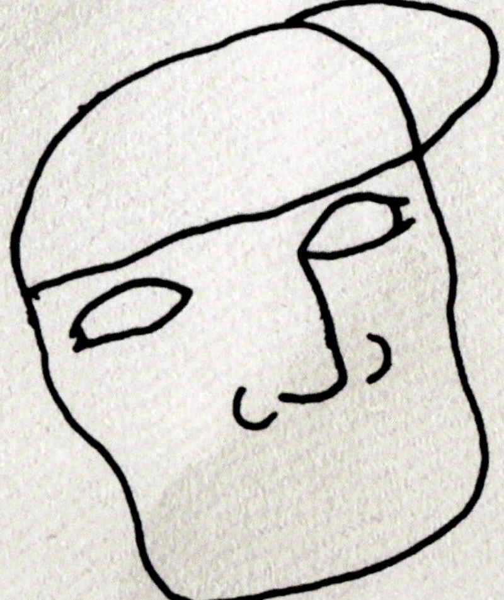

Mark

Tonight may be the last
Tommorow's delay seems ordain
My Friends hooked in, artifial
~~Gland~~
Gonna drain, I should be there
Stick around friend
What I touch, It seems
Seems like 180° Midas.
King tough, might be fatal
Didn't want to, but I did
Love to pull anyone back
~~Rate~~ Be encouragement
It's ok? right?
It ain't
Tell me it's ok to
Sleep again,
Perhaps, it'll be ok!
Be OK?!

DIAMOND
LIE

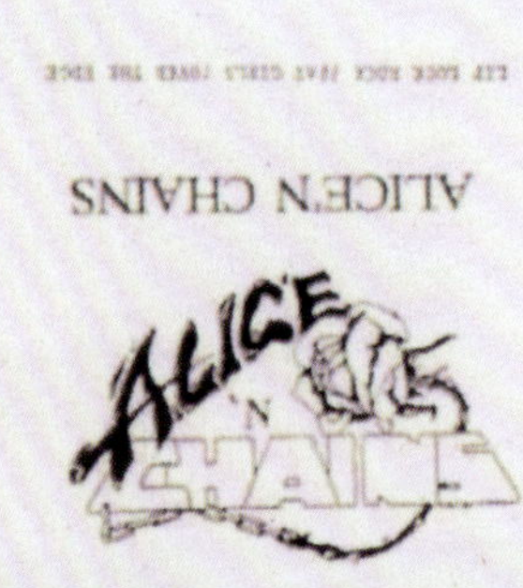

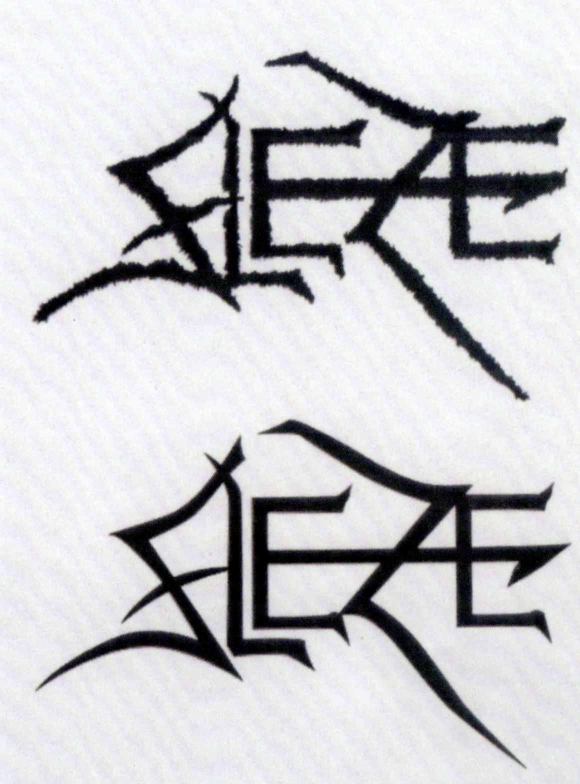

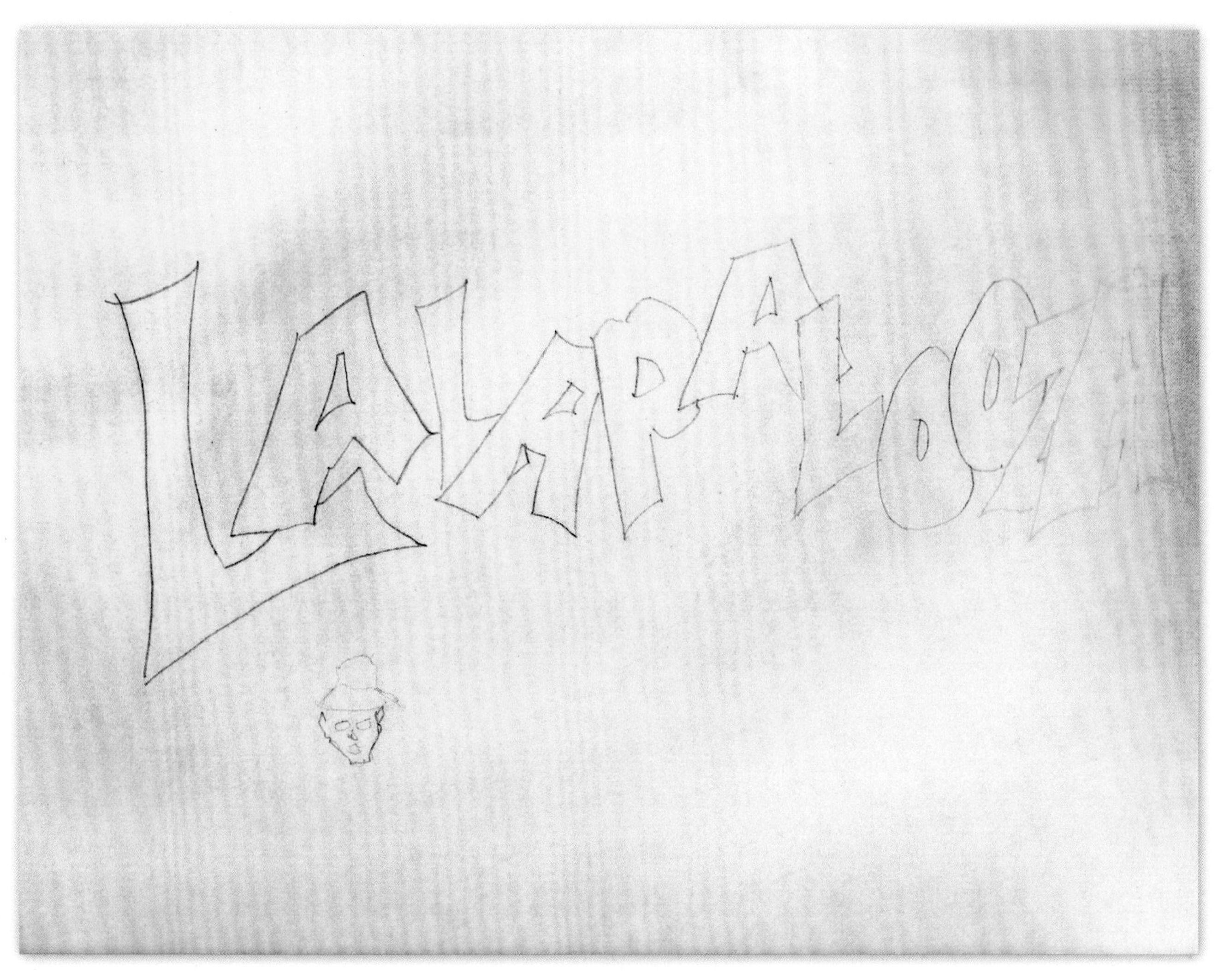
LALAPALOOZ

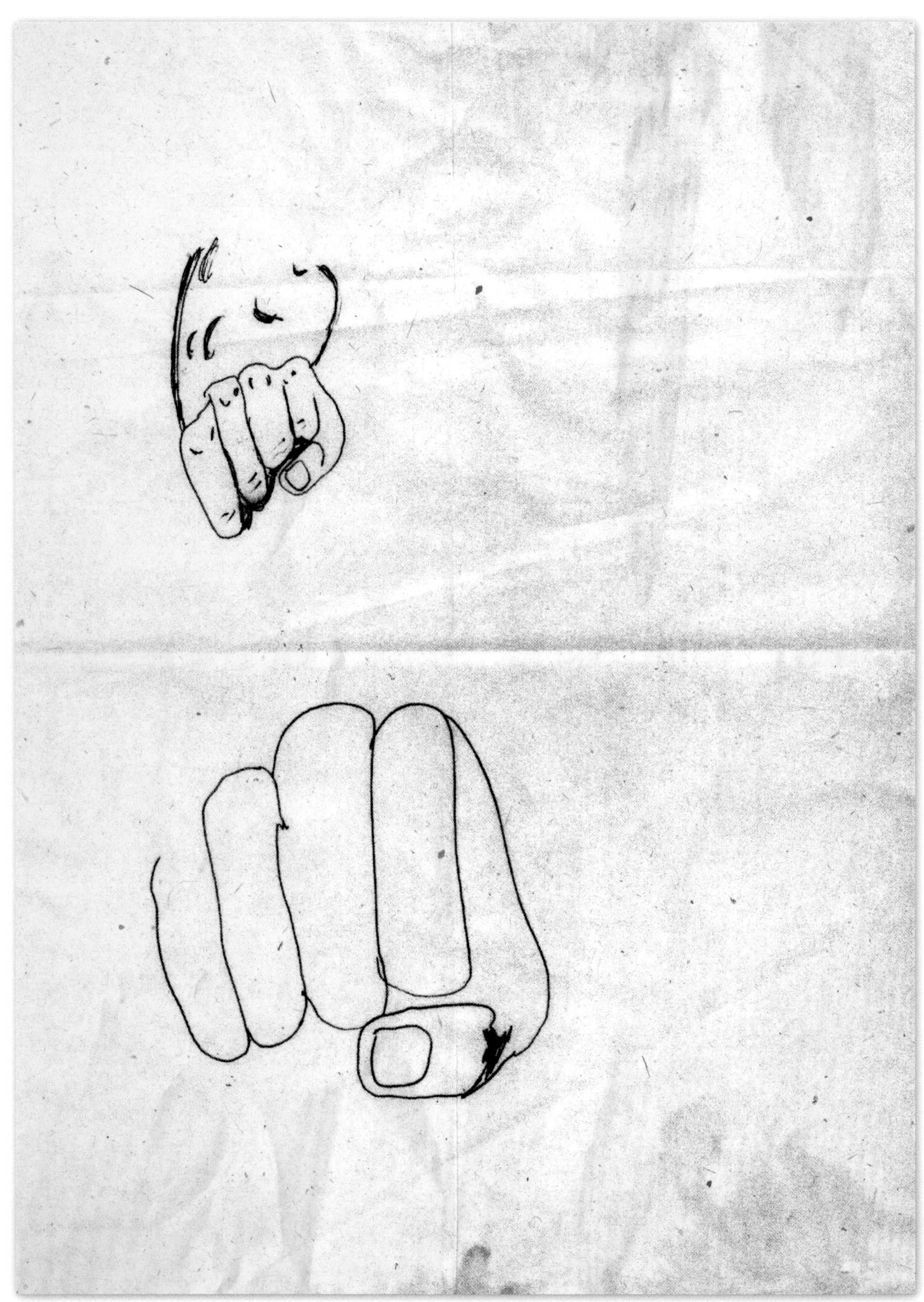

Hands take practice!

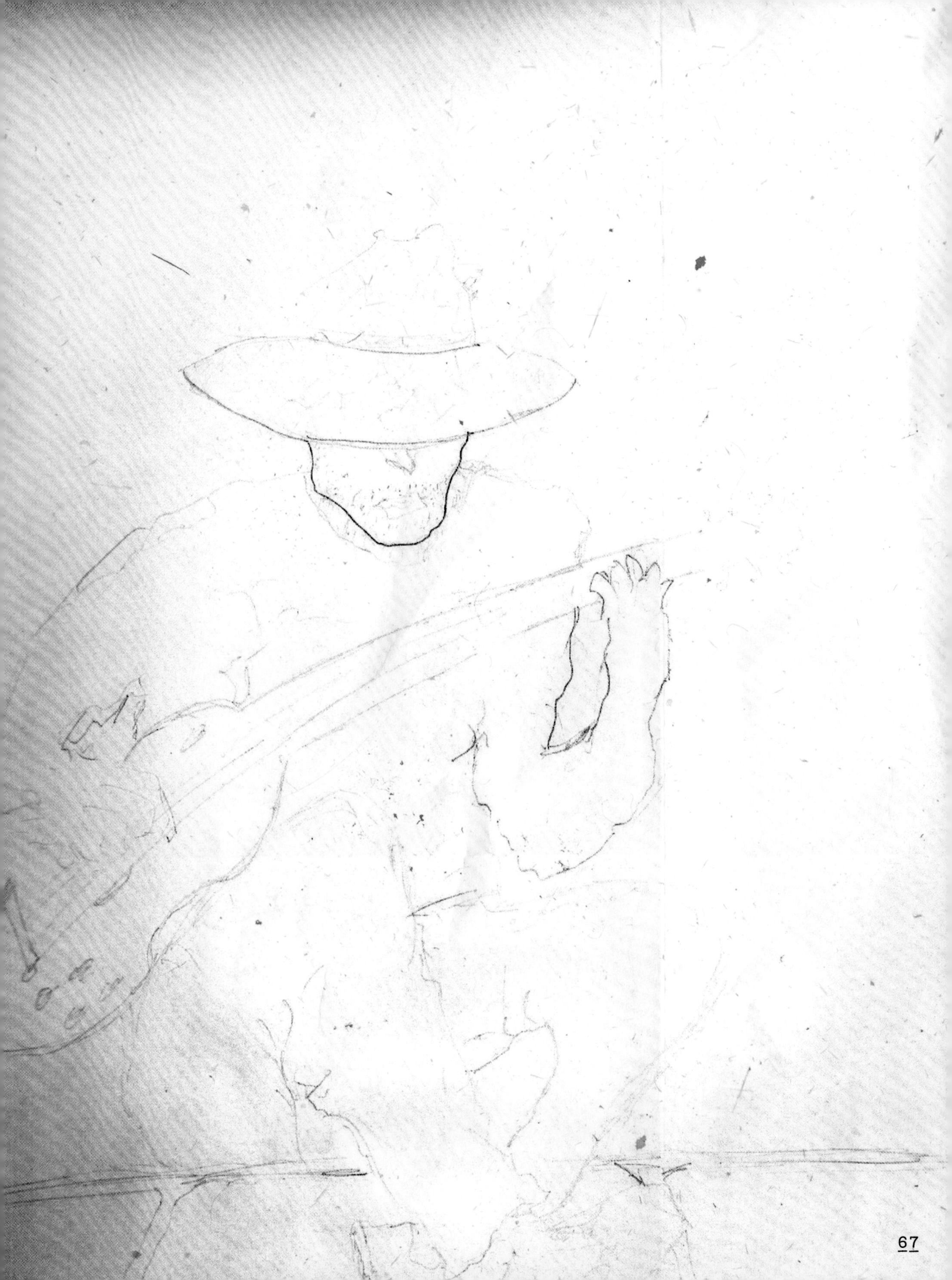

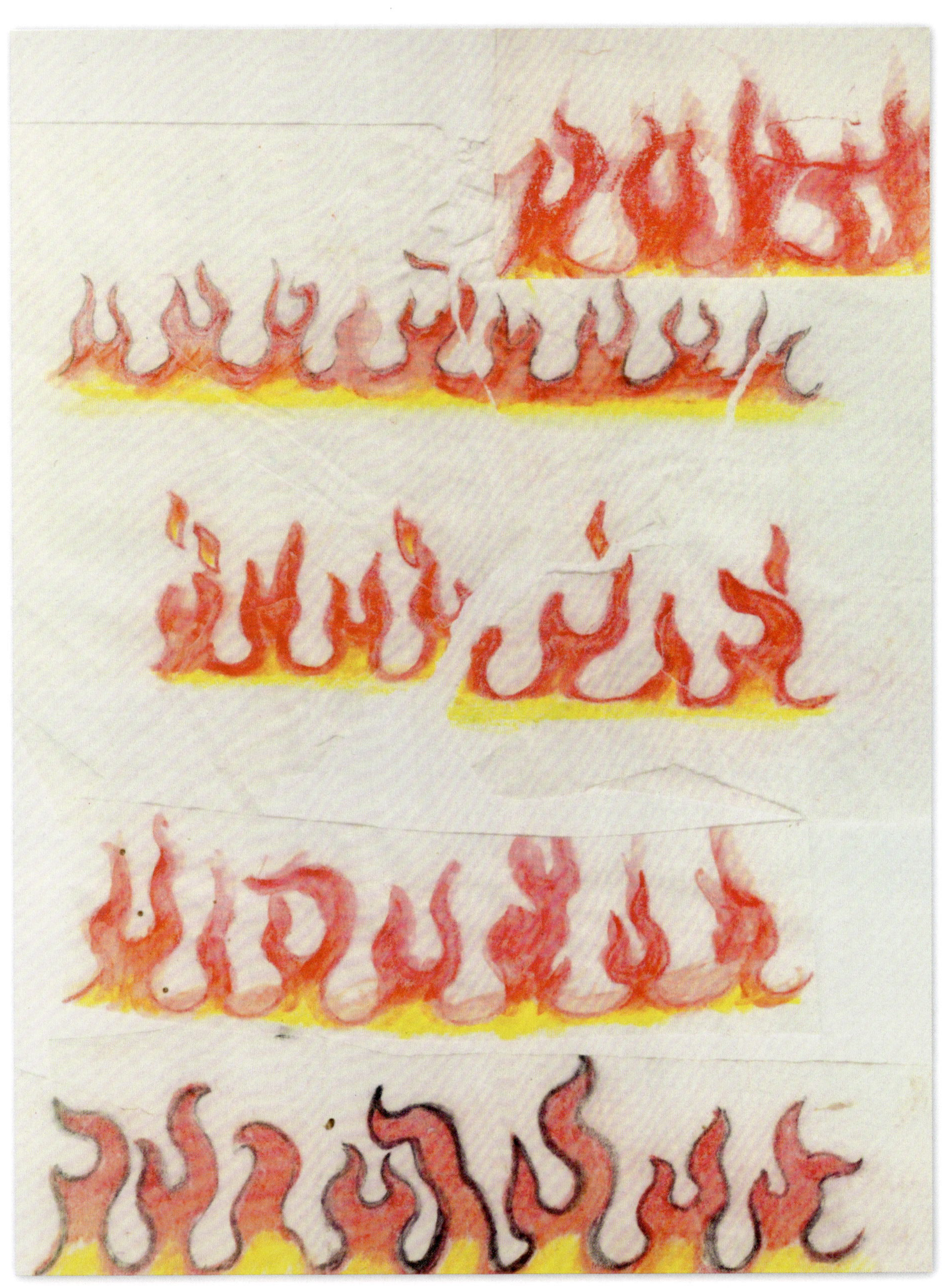

He did lots of flame doodles.

I came - I saw - I conquered
vene-vidi-vici

sieze the day
carpe diem

My journey always begins here
But it seems I'm always thrown
back a little farther
Inching closer to a better destiny
than a written tragedy
With a misspelled name

What a high, with the heavy cold
Of a piece in my hand !
Wouldn't that be grand, with such
Power and all my hate
And I could pull it, too
In slow, watch and feel it break
The skin on your neck
Or the soft of your belly
Double over and see nothing
But your disgusting life pass before you
I hope it lasts forever, pig

Too bad it can't be so easy
Instead It soaks in through
My lying shell of a man at peace
I am not at peace and have great
Doubts that I will ever be
But still I strive as any who are
Like me must
Too change this confused whirlpool
Of disastrous thought
Do you Imagine yourself, in frustration
Rapeing?
Or in anger, harming others?
In depression, ending your life?
All that we know is wrong
So stop, and know again, that it's
allright To Feel.

Rediscovering innocence + humility
My journey always begins here
But it seems I'm always thrown
Back a little further
Inching closer to a better destiny
Than a written tragedy.
With a mispelled name...

Satanoscilatemymetalicsonatas

Satan oscilatemymetalic sonatas

SATAN OSCILATE MY
METALIC SONATAS

~~Get up and~~ dance
~~Roll around~~ on
~~the floor~~
Feel the rythym
of the beat and
then you start
to ~~dance~~ move & get
out of youre
seats

Stole

It happend 14 years ago.
The transformation
An innocent, lonely child
Abandoned himself
And for 14 years now,
His borrowed mind has taken on
Many new identities
Each with their own decided list
Of rules, morals, and wicked habits

This was never an inconvienience
Until that boy of twelve,
Thought to have been left behind,
began spying these atrocities
Fighting to regain the body
That was harboring these monsters
And victory was always his
But not knowing it was given him
With the intention of a soon to be
Broken spirit

He has played witness to some awful things
He has mocked the living dead
Then been forced to live among them
He could only watch
As the body he hoped to regain
Was sabotaged with poisons

I hope to travel, south of
Medicine wheel
Rediscovering innocence
My journey always beg
But it seems I'm alway
Back a little farther
Inching closer to a be
Than a written traged
With a misspelled name

Thousand eyes, a fly
Lucky they'd be
In one day deceased... Sick man

I can feel the wheel, but I can't steer
When my thoughts become my biggest fear

Aaah - what's the diffrence I'll die
Aaah - ~~come~~ to this sick world of mine

What the Hell am I?
Leper from inside
Inside wall of peace
Dirty + diseased, sick man

I can feel the end is getting near,
I won't rest until my head is clear

Aaah - what's the diffrence I'll die
Aaah - ~~come~~ in to this sick world of mine

Bridge
Can you see the end?
Choke on ~~thy~~ me, my friend
Must to drown these thoughts
Purity over rot

"Sickman" by Alice in Chains. Released in 1992 from the album Dirt.

Sits on the lap of leprosy
She is afflicted-
But denies her illness exists

I know a girl who'll
Do anything for a fix
To mend the stomach
which hides the dirty secret

I know a girl who
Lies to be who taught her how
But it's her health first
And the weak continues self [illegible]

I know a girl who ~~would~~ tell
Who would sell her mother
Without first telling her
That she loves her

I know a child
who is trapped underneath
lead weight & someone
unfamiliar

I know a child
Who is helpless
To direct herself [illegible]
To day [illegible]

Some place this is now
One more run could kill
so stay, learn see now
9th day, keep praying

why me? why me? why me? why me

can't you see, oh
fucked your high, up
Getting clean, oh
But my head says
Try again lover
Taste once more forever
~~shoot~~ swallow-drink-smoke-shoot

Those who are starved for salvation
Need not be force-fed a savior.
Proven millions will swallow Jesus
As easily as they would a pill
To numb pains.
Believe in me, you, and that is
Hypocritical faith does not
Wash the soul of that which
Causes guilt,
~~For a clear~~ consciousness
~~Is not bought or achieved,~~
~~It is retained.~~
Accepting forgiveness In ~~God's name~~ the name of the lord
condemning those who don't
Chant your magical oath
~~But~~ the only true goodness + purity
of mind
One cannot demand + declare

Some say you're goin downhill boy
I say I've never been uphill boy
One day maybe I'll know me better
~~Perhaps~~ Someday I'll die and leave a letter

Dying, oh
Inside, so
Confidence, low
I'd like to go
Learning, slow
Lost my glow
What I know
Pain does flow

Rob and I took a break from hell, yeah
Brought a little with us keepin' well
Time to get my head into shape now
Drag my spirit from the clouds now

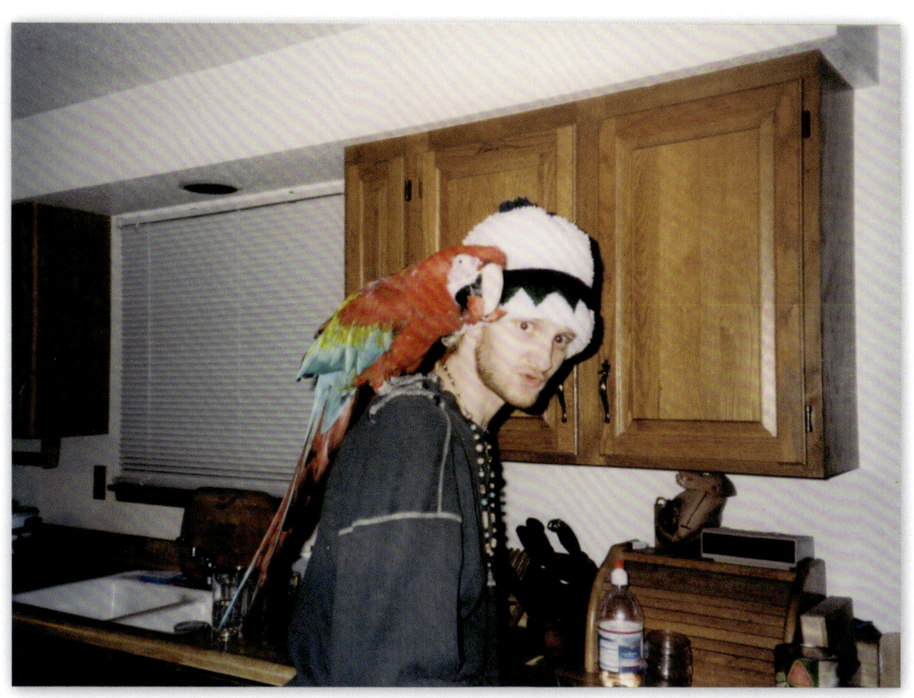

He had many whimsical hats made by his cherished friend, Rachel. Photograph by Nancy McCallum.

convine convene
convienant convienently
convieniantly

Those who would crucify me.
Insanity
Is a short
story, the author
will be remenbred
for a short time
In comparison to
the imensity

Searching for the right spelling.

What I feel right now

Hurt, frightened, alone
Empty, blank, dark, heavy
Hateful, sad, depressed
Confused, disgusted, sick
Worried, insecure, dead
In pain, secluded, psychotic,
Sadistic, lost, withdrawn
Bored, small, unbalanced.
I don't care if I die now
I'd like to know what
it would feel like to
take someone's life.
Stabbing.
Imagine the guilt.
That could keep my
mind busy for a long time
Imagine the high
Surge, rush, sickness, rush
Panic, grief....

My hunger for turmoil is
GROWING

The Dream:

What a high, with the heavy cold
Of a piece in my hand,
Wouldn't that be grand.
With such power and all this hate
I could pull it, too
In slow, watch and feel it break
The skin on your neck
Or the soft of your belly
Double over and see nothing
But your disgusting existence pass before yo
I hope it lasts forever, pig!

Waking Thoughts:

Too bad it can't be so easy
Instead, it soaks in,
Through my lying shell of a man at peace
I am not at peace and have great
Doubts that I will ever be
But still I strive as any who feel
like this must
To change this confused whirlpool of
Disastrous thought
Imagine yourself in frustration, raping.
Or in anger, taking the life of another.
In depression taking your own life.
All that we know is wrong, evil.
Yet, these troubling dreams feel more real
Than the numbness of being awake.
And if the numbness were actually the dreams?

ed 14 years ago.
formation.
nt child

Teeth sink in deep to sicken + kill
Something around us is stirring up pain
A movement, look, or a threat
No control over the hate I have under
My skin to protect me is torn
You ask how I do it, No balls to destroy me
Adrenelyn helps me, I bleed + I'm high

Yeah, Yeah, Disfunction can beat you
He'll fuck with your mind, mind
Mine has been dilluted with mud for some time
Time, time to touch on your senses
Or drown in your pity, pity
Pity the fool who knows nothing more
Than what he's taught

Control is one thing I'm obsessed with having
Why then remorse for the acts I decide?
Blackened thoughts in me, addiction created
Disgust me, Insane? How bout you?
Here I sit nervously digging my callous
Years of repulsion, the search for the core
Rape + religion, not my way to heaven
Search for my self and then, someday,
Above you I'll fly

Lifeless, dead, that unclean bed
Til or when her hungers fed
How he'd wished that they would wed
"I promise on our love" she said."
Promises were never kept
Alone on dirty floor he slept
And although he'd not accept
She was gone and so he wept
Then a demon came to him, said
"Bring your mouth down to the tin,
You must know that I'm gonna win,
I helped her put the needle in"
But he rose out of the shit
So little had even touched his lips
He's tempted for a couple sips
Though Hell would make a better trip

Based on a true story.
by [illegible]

Names, roles, characters are
purely fictional. Any similarities
are coincidental and this [illegible]
unintentionally describing each
readers personal relationship.

Waiting

Lady of another place won't serve
the man downstairs
Man of a million thoughts but
A boy with an empty stare
I require only a little true praise
For who I am
Not who I appear to be.
Generations of Disease
Have left me with the inability
to be myself
He who I have not yet met
Though pointing the finger at any
one thing only
Points three at the man I truly be
Anxiety for the plane
That will take me to another place
Where I will surely see yet
another friendly face
Waiting is most certainly
The worst punishment that can
be bestowed upon me
But I'll wait again
Till the drunken haze
Lowers my face .. to the ground
Only 5 minutes
Till the Lady from another place
Will serve me but another taste
of Disruption

Layne Staley

What I Know

I know a girl who sits
In the lap of leprecy
She is afflicted
But denies she is affected

I know a girl who will do
Anything for a fix
To mend the stomach
That holds a dirty secret

I know a girl who lies to
The one who taught her how
Only, to her self first,
And the confusion is penetrated

I know a girl who would
Sell her mother, and
Never tell her mother
How much she loved her

I know a child, who is
Trapped inside the body
Of Someone unfamiliar

I know a child who is helpless
To direction of foe, willing,
To take the unwilling

I know a devil who does not go away
But, assumes less dominance
When weak from lack of affection

Who am I?
A man that does most truly
Love someone who, most
convieniantly, cannott wait
for the truest she will ever
Find.
Self Pity? Only to be thrown
By those who would crucify
Me or mine.
This insanity is a short story
Me being the author who is
Remembered for, and forgotten in,
Such a short time.
So very short, in comparison
to the imensity of this
madness, but, even more so, for
The imensity of this Love.
But who cares? Who but I?

10-92

Why we have to live with
so much hate every day
Why the fighting they're in the
comin' down am I sane
I don't know
When the teacher puts the
ruler down on my hand
I laugh
Cross my heart and hide
reliever in trails of blood
I love

I don't know anything
I don't who I am
who to be

"I Don't Know Anything" by Mad Season.
Released in March 14, 1995, from the album Above.

Tonight my buddie's sedated
~~[illegible]~~
So I decline to my bunk
Humid, sticking to my sheets
Buddy's got a problem and
~~It~~ I ain't me
Tonight long hair's frustrated
So I leap into nuetral
Angry, amused I hit him
Worm needed a hand and
It was mine

~~So if you let me [illegible] It hurt you~~
~~Beat you to dirt before masses~~

Well, you can't get by without a little shove towards hell from your "friends."

I never think the people I choose to be around could be capable of anything truly, knowingly evil.

Everybody gets wicked, and nasty from time to time, but some of those who dont, those who act shocked by our mischievious acting out, might just be the witch in fair maiden's cloth.

Being a firm believer in Karma, I know that those who dish it out, get a pie back in the face.

I consider myself blessed with the gift of witnessing a full circle of Karma returned in full force to the original giver of grief.

See, There was this girl, who, in her profession, started where they all do, stealing, & soliciting ~~sometimes~~, borrowing money for drugs & the~~n selling small amounts to support the habit~~

Well this one girl inparticular (who shall remain nameless) started at the bottom, and worked her way up to a small empire (well maybe not empire) in a short amount of time and made many friends and seemed very good hearted.

One of her friends was a friend of mine as well, who was also stealing, borrowing, and eventually soliciting.

When girl number one got hooked on crack.

Feb 10 1992

Me + Dem did our last shots this morning but I can't feel it anymore. At the airport, on our way to drug treatment. It'll be great not to rely on this shit anymore. I'm excited to be healthy again, mentally and physically. Physically I'm skinny, I've lost alot of weight and I'm weak. Mentally I'm dead inside, and have no creative energy - I need to get it back. I'm excited to get all my strength back. I've heard that detox-ing in a place like this is pretty cushy, but I'm so strung, I can't imagine I will feel no pain at all. I just hope I can sleep. I hope it's easy on Dem too. She doesn't like hurting and she feels sick alot, I'm sure it won't be cushy enough for her. I just hope she doesn't run away like she has before. I want us to get healthy together, but if she decides she's not ready again, I will still continue my program, but I love and care about her alot, and I want her to feel good, especially about herself.

Morning Glory

Andy

You been thinkin' too much
You been worried for too long
I like this space,
Can I give you some?
Thousand miles from home
Lord shall I ask you again?
Long ago, So long
But your smile still means the
World to me

(oh) That smile, enough to build a dream on
That pretty, pretty face
(oh) That smile, enough to break down walls
But not your own

You been countin' the days
Can I call you sometime?
Baby, stay young and brave
And be forever mine
You may be thinkin' this is bullshit
And not pertaining to you
But denial and resentment
Will keep you off your food -

* I'm to blame for the morning glory days:

I been dancing all alone
Not wearing pants at all
I am more than just confused
My words "not now, not now"

A good night, the best in a long time
A new friend turned me on to an old favorite
Nothing better than a dealer who's high
Be high, convince 'em to buy

What's my drug of choice?
Well, What have you got? chorus
I don't go broke
And I do it alot

Seems so sick to the hypocrit norm
Running their boring drills
But we are an elete race of our own
The stoners, junkies, and freaks

Are you happy, I am man
Content + fully aware
Money, status, nothing to me
'Cause your life's empty + bare

-chorus-

You can't understand a user's mind
But try with your books and degrees
If you let yourself go and opend
Your mind, I'll bet you'd be usin'
like me and it ain't so bad

"Junkhead" by Alice in Chains. Released in 1992 from the album Dirt.

Can you see the end?
Choke on me, my friend
Must, to drown these thoughts
Purity over rot

I can feel the end is getting near
I won't rest until my head is clear

Aaah - what's the diffrence I'll die
Aaah - come to this sick world of mine
Aaah - each day in fear of myself
Aaah what's the diffrence I'll die

What the hell Am I
Thousand eyes, a fly
Lucky then I'd be!
In one day deceased
Sickman, sickman, sickman

What the hell Am I
[illegible]

"Sickman" by Alice in Chains. Released in 1992 from the album Dirt.

What the Hell am I?
Thousand eyes, a fly
Lucky then, I'd be
In one ~~deceased~~
Sickman, Sick man, Sic

I can feel the wheel but
When my thoughts become m

Aaah, what's the diffrenc
Aaah, Come to this sick

What the Hell am I?
Leper, from inside
Inside wall of peace
Dirty + diseased

I'll not live for any one
Selfish maybe but from th

"Sickman" by Alice in Chains. Released in 1992 from the album Dirt.

Straw that broke your back, you're under
Cast all them aside who care
Empty eyes and dead end stare

Don't you know, none are blind
To the lie, And you think
I don't find ~~shit~~ what you hide?
~~Answer me~~

What in God's name have you done?
Stick your arm for some real fun
So your sickness weighs a ton
And God's name is smack for some

For the horse you've grown fonder
Than for me, That, I don't ponder
As the hair of one who bit you
Smiling, bite your own sElf too?

And I think you're not blind
~~To~~ To the one's you left behind.
I'll be here ~~or very near~~
~~Always~~

"Godsmack" by Alice in Chains. Released in 1992 from the album Dirt.

So crazy feel my pain
So lazy drunk and drain
So angle will it rain
So let me be the same

Lonliness follows me, unshakeable
Much quicker than the darkness
Crawls to the surface of my skin
Visibly surrounded by it

Surrounded by empty souls whose
Courage is found only in bottles
And because so was mine once found,
I walk this maze alone ... alone

Black is all I feel, so this is how
it feels to be free?

The man is beside himself
Man is below himself
Man is behind himself
Am I inside myself?

Chaos & hate shadow me
Pain, it fills me up
Only one thing makes me feel
Missing better half of me

"Am I Inside" by Alice in Chains. Released in 1992 from the albums Dirt *and* Sap.

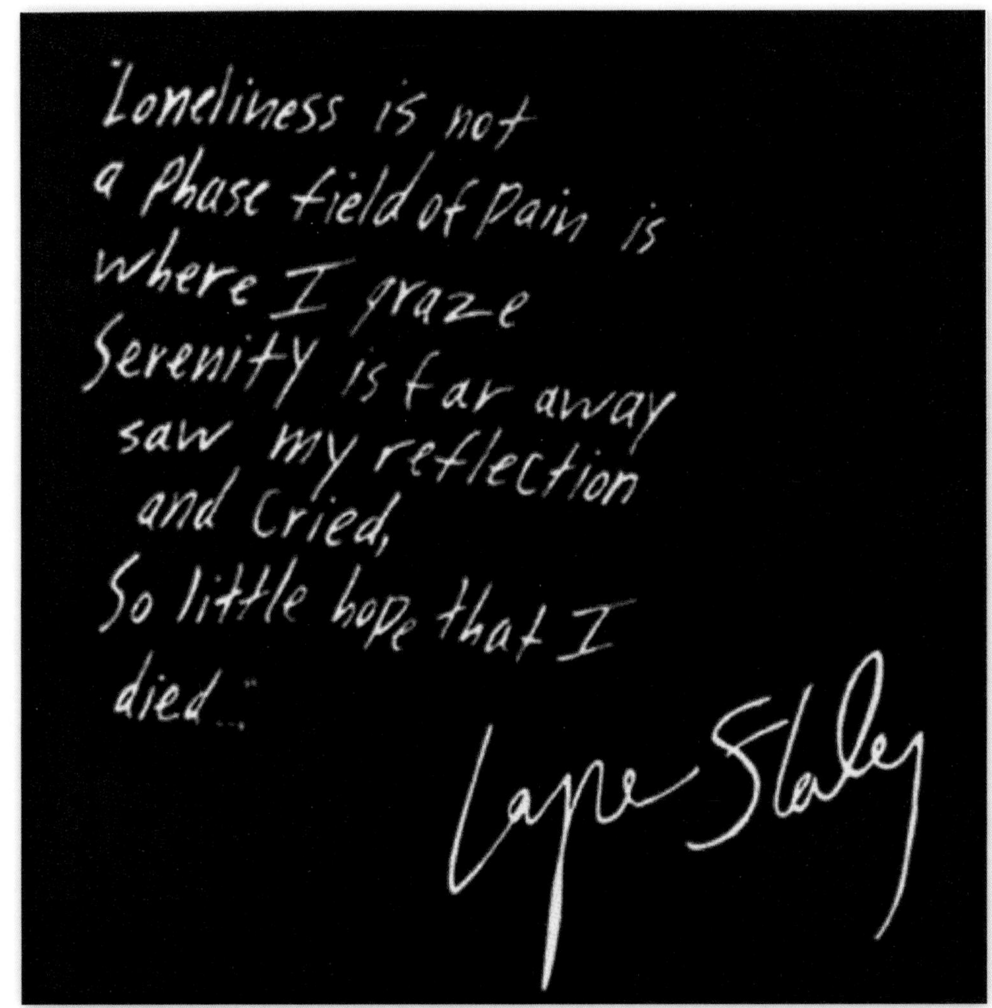

"Angry Chair" by Alice in Chains. Released in 1992 from the album Dirt. *Note Layne's correct signature.*

seen the brightest light
put up such a fight
hing all your life
urhing like a knife

now the reasons why
high or you will die

"Godsmack" by Alice in Chains. Released in 1992 from the album Dirt.

The greatest gift in
Living, is knowing you will
Someday Die
The hardest part is finding
a way to kill time while
waiting...

Layne rarely dated his work. Dating meant something significant to him.

Thousand eyes, a fly
Lucky then I'd be
In one day deceased... Sick man

I can feel the wheel, but I can't steer
When my thoughts become my biggest fear

Aaah - what's the diffrence I'll die
Aaah - ~~come~~ to this sick world of mine

What the Hell am I?
Leper from inside
Inside wall of peace
Dirty + diseased, sick man

I can feel the end is getting near
I won't rest until my head is clear

Aaah - what's the diffrence I'll die
Aaah - ~~come~~ to this sick world of mine

Bridge Can you see the end?
in
Choke on ~~thy~~ me, my friend
Lust, to drown these thoughts
Purity over rot

"Sickman" by Alice in Chains. Released in 1992 from the album Dirt.
Compare different versions of the same lyrics/poem to see the writer's progression.

Stripper -

Yeah YeahYeah
Fat Girls - Rap after first chorus
Sealed - rap before song
Over the edge
Don't be - quick rap
Queen of the rodeo - Intro
Hush Hush
Lip Lokk Rokk
Crowd participation
Bass Solo
Lip Lokk - Trumpets
Tracy - Hike football
Football
Glamourous Girls
out w/ Don't be - Picture, Party

Fat Girls
Lip Lock
Hanky Panky
One way
Don't be
Glamourous
Boys in Blouses

Sealed with a Kiss
Hush Hush
Alice in Chains
Nasty Letters
Fairy Nuff
Boy/Girl Boy
I Play Doctor
Cuttin Class
Girl Next Door
Pleasure Island
Maid of Honor

Set lists for shows.

I live high up on a hill now,
Nervously waiting for my new sanctuary
To come crashing down, Knowing full well

Layne had just moved into his University District condo.

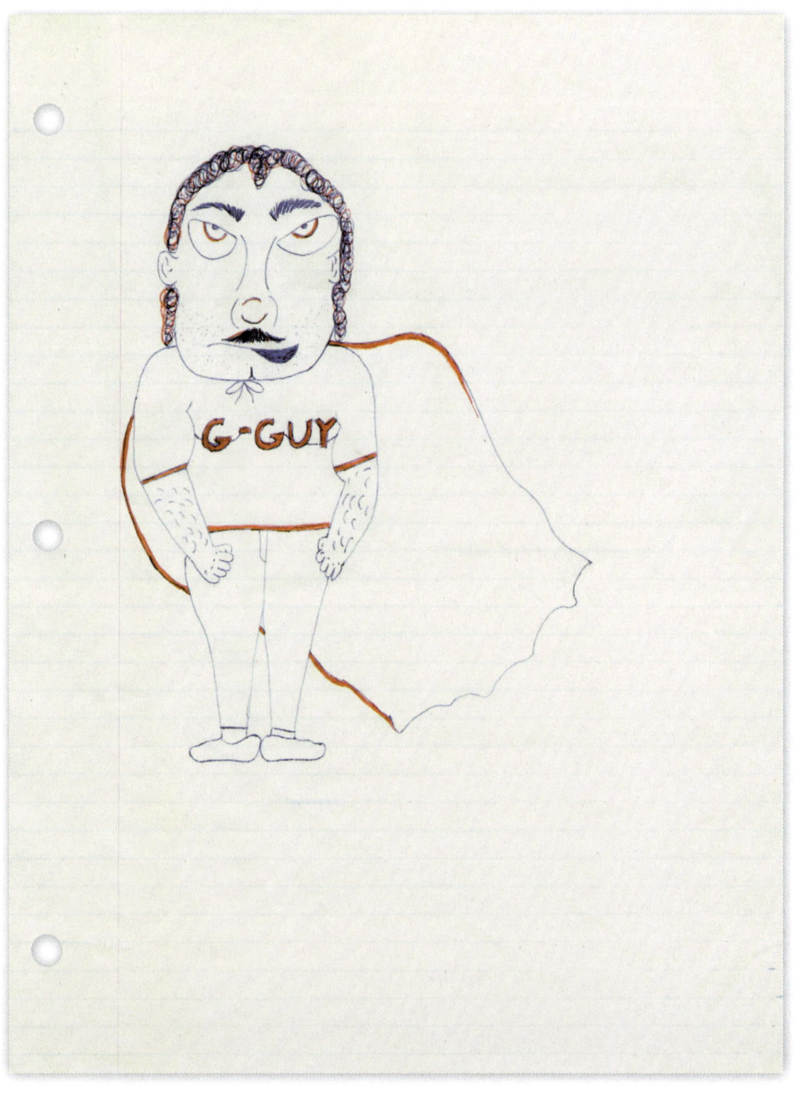

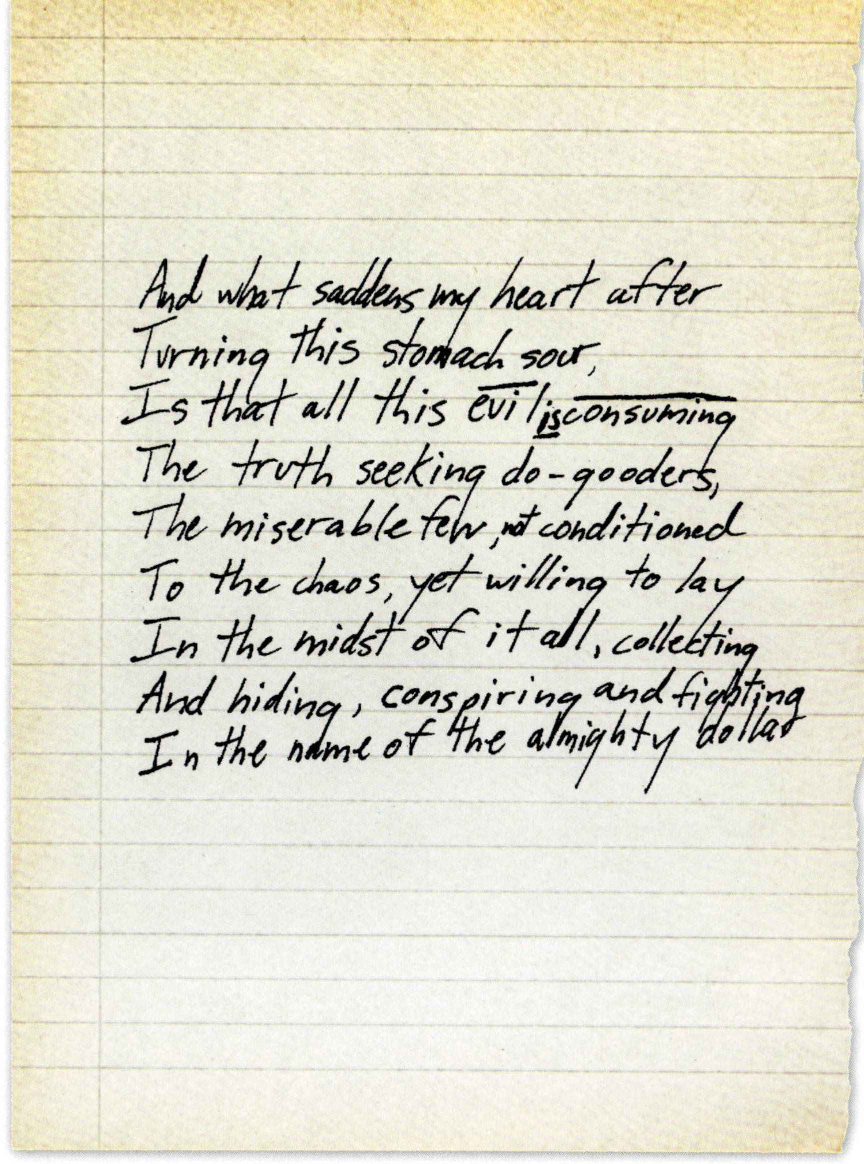
And what saddens my heart after
Turning this stomach sour,
Is that all this evil is consuming
The truth seeking do-gooders,
The miserable few, not conditioned
To the chaos, yet willing to lay
In the midst of it all, collecting
And hiding, conspiring and fighting
In the name of the almighty dollar

He had similar musings in "I'm Above," Mad Season.

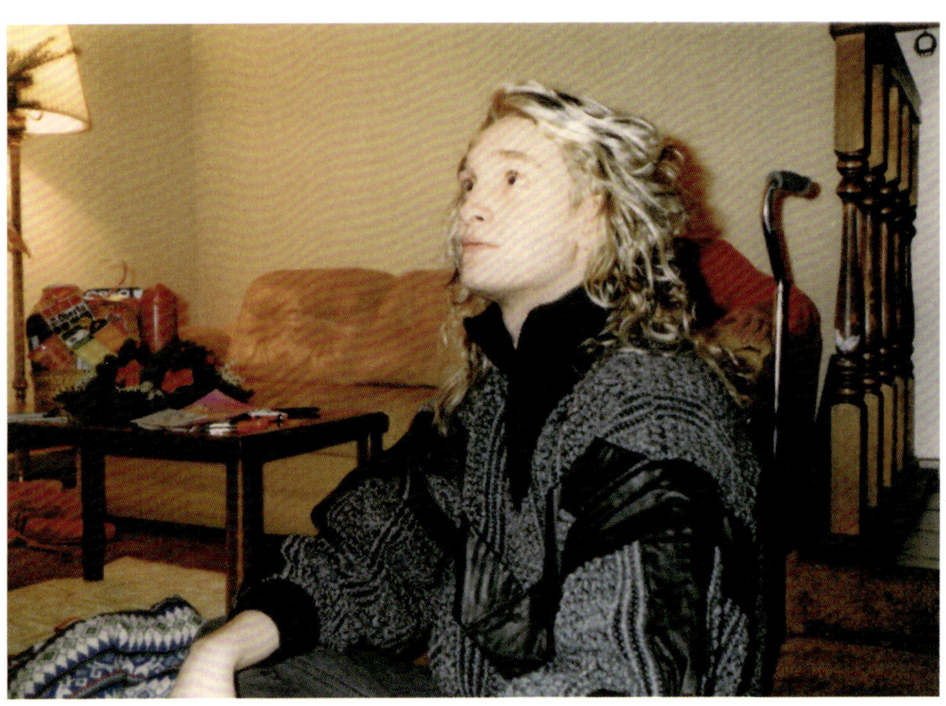

Christmas at the Elmers' house. Grandpa Layne in background.

An early version of lyrics . . . compare with ongoing versions.

Betzold 328-0718

Was it something I said, or was it our bed, or the roof I so selfishly put over your head?

~~that turned you into~~

I don't lose track of their names when the story's the same, and a freeway of dirt coarses through the veins of a tainted soul, where perhaps the remains of a beautiful innocence still lies dormant. Your body is a temple, and your mind an alter to where infantile men and children, rich in materialism and poor in self worth and individuality, kneel in front of you and lie inside you, buying penance and purchasing a place in heaven with just enough poison to build on false character while slowly chiseling away at true beauty.

These parasites have adapted to my pain. Before,

Core

Self Imprisonment.
I suppose somewhere inside me
I yearn for freedom from
That which holds me stagnant
Over exagegeration turns under estimated
Emotion...
Emotion. Why the urgency to hide and
Slow the flow of, that which could,
And perhaps will, Improve and
Heal the burning inside?
I am protecting my pain
It is mine!
And I so badly want to keep my
Pain to myself
But, in doing so I am hurting
So many who cross, or care for me.
Aching for love and acceptance
Only to throw you down in the latter
of our shared love
Yet anger and guilt not shared between
Me and you
You are blamed for all that is a mystery
Whithin myself - Burning
Oh I pray that I might someday
Throw a blanket over that angry child
If the strength is found within the
Core of my being
His tears soak my **heart** and weigh
it down
I am tired, I am numb, and I am so
very, very lonely
I am...

May 93

A final copy was delivered to The Rocket *for publishing.*

Set The Sick Ones Free Andy

Nothings free when you got bad habits
I been there, I been down
Look to me when you need company
Ain't got no time too precious to share

Nothings gained when you get on a rollerride
You can lose it all if you don't
watch yo' ass
Call me morning, day, or night
I'd give my life to free you from disease

Set the sick ones free {chorus}
Ooh Set the sick ones free
God Set the sick ones free - including me

In my life there's been sorrow
There's been joy and incontested love
I beg of you please do the footwoork
Bless the one who tries to help themselves

'Cause no one wins with a needle
As we know, though who will try
Fight the sickness, the illed weakness
Cause God loves ya children, loves you all

{chorus}

Signs of treatment, and hopes for recovery and sponsorship.

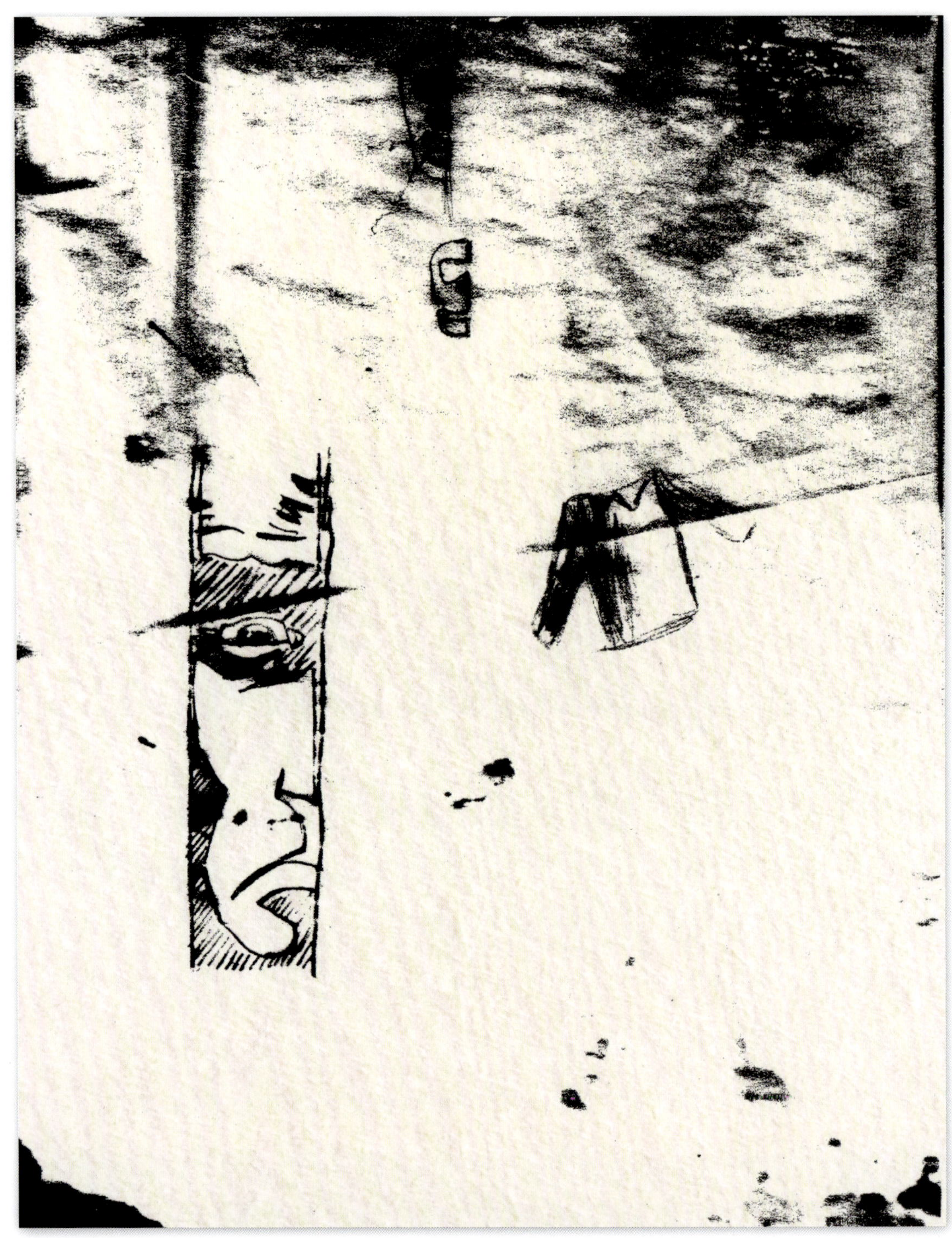

"Here's looking at you."

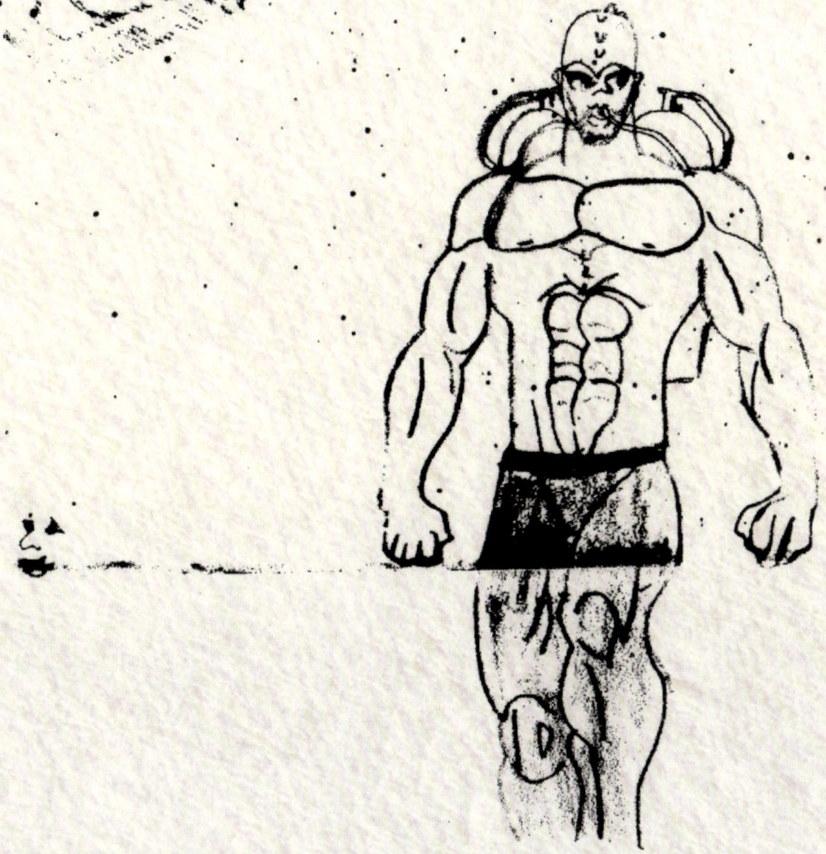

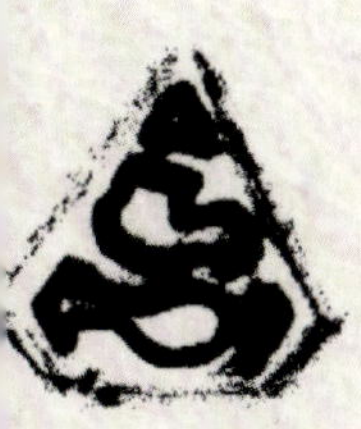

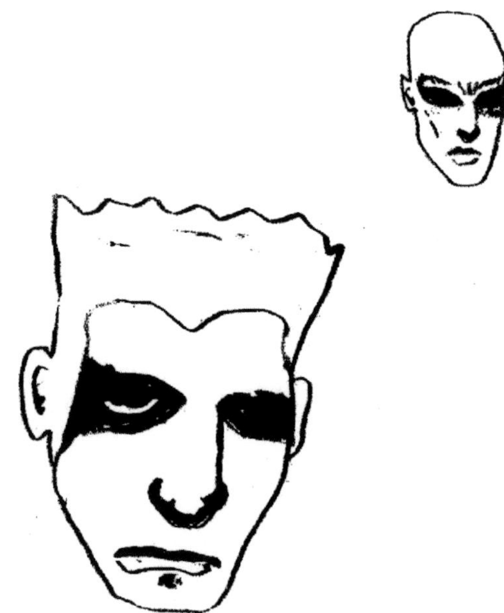

Layne collected comic books and action figures.

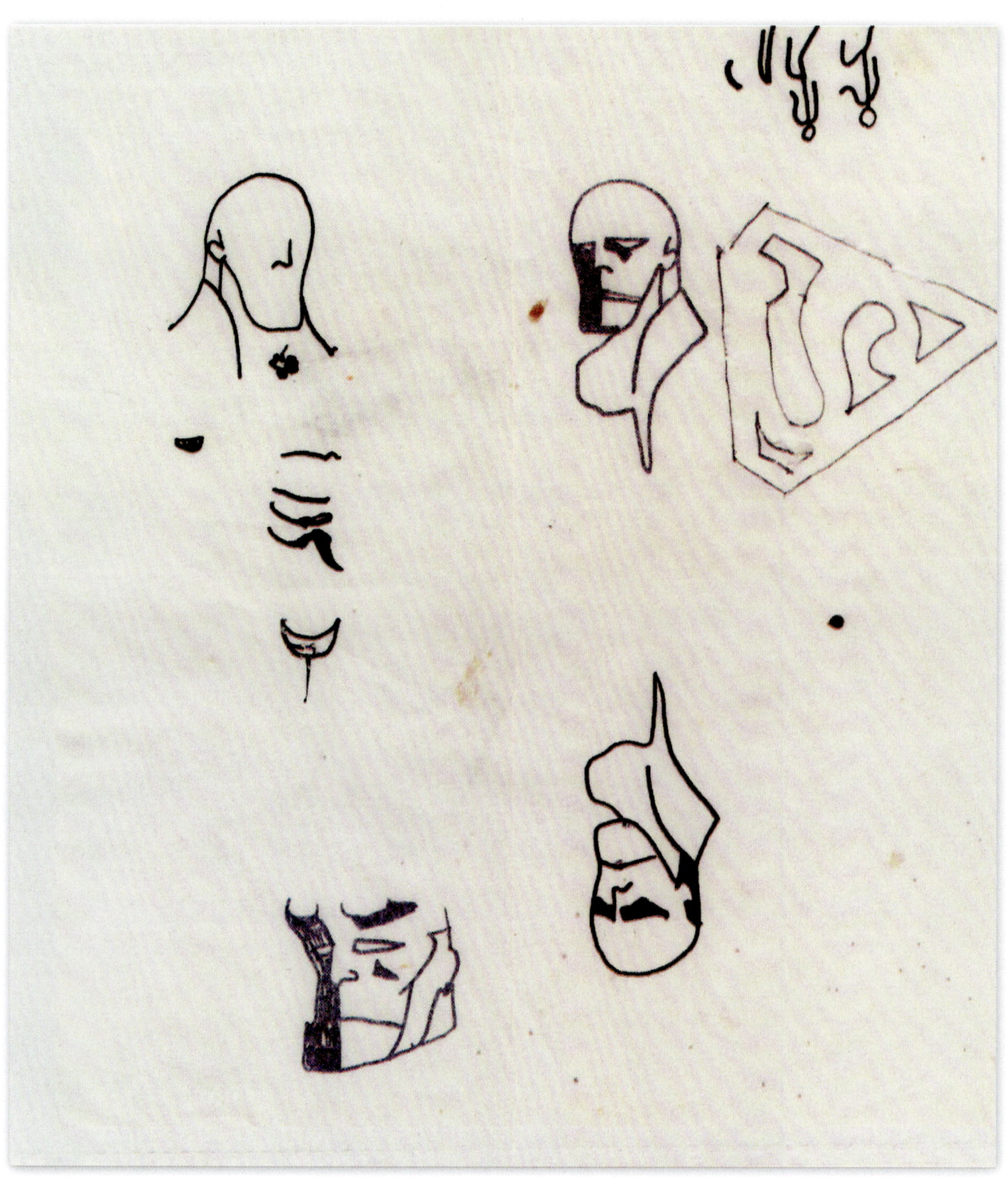

His drawings were structural along bone and muscle lines.

How the mind does shout for rest
When the body is shaky
And the stomach is weak
My endless search for a description of
my nightmare
Ɏ

"A Little Bitter" by Alice in Chains. Released in 1993 from the soundtrack to Last Action Hero.

Disentegration
How the mind does shout for rest
When the body is shaky
And the stomach is weak
My endless search for a description of my
Nightmare
Is in actuality just a pitiful search
for a self centered pardon,
For a self destructive pattern.
Silently I cry out to a mind decidedly deaf
To the one who cried wolf once to many
With the exception of the voice of foul substance
Though knowingly longing,
for self destruction comes in many well
thought out ways—
Had it not been this
Had it not been now
That, would eventually come then,
When, is the only flaw in the master plan

Nov. 92

"A Little Bitter" by Alice in Chains. Released in 1993 from the soundtrack to Last Action Hero.

Disintegration

How the mind does shout for rest
When the body's shaky and the stomach, weak.
My endless search for an explanation
Is in fact just a pitiful search for a self centered pardon
For a self destructive pattern.

Observing the process.

Disentegration

How the mind does shout for rest
When the body is shaky, and the stomach, weak
My endless search, for a description of my
nameless suffering.
It Is really just a pitiful excuse, the reward
of a self centered pardon,
For my self destructive pattern.
Silent, I cry out to a mind decidedly deaf
to the one who cried wolf once to many,
With the exception of the voice of foul substance
Though Knowingly longing, for personal disentegratio
Comes to one in meny ~~th~~ well thought out way
For had it not been this,
And had it not been now,
That, would eventually come Then,
When, is the only flaw

"A Little Bitter" by Alice in Chains. Released in 1993 from the soundtrack to Last Action Hero.

Mother said come home
Father said come home
Sisters said come home
So my friends said come home

I said

chorus
Let me be, I'm alright
Can't you see, I'm just fine
Little Skinny, OK
I'm asleep anyway

Then I heard a voice
Said "son you have a choice"
I then slapped my face
Allow me to taste

2nd chorus
Let me be, I'm OK
I'm awake anyway
~~It's too bright over here~~
I can shift cannot steer
So I drive them away
For Awhile, then I stay
~ Solo ~

Little Skinny, OK
I'm awake anyway

Now I have to go home
Do as, when in think

Let me be I'm alright
Can't you see I'm just fine
Little Skinny, OK
I'm alseep anyway
Let me be I'm OK

I'm awake anyway

4.00
6.00
4.00
7.00
1.00
2.00

24.00
15.00
43.00
12.00
20.00
22.00
45.00

Acheived

“Swing on This” by Alice in Chains. Released in 1994 from *Jar of Flies*. Notice Layne’s expenditure totals. He stuck to his budget. If he went over, he’d pawn something!

mother said come home
father said come home
sisters said come home
So my friends said come home

And I said

let me be, I'm allright
Can't you see, I'm just fine
Little skinny, OK
I'm asleep anyway

~~One day I~~
Then I heard a voice
Said Son, you have a choice
I then slapped my face
Live to fast a pace

let me be, I'm OK
I'm awake anyway
It's too bright over here
I can shift, just not steer

"Swing on This" by Alice in Chains. Released in 1994 from Jar of Flies.

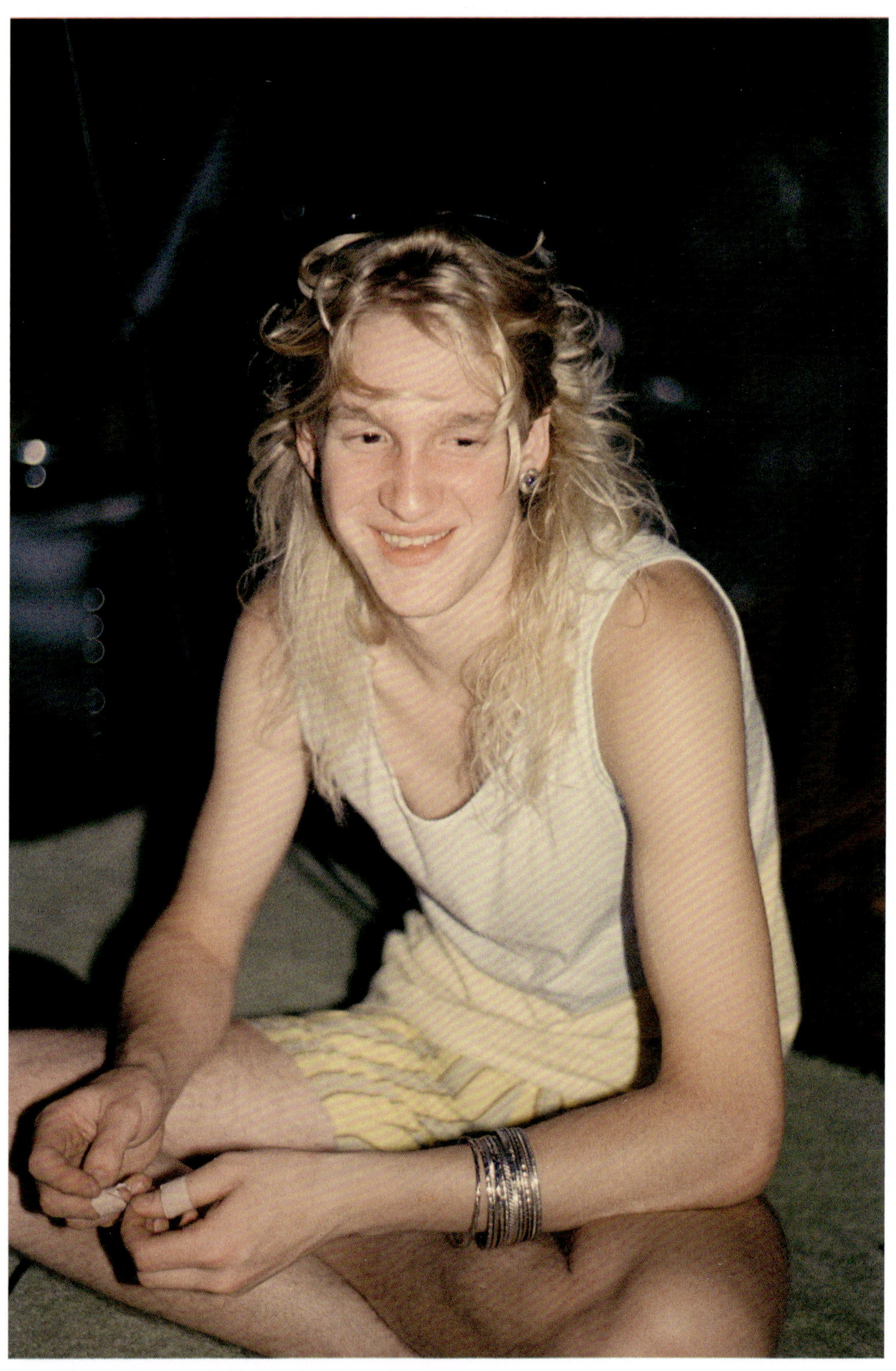

Layne enjoying a moment at the Music Bank while practicing with his band Alice 'N Chains. © 1987 Carolyn M. Cawrse

Yeah hey ~ I hope to travel
south this year
Ah woah ~ Won't prevent safe
passage dear

Why you always tracking around
Points are in a trail on the ground
~~Imitation strength in the voice~~
~~Masturbation/Drama, the choice~~
Another sick room with your name
The trauma's ~~set~~ just a play in the game

"I Stay Away" by Alice in Chains. Released in 1994 from Jar of Flies.

The Poisons Andy

There's a hole in my stomach
For when the whole shibang falls in
I've laid it on thick with the poisons
And this time it's kicking my ass
(so I wonder why the phone scares me to death)
(repeat again)

I'm lookin' for a friend
Or a familiar face
Excuses turn into fair game
And you know that can kill a man
So I wonder why the phone scares me to death,
(repeat again)
So your alone - big deal - Can't you love yourself?
You ought bestl be ashamed - Dying boy'
~~There's a hole in my~~

There's a hole in my stomach
For when the whole shibang falls in
You see - I've laid it on thick withe the poisons
And this time it's kicking my ass
(so I wonder why the phone scares me to death)
(repeat again)

Just love yourself
And make the difference
Just love yourself
And love the change

Recovery thoughts in lyric form.

Yeah
Uh, huh

I can't help but to feel that I've been betrayed,
I'm high, you'll die before me I think
I'm so far in debt I should blow out my head
I could, I should, would you miss me for long
Cold + shaking aching to wait for the meds
I'm out, sedated, but my hate is as strong

Why you act crazy?
Not an act maybe
So close, daddy
Shifty eyes shady

"I Stay Away" by Alice in Chains. Released in 1994 from Jar of Flies.

I'm above

M = Mark
L = Layne

L ~~Four~~ For clear space and soundness of mind
M I've let you play me for some time
L One can only recieve and retain
M But the lies you recite for ~~self~~ own gain

L And so you rely on my faith in your kind
M Or rather continue to pretend I am blind
L You say I made your life a living hell
M And yet still let me pay you more when I fell

1st
How is it your feeling so uneasy
How is it that I feel fine
Life reveals what is dealt through seasons
Circle comes around each time
M 2nd
I have been blessed with eyes to see this
Behind the unwhole truth you hide
Bite to remind the bitter, bigger
Mouth repaying 10 fold wide

I'm above
Over you I'm standing above
L Claiming unconditional love
Above

Lyrics for Layne and Mark Lanegan. "I'm Above" by Mad Season. Released in 1995 from the album Above.

L Try to keep bad blood in the past
M Never thought a chance it would last
L I have strength enough to forgive
M ~~Because~~ I desire peace where I live

L Fear alive and strong of a just loss
M No one can own me If I am lost
L There can only be one of me
M Best ~~release~~, consequence, you'll agree

Mark {Sabbath part}

Layne {chorus}

Above

For clear space and soundness of mind
I've let you play me for some time
One can only receive and retain
But the lies, you recite for your gain

So, you rely on my faith in your kind
Or, rather, continue to pretend that I'm blind
You say I made your life a living hell
And yet, still let me pay you when I fell

{Hard chorus}

How is it your feeling so uneasy?
How is it that I feel fine?
Life reveals what is dealt ~~that~~ through seasons
Circle comes around each time
I've been blessed with eyes to see this
Behind the ~~untro~~ unwhole truth you hide
Bite to remind ~~the~~ the bitten, bigger 10-fold wide
Mouth retaining

{Soft chorus}

I'm above, over you I'm standing above
Claiming unconditional love, above

Try to keep bad blood In the past
Never thought a chance it would last
I have strength enough ~~for~~ to forgive
I desire peace ~~#~~ Where I live

{Hard Chorus}
{Soft chorus}

"Never thought a chance it would last."
"I'm Above" by Mad Season. Released in 1995 from the album Above.

And I'm sick of it
Still I'm stuck in it
Can't get rid of it

Air conditioned, on a bed
that's mine but only for
the moment

On a cloud of pink has
turned to gray and I'm
alone again

Someone to hold untouched
against my own is what I
crave

~~Just for a~~ while
Like a dream, I wake
and shaking, aching
fore

". . . on a cloud of pink turned to gray . . ."
"Artificial Red" by Mad Season. Released in 1995 from the album Above.

Artificial red, smoke, poison consumed
In the House of Ill Repute
Is this the way I spend my days
In recovery of a fatal disease?
Whores tease you for a dollar
Turn you on for a few more
Doubting I'm good enough, again,
My hateful mind blames it on her

Air conditioned on a bed,
That's mine, but only for the moment
On a cloud of pink has turned to grey
And I'm alone again
Someone to hold ~~one~~ untouched
Against my own is what I crave
And like from a dream, I snap out
Cold and shaking, aching like before

On the Television I focus
On the Television ~~for~~
bad 70s ~~Psycadellic theme music~~ spastic mood music
~~the feeling~~
Adding more chaos to the sick visual
Almost comical, but I don't want to laugh.
I just want to throw up
I just want to sleep
I just want to dream of a time
When my most difficult, fidgety moment
Was telling mom I said "Fuck" to the neighbor kid
... And life after the truth wasn't ~~that~~ so bad.

"... dream of a time ..."
"Artificial Red" by Mad Season. Release in 1995 from the album Above.

Crazy - Feel my pain
Lazy Drunk & Drained

Time to tell my daddy off
Tired of a shootin man
Slide me to the side again
Slapped in the face again

Angie will it rain
Let me be the same

Time to call the doggies off
Tired . . . shadow

"Head Creeps" by Alice in Chains. Released in 1995 from the album Alice in Chains.

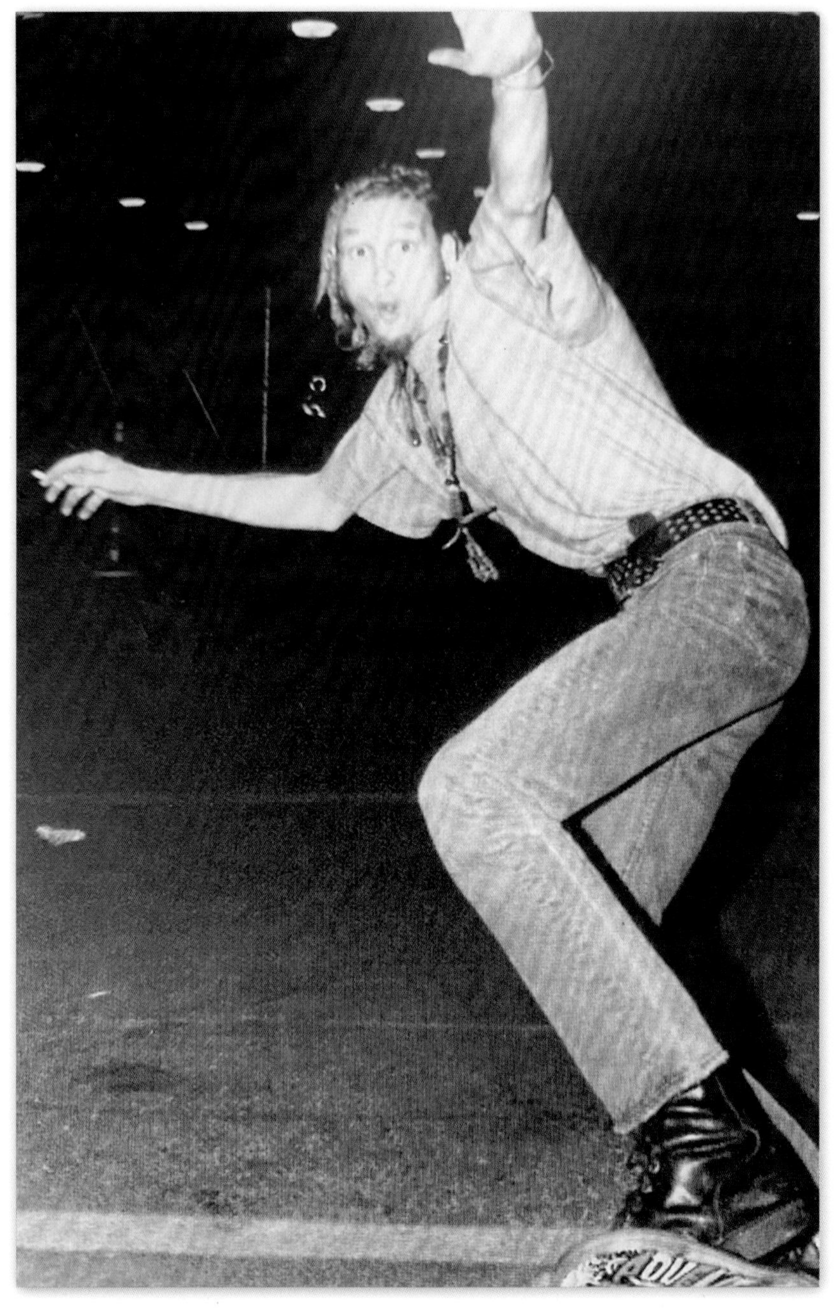

Do the laughs die when
One such as I run,
And allow myself
Time for own Love need
When convincing me
That your on my team
May not lie to me
But not mentioning

X-ray mind reads plenty
Worth no more than pennies

So sit back and have
An hysterical
Laugh at tiny holes
Buy and trade men's souls

Hire a spy and bug me
Pimp your friends for money

You, they, It or what
Have been fair I thought
May you never free
You from you or me
See the more I think
I'm afraid to blink
I don't move an inch
Slowly draining me

Rich and growing sicker
Sell the dead ones quicker

"X-Ray Mind" by Mad Season. Released in 1995 from the album Above.

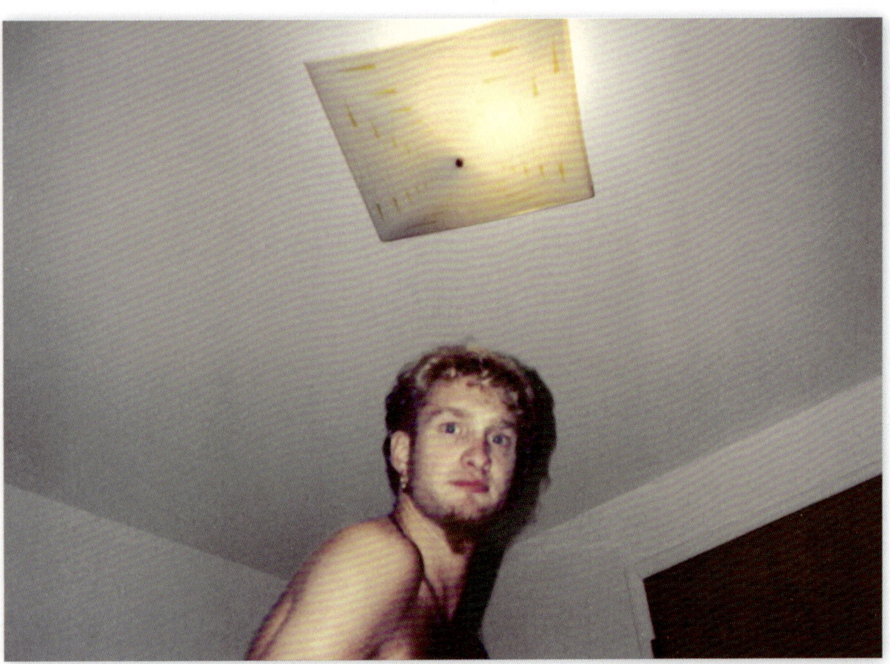

Layne, shirtless, possibly in one of his apartments, in his twenties. Not a family photo.

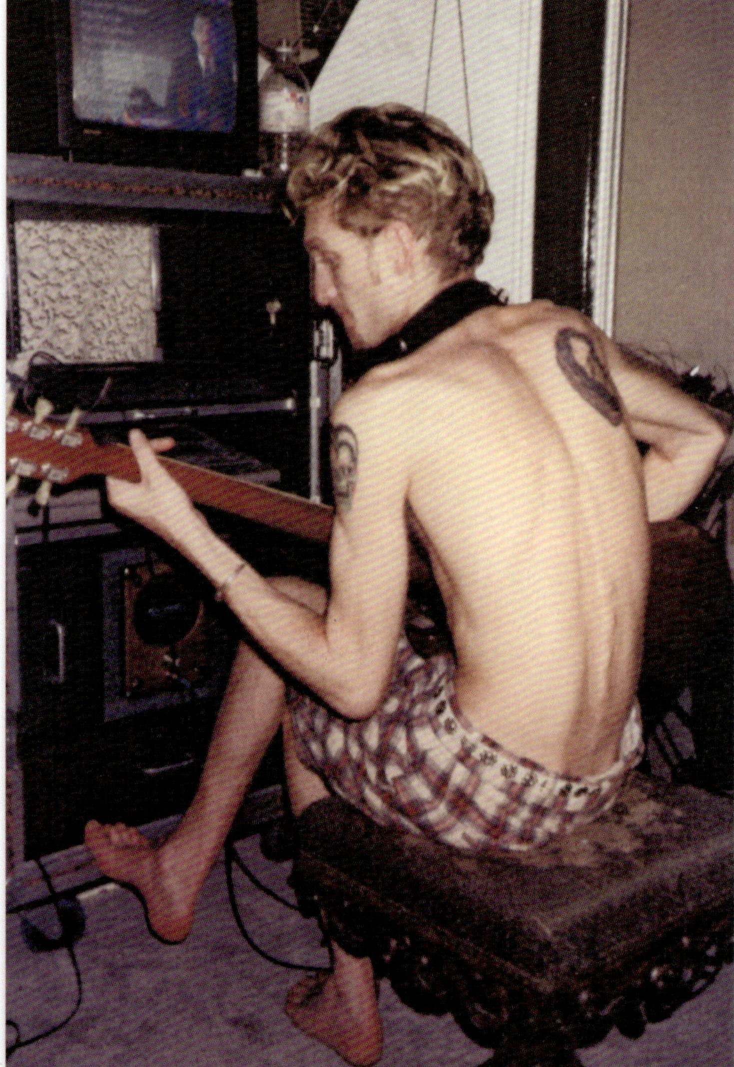

Layne in his Ward Street apartment near the Seattle Center's old Armory. He sports a "Man in the Box" tattoo, a playful claim to the Alice in Chains lyric. Note the matching (or perhaps intentionally mismatched) Elvis skeleton tattoos he and Jerry share. Layne, brimming with youthful enthusiasm, proudly displays his progress on the guitar. Photograph by Nancy, date unknown.

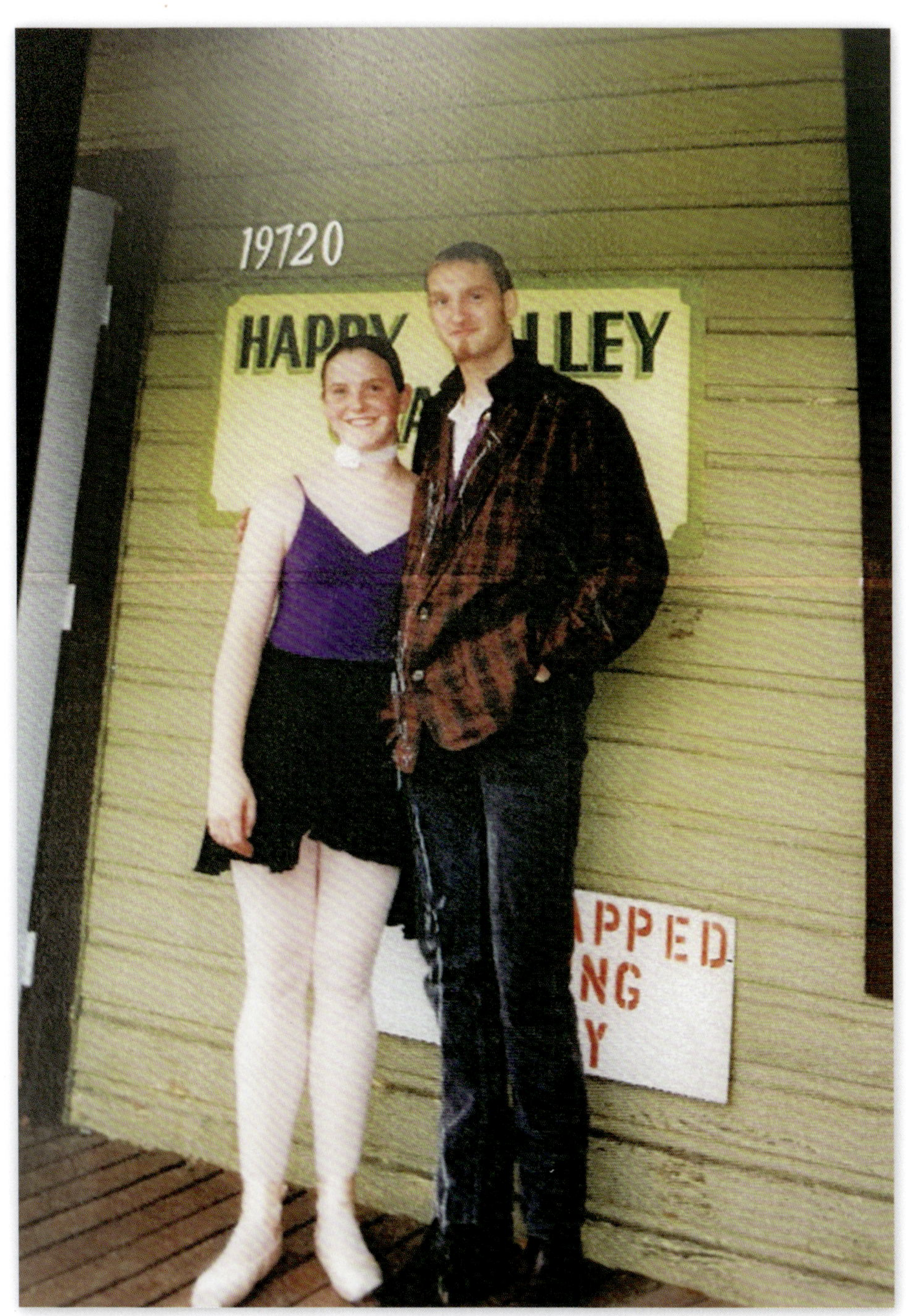

A proud Layne with his sister, Jamie.

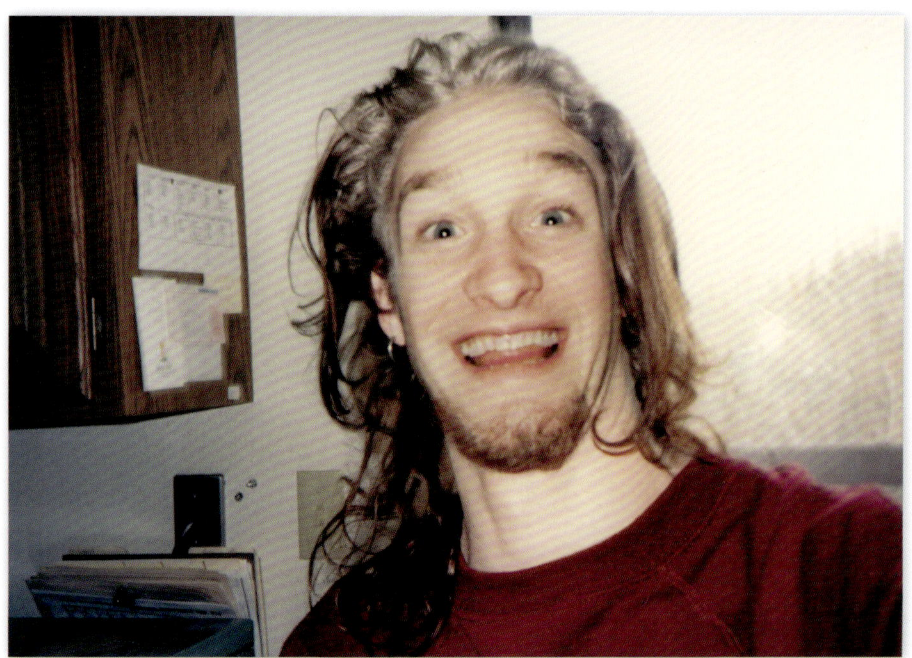

Layne, in his mid-twenties, visiting the family home on SE 7th Street in Bellevue, WA, around 1987. Always ready with a smile, a funny face, or a silly gesture, his playful spirit is evident. Photograph by Nancy McCallum.

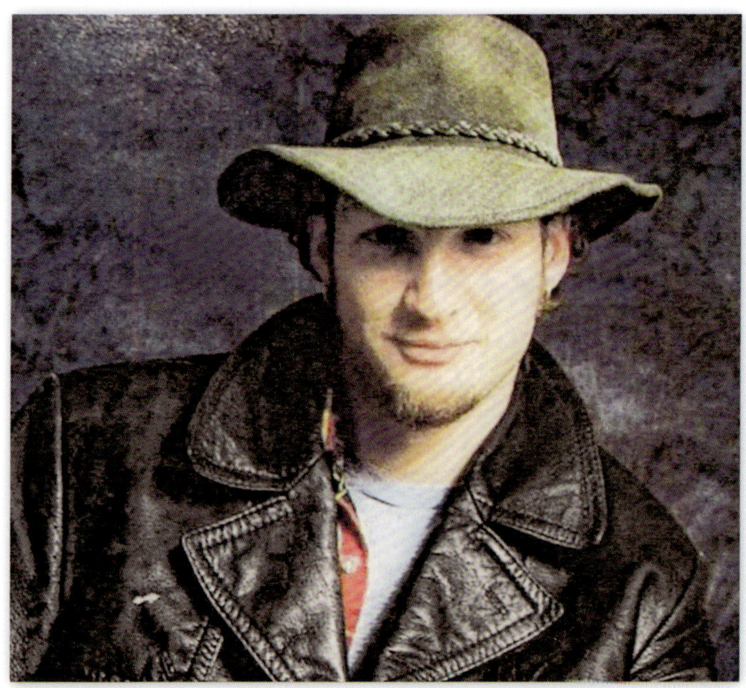

From a Paul Hernandez photo shoot.

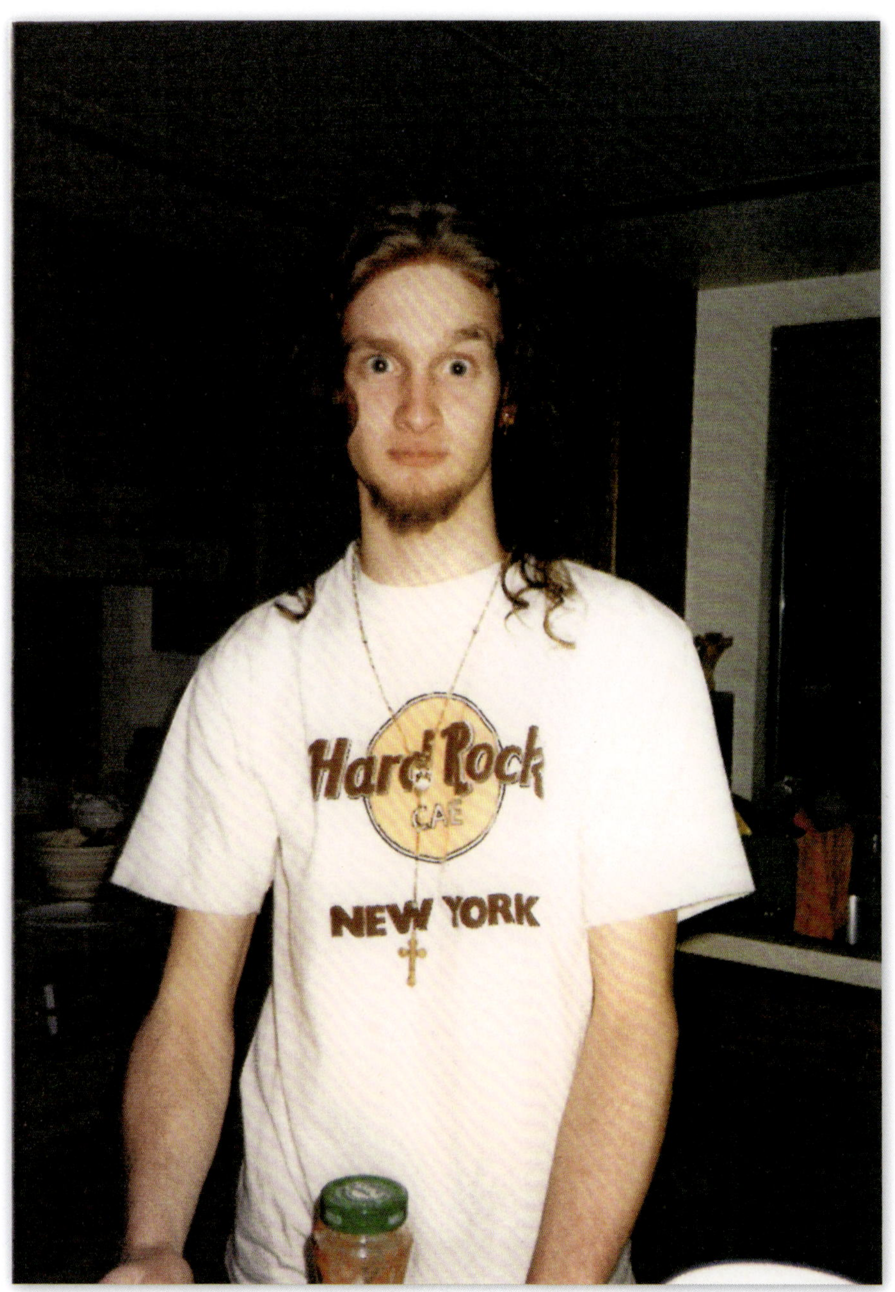

Layne, in his early twenties, in the kitchen of the Bellevue, WA, home on SE 7th Street. Photographer likely Nancy McCallum.

People often misunderstand Layne's life. What many don't know is that I never spoke negatively about his father to the kids. His dad was struggling, but Layne had a wonderful life. He was a really lucky boy and much luckier than some children whose parents stay together but fight or don't communicate. When people email me suggesting his dark music or stage presence was due to his father's absence, they're missing who Layne really was.

I remember at his 20th high school reunion—after Layne had passed—one person told me, "Layne Elmer is Layne Staley? Layne was the quietest boy in our class." I knew he was quiet, but that was his personality. Later that night, I spoke with his friend Calvin in the hallway. When I mentioned how quiet Layne had been, Calvin looked at me straight on and said, "Nancy, he did it for us all." The stage gave Layne permission to express feelings he couldn't in everyday life.

One of my favorite memories is of Layne at about twelve years old. It was a sunny Saturday morning, around seven, and I looked out the bedroom window to see him riding his Huffy bike in the cul-de-sac—shirtless, wearing a black cape, a black Zorro cap, and a Zorro mask. He was in another world entirely.

He once told me it was so much easier for him to draw his feelings than to find the words. He was about 30 then, writing for Alice. Fortunately, he was in an environment that encouraged creativity—the Seattle music scene wasn't competitive but more like a brotherhood where musicians supported each other.

Despite the darkness that came later, the extent of his addiction wasn't the boy I knew. It's not the boy I think of, not the boy I hold in my heart, and not the boy I have hopes for. I believe his spiritual awakening will take place like all the rest of us, and he will be able to leave all that behind and be Layne again.

That's how I choose to remember him—not as he appeared in those later years when he flew me to the Grammys in New York, looking pale and worn, fulfilling contracts and trying to hide his poor health. I remember instead the sweet, quiet boy with the tender heart who was good with babies, pets, and animals. I remember the child who, even at five years old during a fever, saw a hand coming out of the ceiling—already having the vivid imagination that would later fuel his art.

Layne had a wonderful life, and I want people to really understand that. It doesn't take away from the pains—we all have those—but he was loved, he was special, and he touched so many lives. That's the legacy I choose to carry forward.

—Nancy McCallum

Do the laughs die
when one such as I
desides to wait long
enough so that I
may sit back and
have an hysterical,
internal warming
laugh of my own
at such designers
of such an infantile
game or test.

You, They, It, or What,
have given me fair
warning to the idea
that I may have been
here to long.
Although, I may, no, I will
cheat you until I get
what I want of the
game. And my will, will
crush any rule unsuitable
to the one who resides

"X-Ray Mind" by Mad Season. Released in 1995 from the album Above.

No more time
1st No more time
No more time

Time to call the dummies off
Tired of the shadow men
Slightly push aside again
Slapped in the face again

1st

One day my plane leaves
Some way my head creeps
Some lay filthy seeds
One way my head creeps

Now I lay me down to bed
Pray for my soul to keep
If I die before I wake
Leave my soul for heavens sake

A rewrite of "Now I Lay Me Down to Sleep."
A childhood poem, but not used in our home.

My pain is self chosen.
Or at least I believe it to be
I can either drown and
Wonder where I'll go.
Or pull out of this given skin
And drag myself ashore
Where I can now begin
The spiritual cleansing
And patiently await the
Growth of a beautiful
New shell for all to see
~~And~~ Then, I, and all
will see.
That My pain
Once disclaimed
Isn't me.

Thoughts inspired by The Prophet *by Kahlil Gibran.*
"River of Deceit" by Mad Season. Released in 1995 from the album Above.

My pain is self chosen
At least, so the Prophet says
I can either burn, and wonder
Where I'll go,
Or cut off my pride and buy
Myself time
A head full of lies is
The rock tied to my waist
Heavy enough to pull me to the bottom
Of the River of Deceit,
Who's only direction of flow
Is down

I chew at my rope.
I've done so for as long as I remember
Struggling to free my self and rise abov
But a fist of hurt
Will always be the lack of streng
In my defense... my pain

(cont.)

"River of Deceit" by Mad Season. Released in 1995 from the album Above.

My Pain

My pain is self chosen
At least, so the Prophet says
I can either burn, and wonder where I'll go
Or cut loose my pride and buy myself time
A head full of lies is the rock tied to my waist
Heavy enough to pull me to the bottom
Of the River of Deceit
Who's only direction of flow is down

I chew at my rope
I've done so as long as I can remember
Trying to free myself and rise above
But a fist of hurt
Will always be the lack of strength
In my defense... My pain

My pain is self chosen,
At least I believe it to be
I can either drown, and wonder where I'll go
Or pull out of my skin, and drag myself to shore
Now I can cleanse myself inside
And patiently grow a beautiful new shell
For all to see

"River of Deceit" by Mad Season. Released in 1995 from the album Above.

The pain is increasing at an
overwhelming pace
I coven the rats that find
the poisoned cheese
Quicker than I can find the
strength to either kill you
And myself quickly, or more
Needed, just the quick death
of a man that most truly
does love someone
Who, because of circumstances
Uncontrollable, cannot
wait for the truest she
will ever find.
Self pity? Only to be thrown
by those who would crucify
me
Insanity is a short story.
The author will be remembered
for a short time
In comparison to the intensity
of his love for just one
If there only be one.
And she is here only
when I sleep

Layne had just one great love.

Resume for desired residency

Name: Layne Thomas Staley Age: 26 Male

Occupation: Professional Singer/Songwriter
Currently employed by Columbia Records w/ contract for delivery of 7 full length LP recordings and videos for all singles

Current Residence: Renting ½ of basement of house owned by father.

Desired move in date: Immediately!

Number of roommates: Self only

Work schedule: No set schedule/tours
Have just released miNi-LP + will do small amount of promotional work (Phone interviews, some out of town shows) to support it –
Make new full length LP, tour this summer

Work related successes: 1 gold; 2 platinum records
2 platinum Motion Picture Soundtracks
2 MTV Award Nominations
3 Grammy Award Nominations
1 Grammy Award

Self discription of character: I am very considerate of others needs/comfort, for example; I don't enter another one's home and assume it's ok to smoke, or eat their food. I ask and abide.

Layne in his own words.

I am considerate of other people's schedules; Because I generally keep varied/odd hours, I do not assume others share my schedule and watch television at an obnoxious volume or Turn stereo up above a level that is comfortable for all those living above, next to, or below my living space. I will establish Acceptable volume for sleep schedules, and during the hours others are awake.

I hold high respect for the situations of others, and accept others rules and differences of opinion, and generally am given the same respect in return.

I am very friendly, helpful, supportive, and generous and enjoy extending help if opportunities arise.
I work very, very hard at what I do, it is more work than it is fun + games, and find that other people can't see that it is work sometimes.

I am a private person. I like to have alot of time to myself, and work without disturbances on my writing, drawings and song writing.

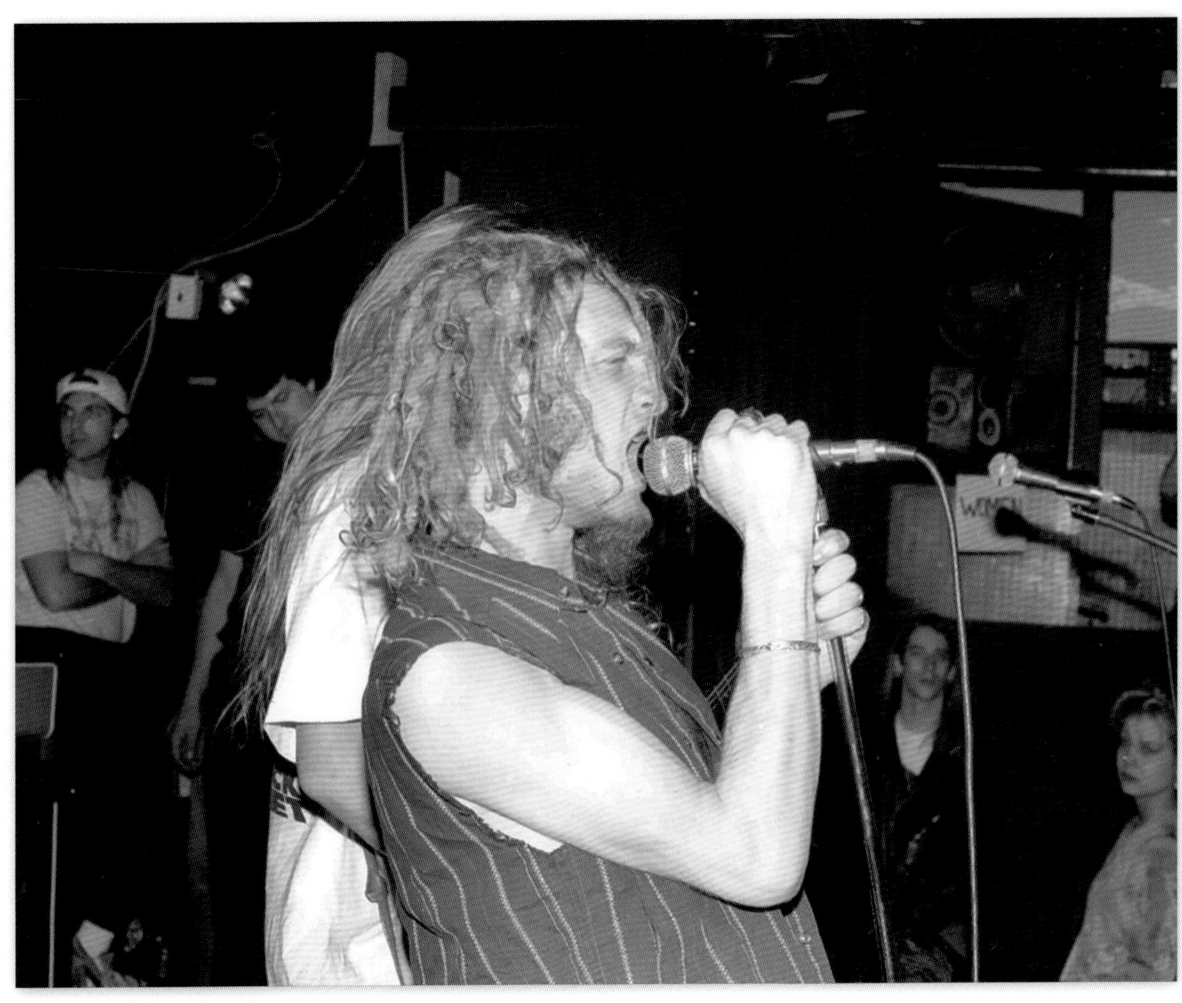

Alice in Chains at the Off Ramp, Seattle, April 1991. Photograph by Alison Braun.

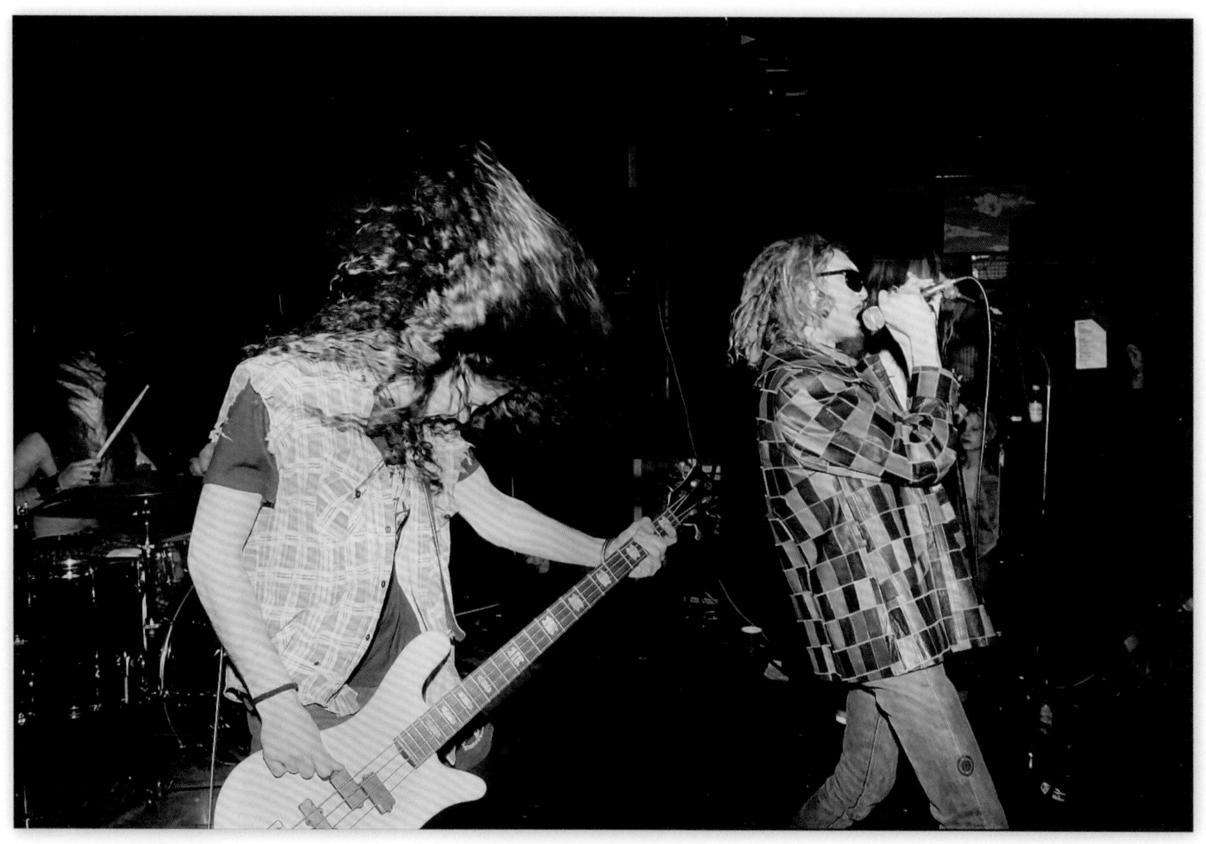

Alice in Chains at the Off Ramp, Seattle, February 1991. Photograph by Alison Braun.

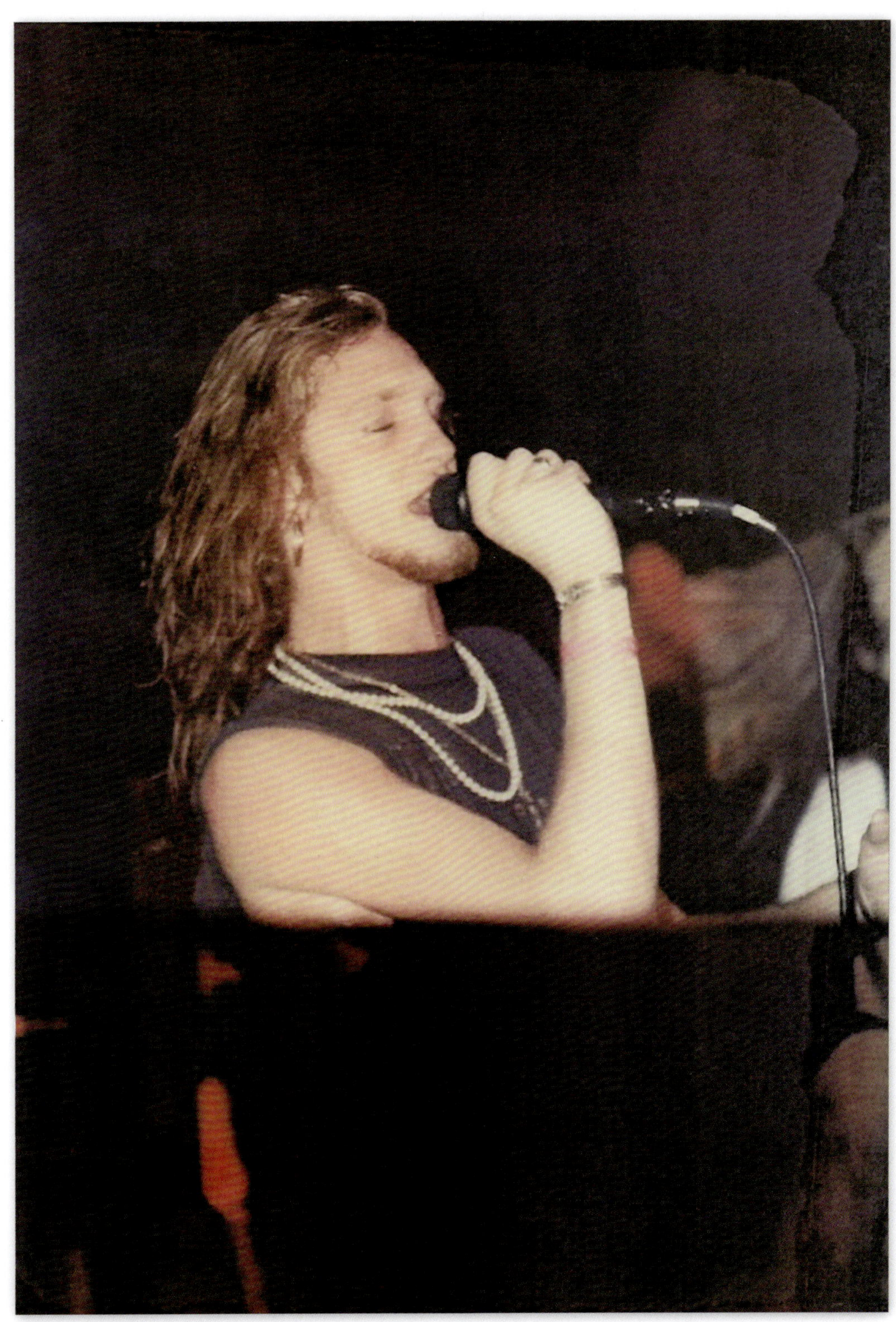

Performance from Central Tavern, 1989. Professional portrait. Photographer unknown.

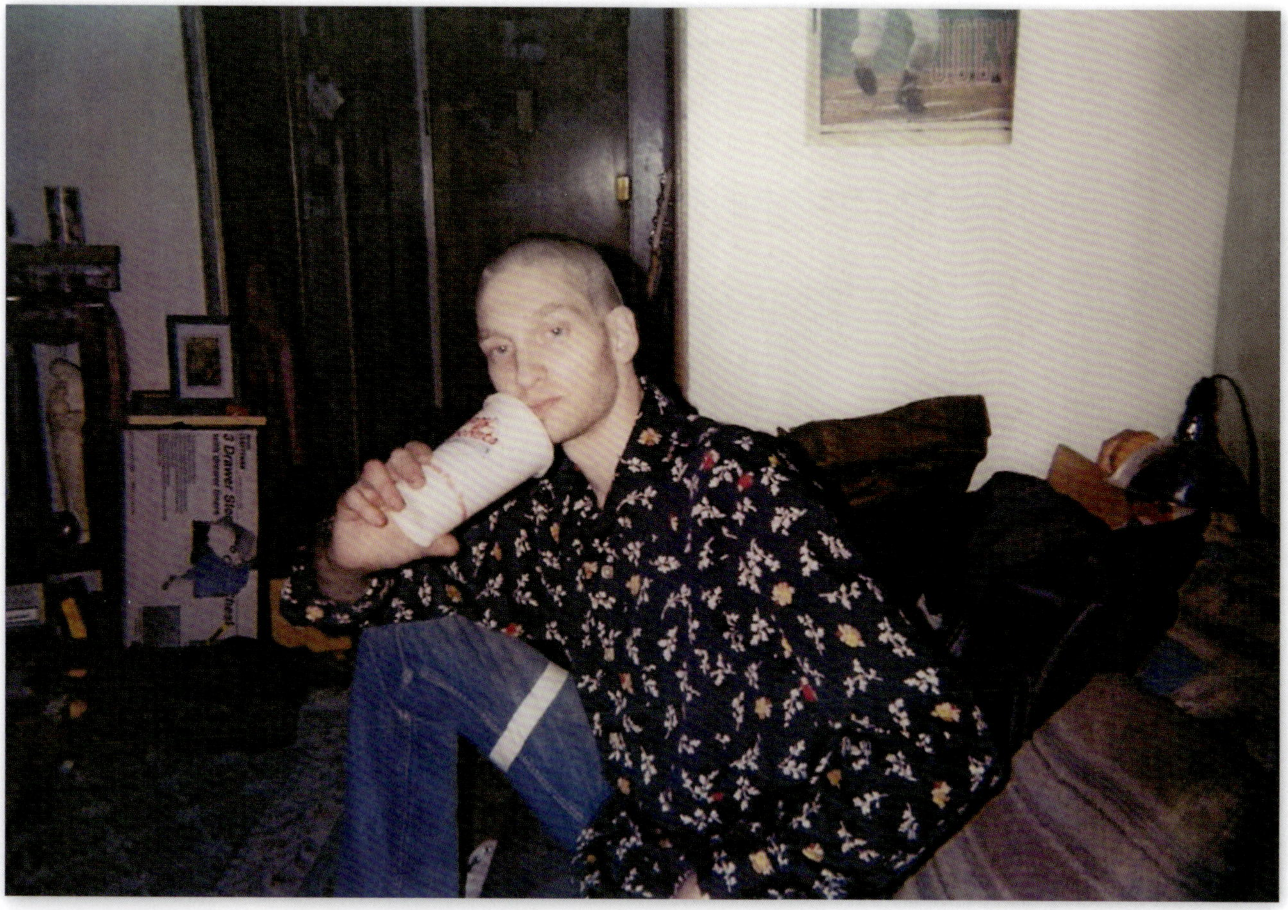

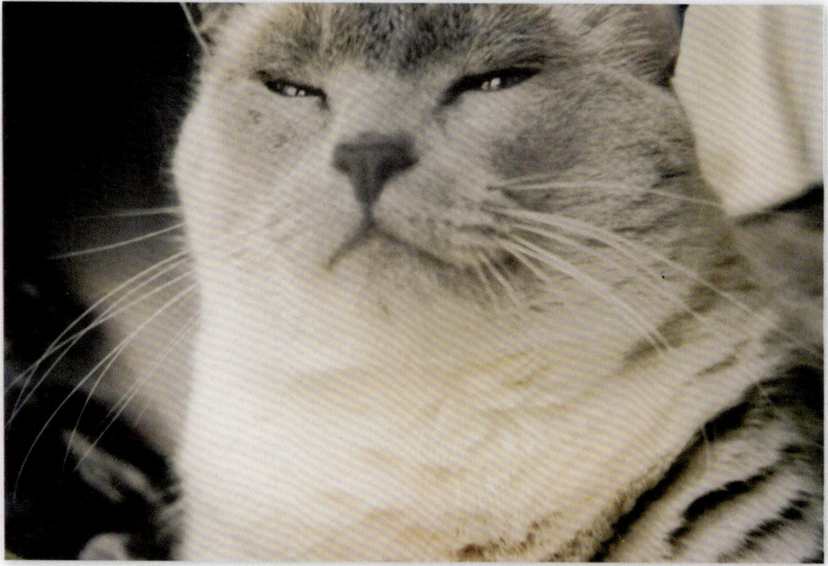

Layne's adorable cat, Sadie, had a litter of kittens that were given to some of Layne's friends. When Layne passed, Sadie went with David Cantrell to live a farm life.

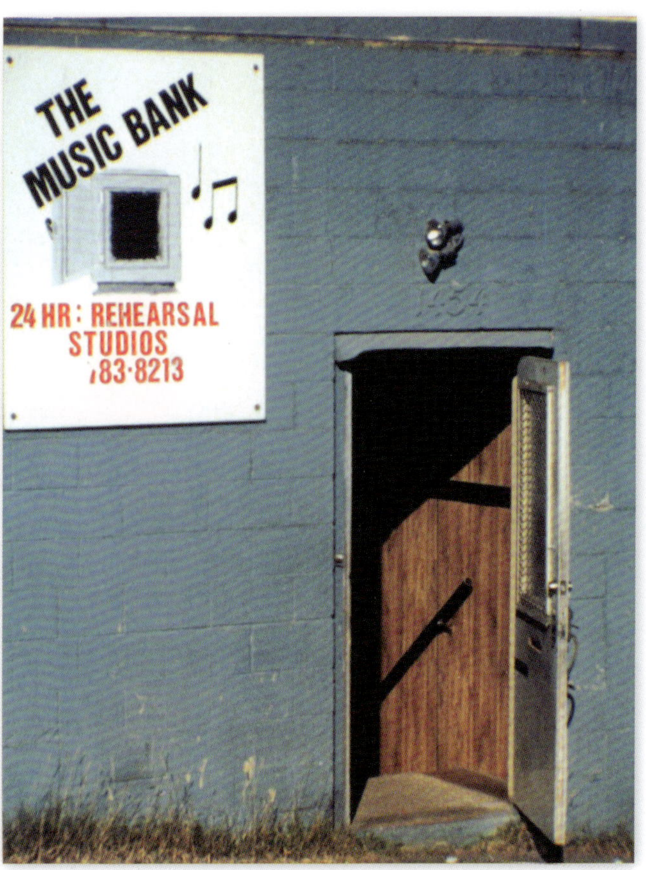

Layne Staley's connection to the heart of the "Seattle Scene": the Music Bank. Beyond its walls filled with practicing bands in rentable cubicles, Layne held down the front desk. It was a space where he could control the flow, squeeze in his own practice, or even unwind with a movie during his shift.

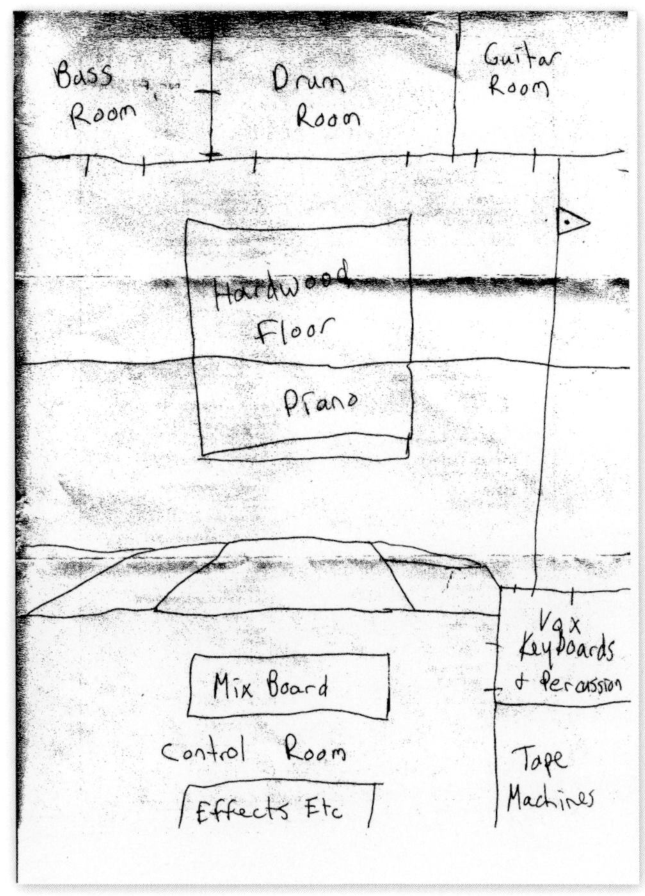

Dreams of a personal recording studio.

I know a demon
Good at convincing
The sick to anaesthetize
The little amount of hurt

I know a pain
That will not go away
But will ~~[illegible]~~ assume its dominion
When weak from lack [illegible]

At least so the Prophet says
I can either burn and wonder where I'll go
Or cut off my pride and buy myself time
A head full of lies is the rock tied to my waist
Heavy enough to pull me to the bottom
Of the river of deciet
Who's only direction of flow is down

I chew at my rope
I've done it as long as I can remember
Trying to free myself and rise above
But a fist of hurt
Will always be the lack of strength
In my defense ... My pain

My pain is self chosen
At least I believe it to be
I can either drown and ~~at~~ wonder where
I'll go
Or pull out of my skin and drag myself to shore
Now I can cleanse the inside of me
And grow a beautiful new shell for all to see

"River of Deceit" by Mad Season. Released in 1995 from the album Above.

Wake up young man, it's time to wake up
Your love affair has got to go
For 10 long years, the leaves to rake up
Slow suicide's no way to go

Yeah, Twisting, Painful, Breathless slow
While buried boy who's not yet died
They tried to steal his soul away
Yeah, self infliction not today

Blue, clouded gray, you're not a crack up
Dizzy and weakened by the haze
Moving onward, urges to back up
So a disease and not a phaze

Yeah, blinding, Crazy, hateful place
Hole's in my boots that need repair
I'm the ~~on~~ only one I can save
But, in the mirror not so brave

"Wake Up" by Mad Season. Released in 1995 from the album Above.

Wake up

Wake up young man it's time to wake up
Your [illegible] has got to go
For 10 long years [illegible] leaves to
wake up
Slow suicide's no way to go

Blue [illegible] you're not a
crack up
Dizzy and ~~wake up~~ weakened by
the Haze
~~urges to [illegible]~~
So an [illegible] infection not a phase

The cracks + lines from where you
gave up
They make [illegible] easy man to read
for all the times you let them
bleed ~~[illegible]~~ you
For little peace from God you plead
" " "

"Wake Up" by Mad Season. Released in 1995 from the album Above.

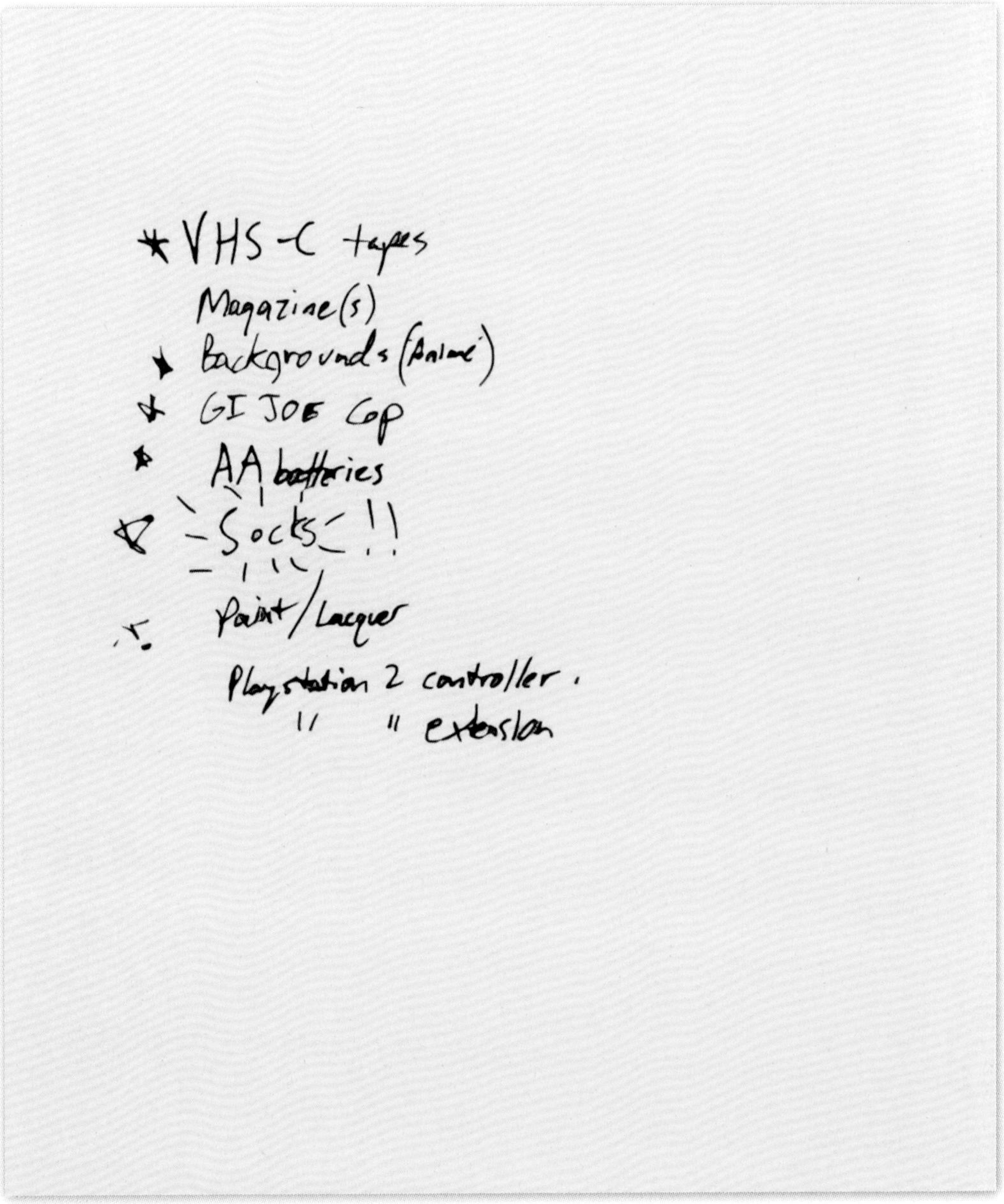

* VHS-C tapes
Magazine(s)
* Backgrounds (Anime)
* GI JOE Cop
* AA batteries
* Socks !!
* Paint/Lacquer
Playstation 2 controller.
" " extension

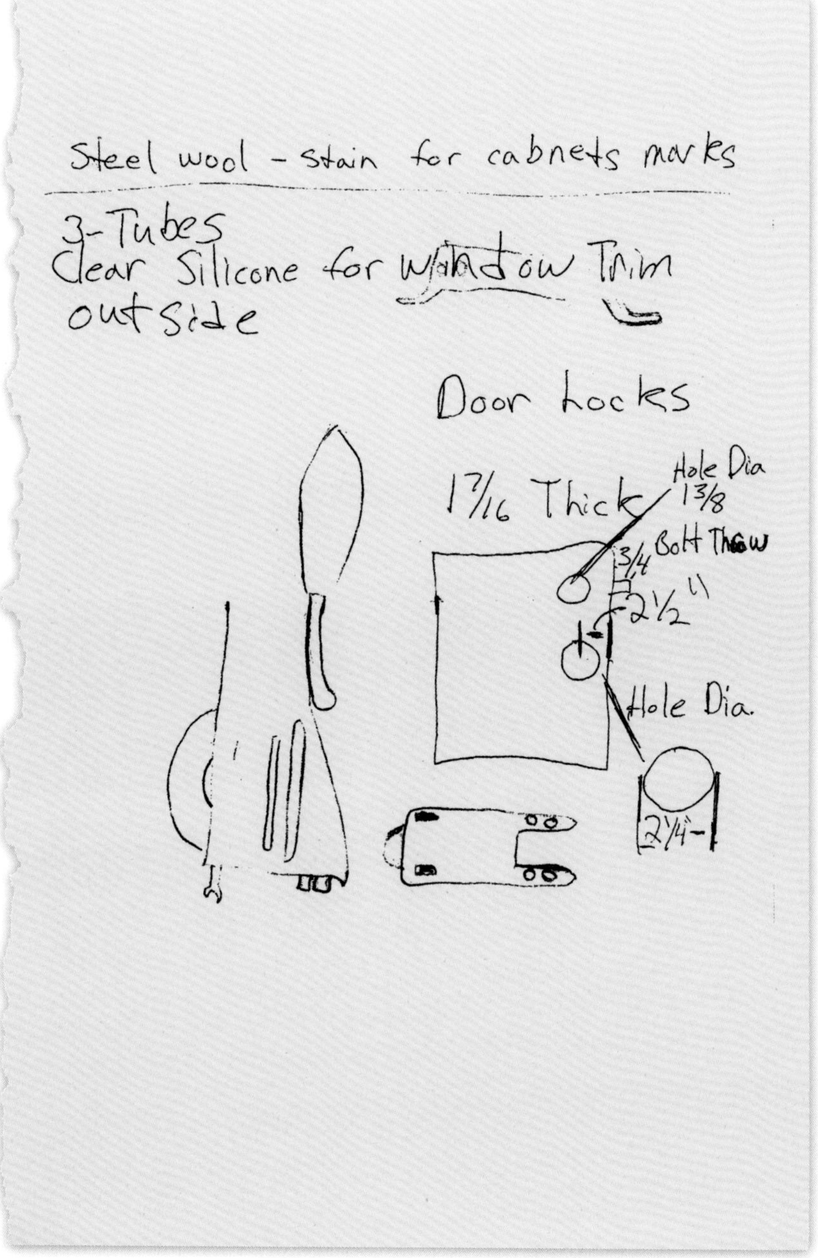
Steel wool - stain for cabnets marks
3-Tubes
Clear Silicone for window Trim
outside
Door Locks
1 7/16 Thick
Hole Dia
1 3/8
3/4 Bolt Throw
2 1/2"
Hole Dia.
2 1/4

RABBIT STAT PHOTOS

1313 Western
in the Northwest Industrial Building
corner of Denny Way and
Western

2929 Western Broad Street
Purple Building

Over Ballard Bridge (15th
turns into Western when you
hit Denny Way the building is
on the right!

(WELCOME TO WONDERLAN
(in bold Black Letters, Large)

pictures in this order like this ↓

Wayne | Nick
Johnny | James

WELCOME
TO
WONDERLAND

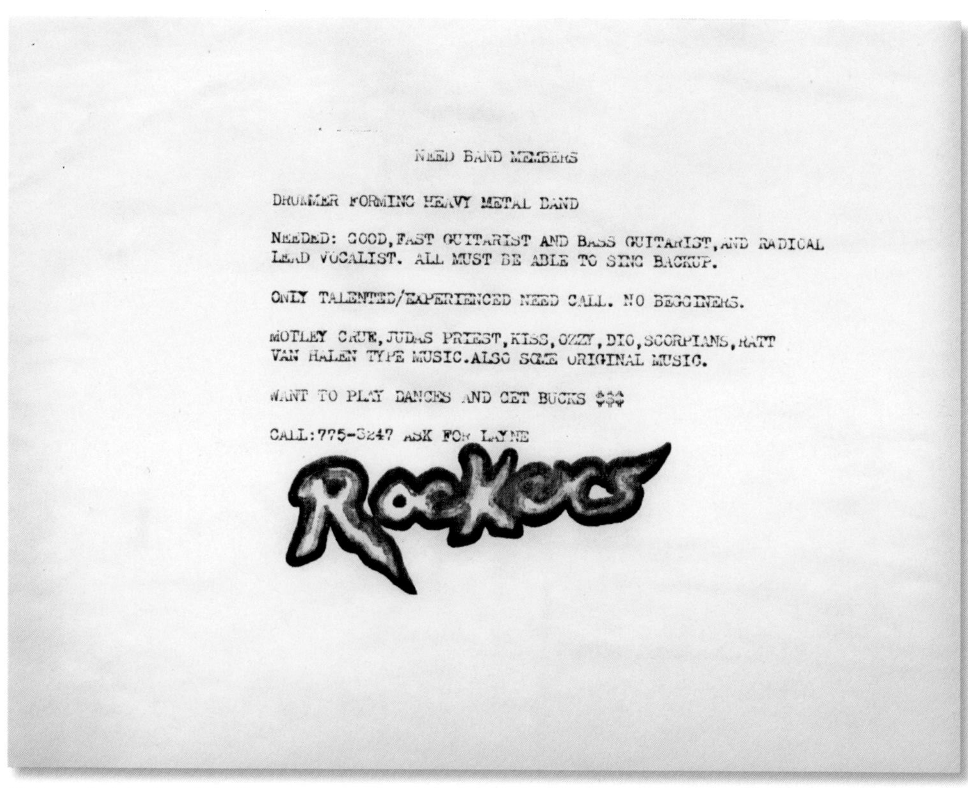

NEED BAND MEMBERS

DRUMMER FORMING HEAVY METAL BAND

NEEDED: GOOD, FAST GUITARIST AND BASS GUITARIST, AND RADICAL LEAD VOCALIST. ALL MUST BE ABLE TO SING BACKUP.

ONLY TALENTED/EXPERIENCED NEED CALL. NO BEGGINERS.

MOTLEY CRUE, JUDAS PRIEST, KISS, OZZY, DIO, SCORPIANS, RATT VAN HALEN TYPE MUSIC. ALSO SOME ORIGINAL MUSIC.

WANT TO PLAY DANCES AND GET BUCKS $$$

CALL: 775-3247 ASK FOR LAYNE

Rockers

Trying to find members for a "heavy metal band."

Mickey Mouse Hat
P.N.T.A. Rentals
Tea

PART TWO: VISION

ART AND IMAGES

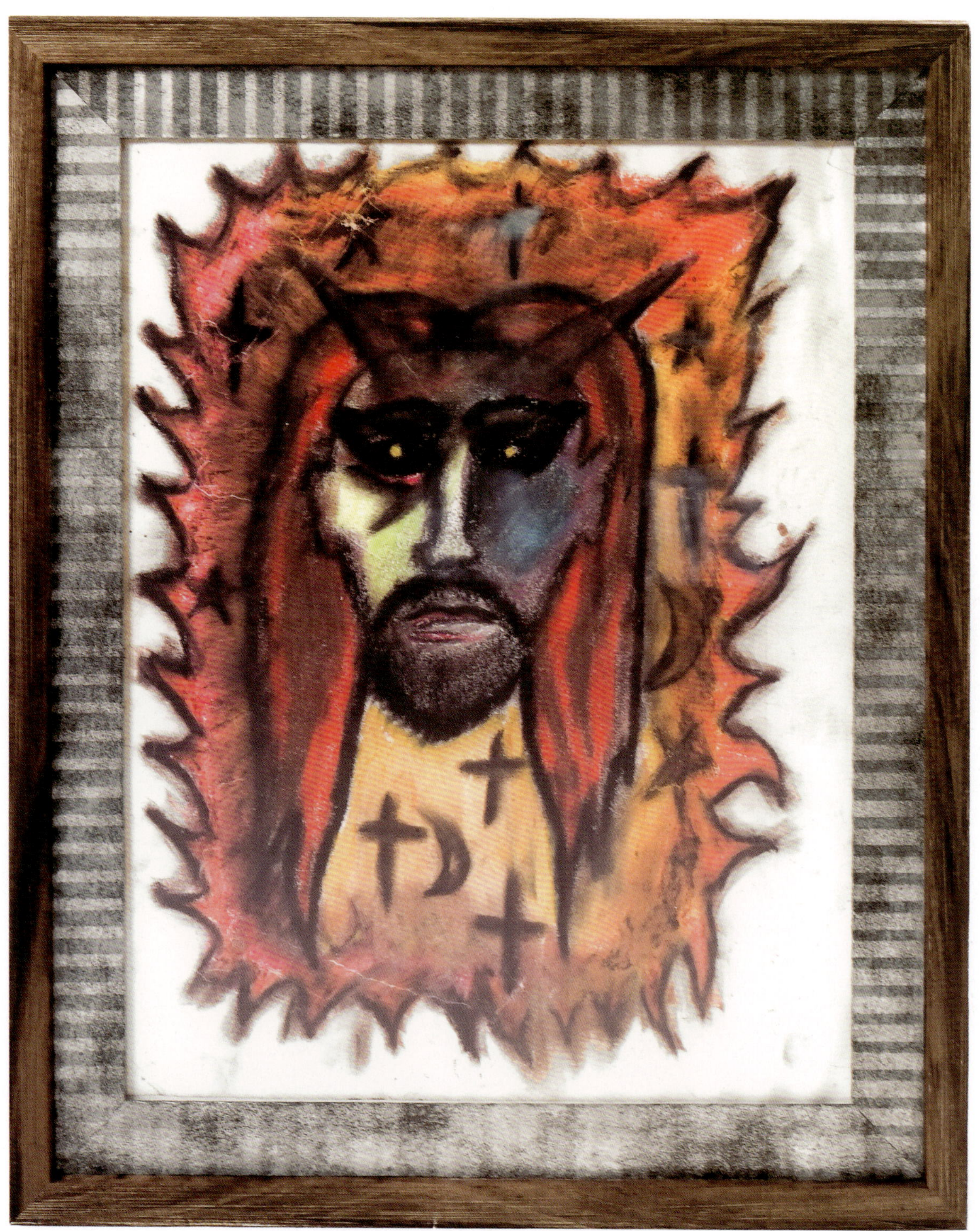

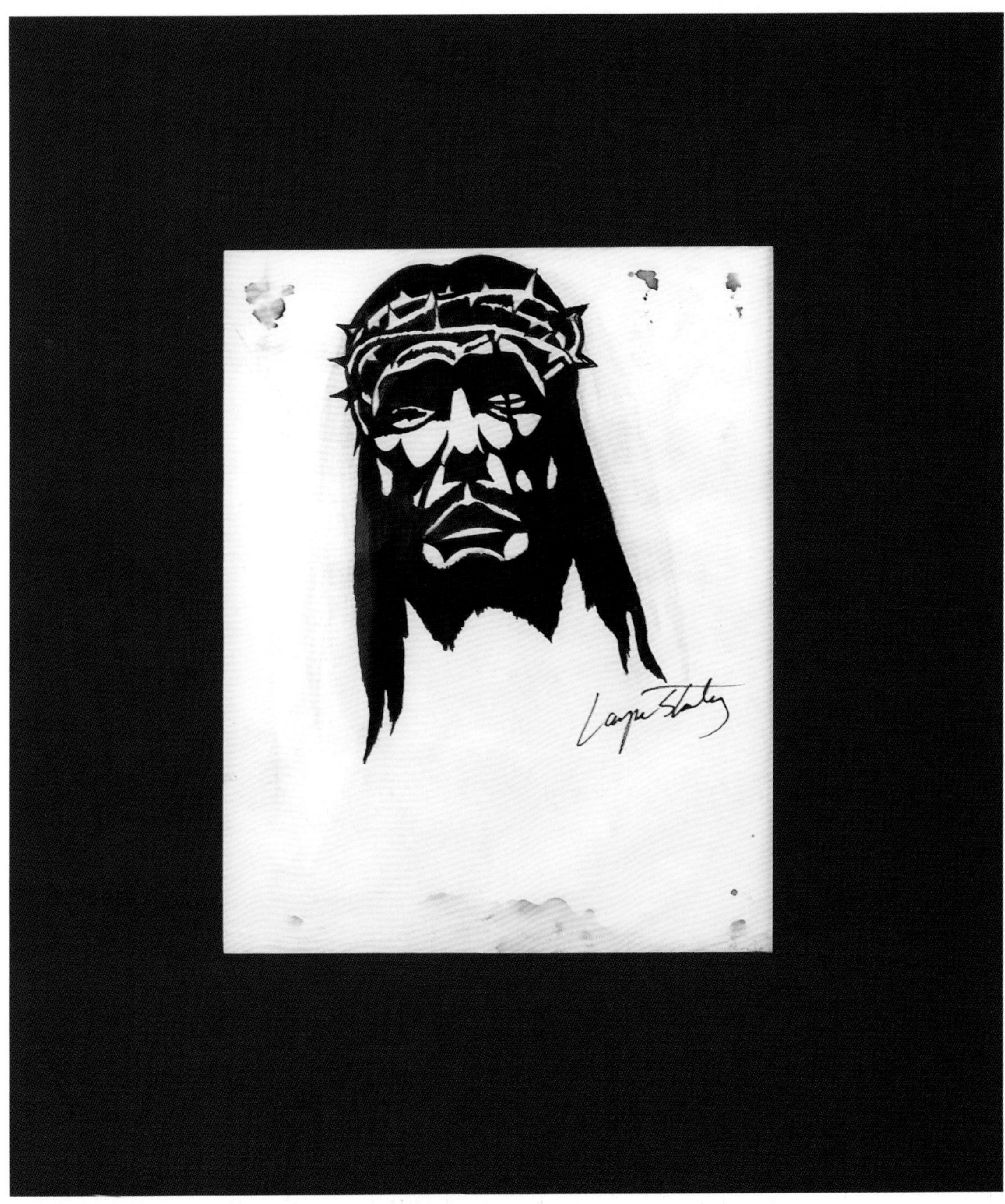

Self-portrait #2.

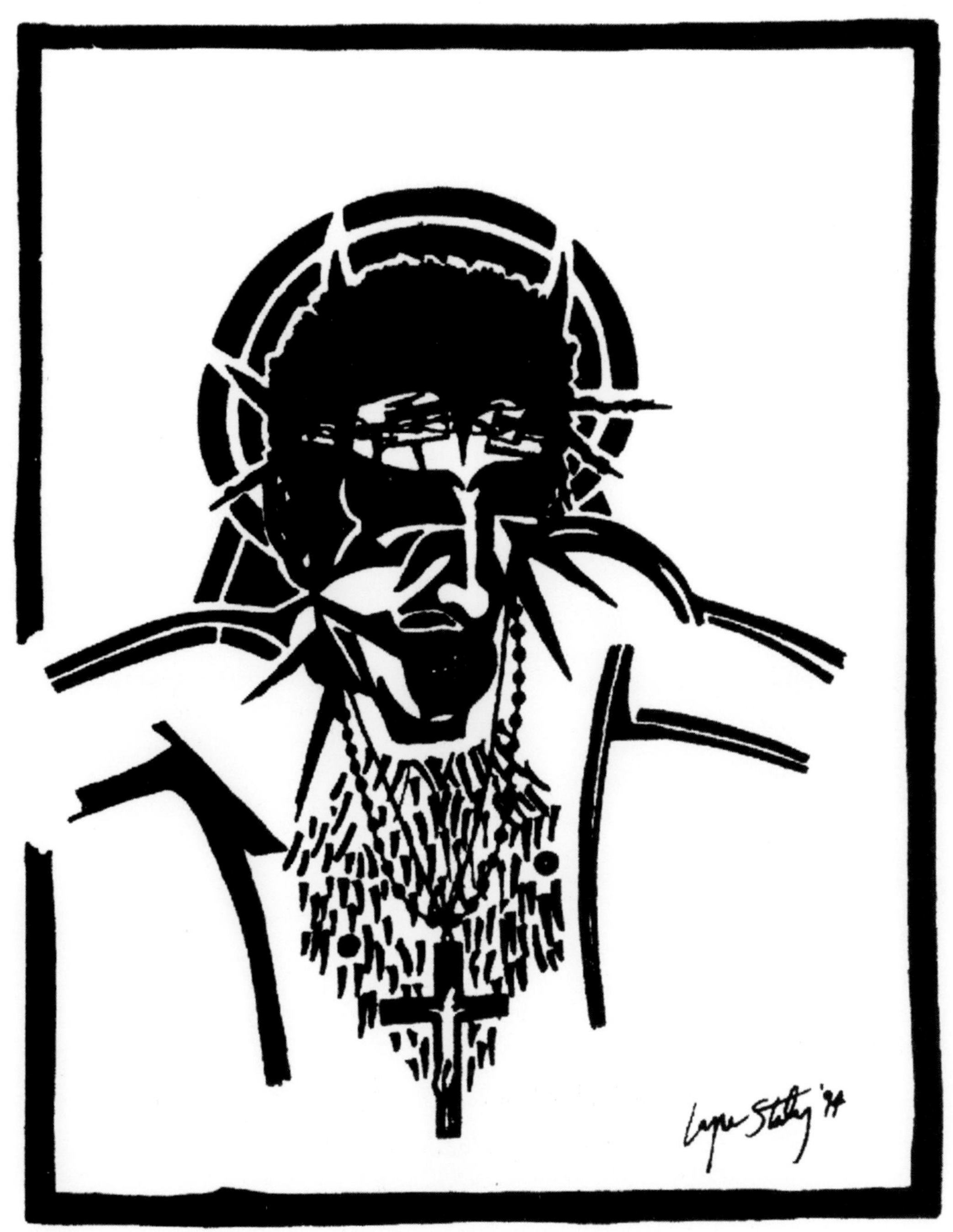

Self-portrait #3. Part of a series of eight "self-portraits" created at different times, this pen-and-ink drawing captures a phase of an experience or feeling. Chosen for a gallery show, it has also appeared on tribute T-shirts, a quilt, and countless fan reproductions. The meaning of its symbols remains open to speculation, imagination, and personal interpretation.

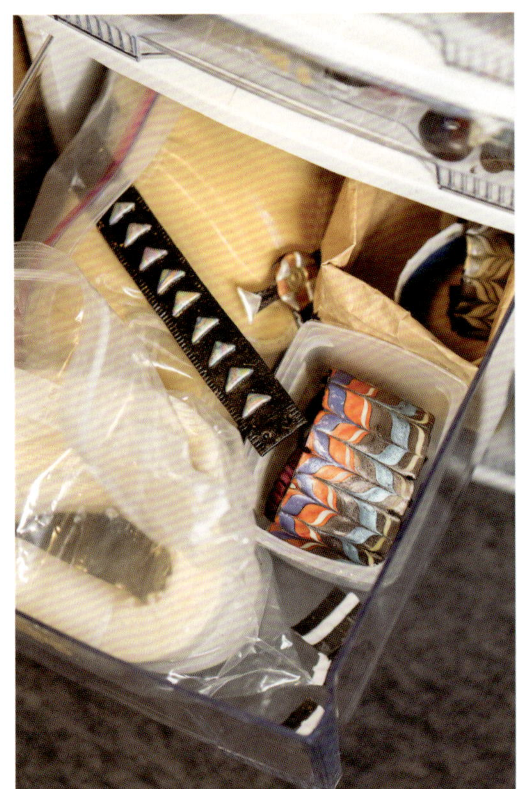

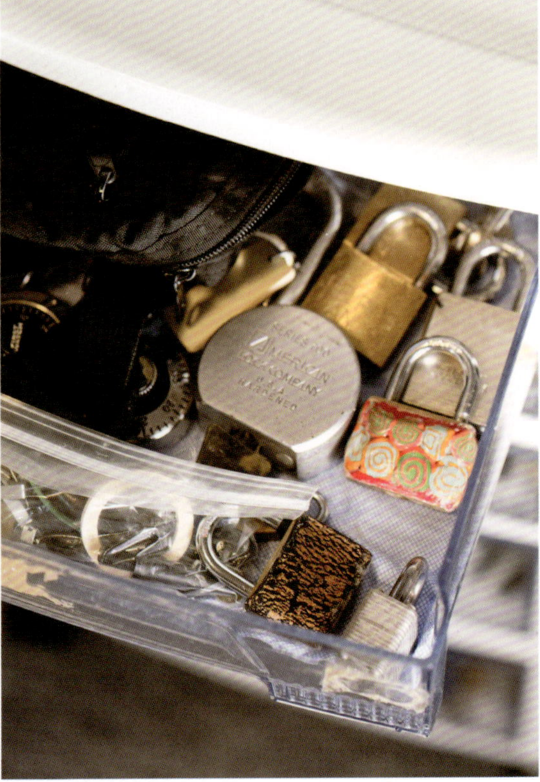

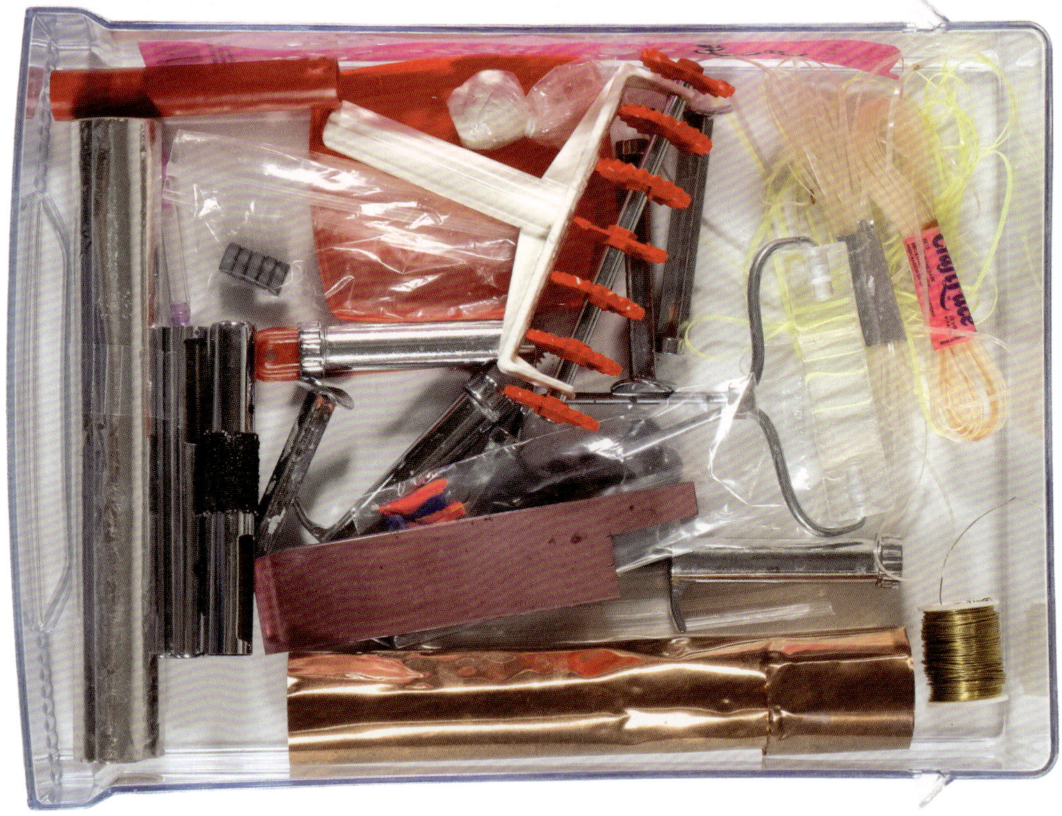

above: Layne's art drawers and a drawer filled with designed locks.
opposite: Drumsticks as works of art.

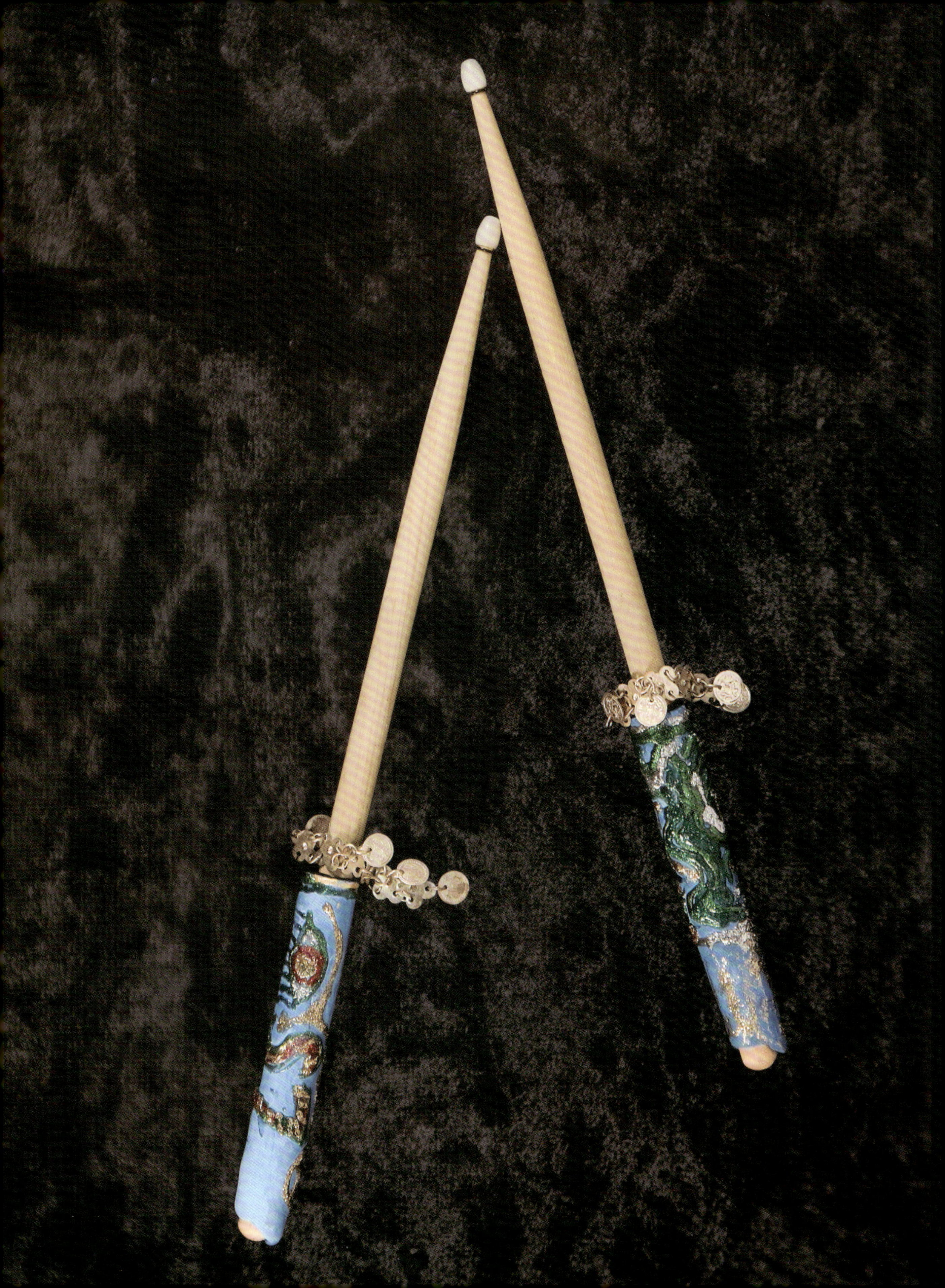

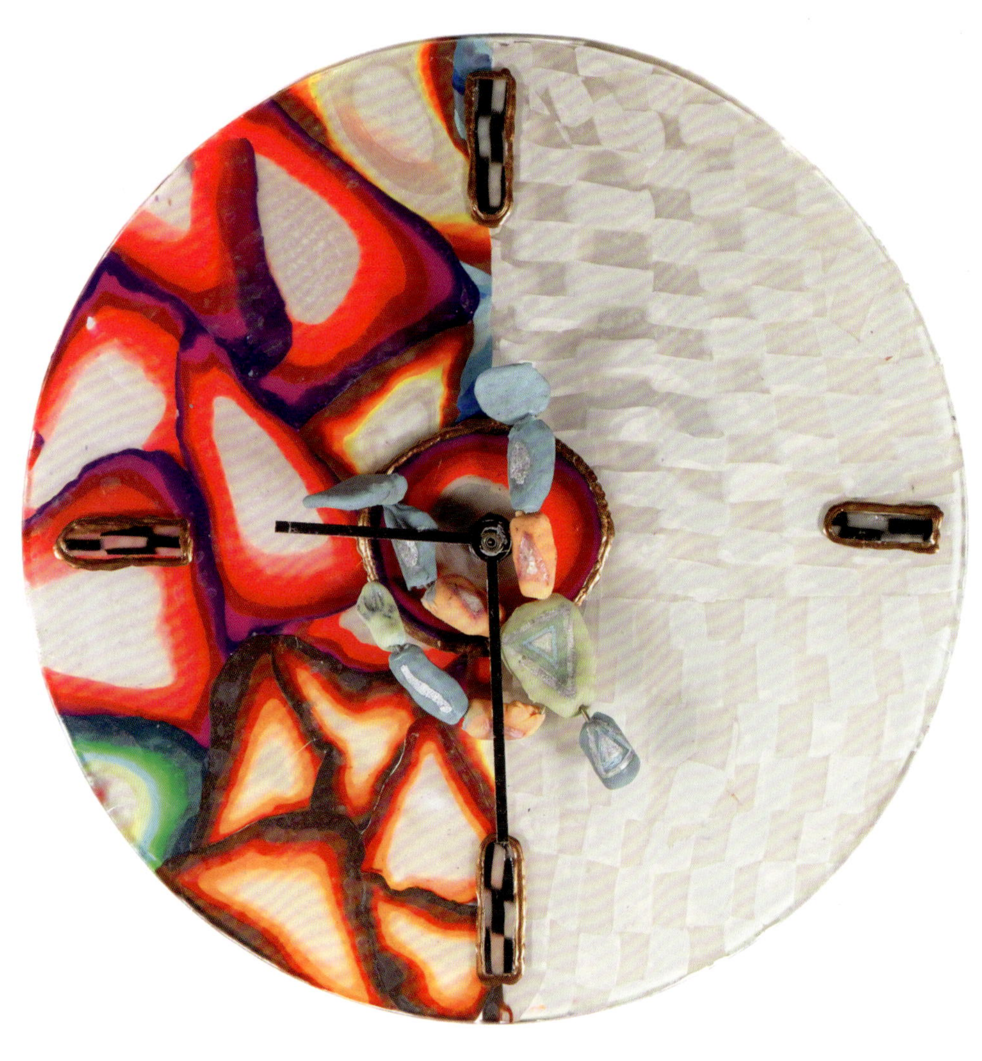

Clock with multicolored Sculpey clay figure and glow-in-the-dark colors.

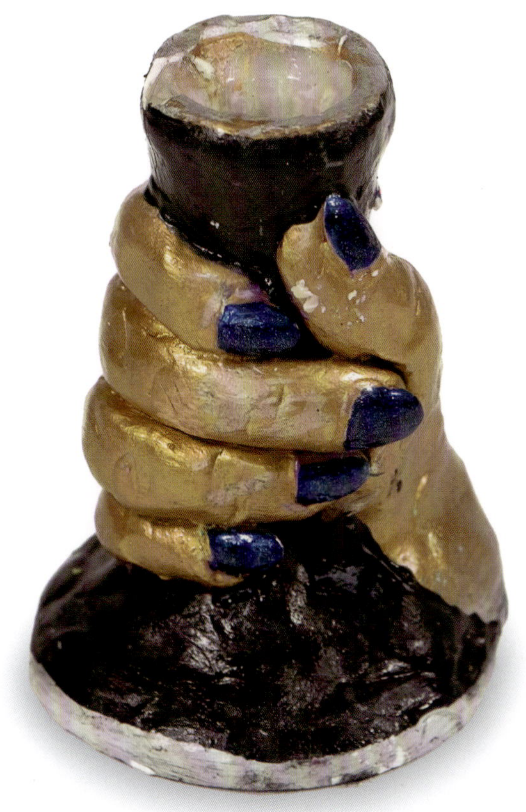

Candlestick.

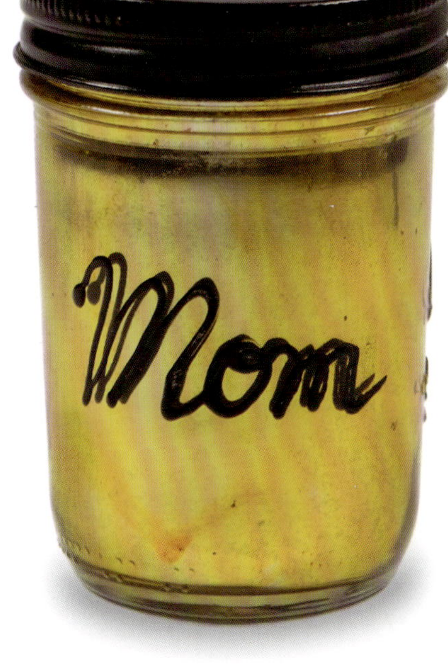

Handmade Christmas gift,
a family tradition.

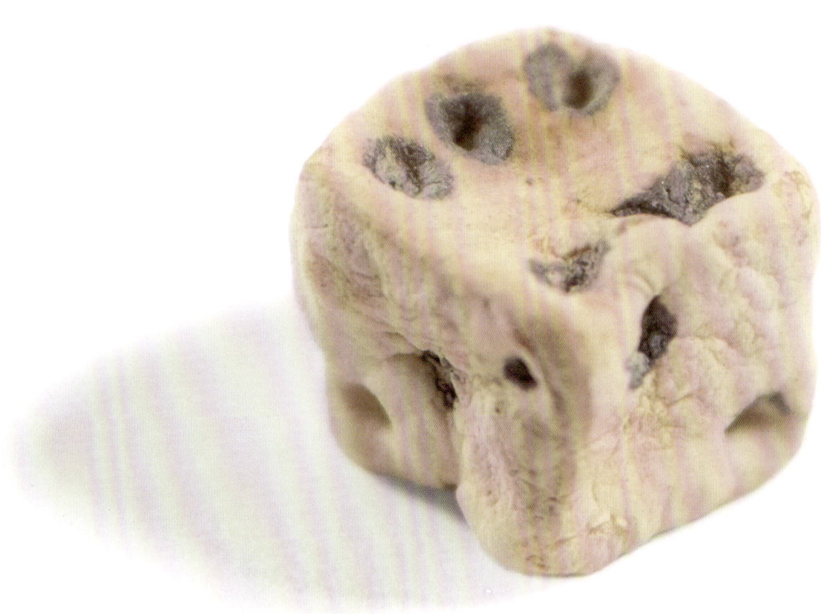

Experimenting with clay.

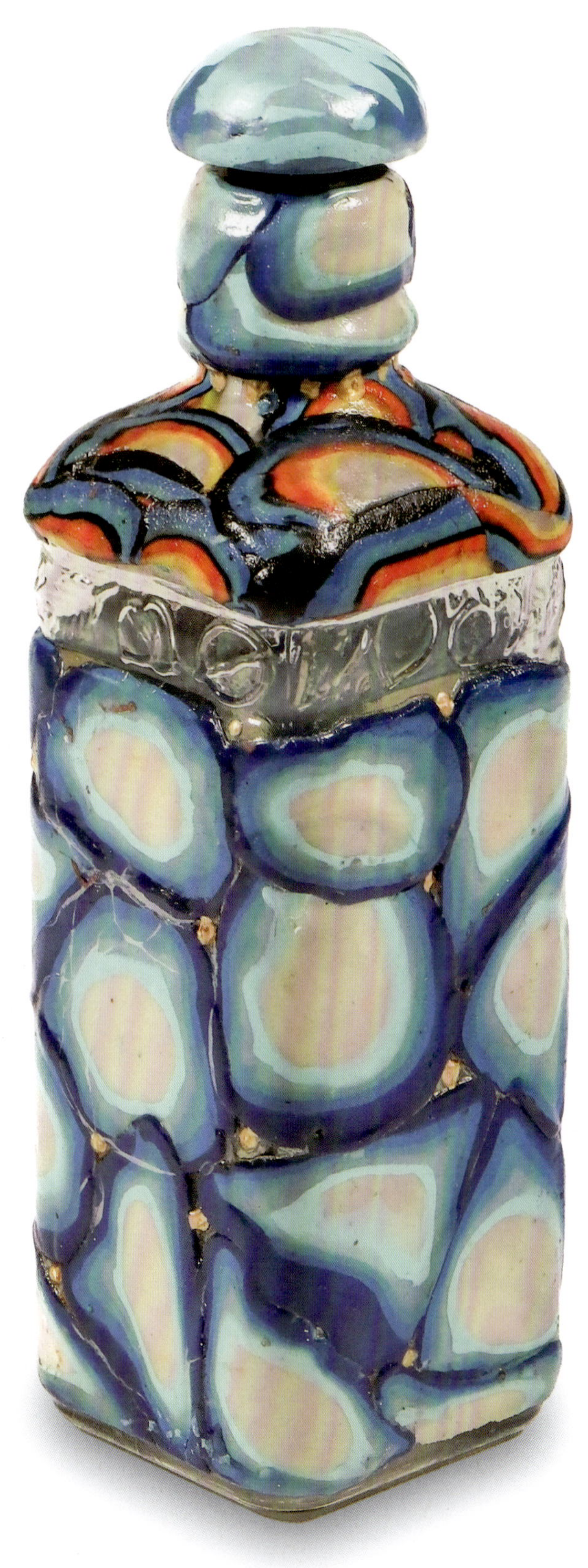

above: A gift for mom.
opposite: From Minnie's Bar by Layne and Demri.

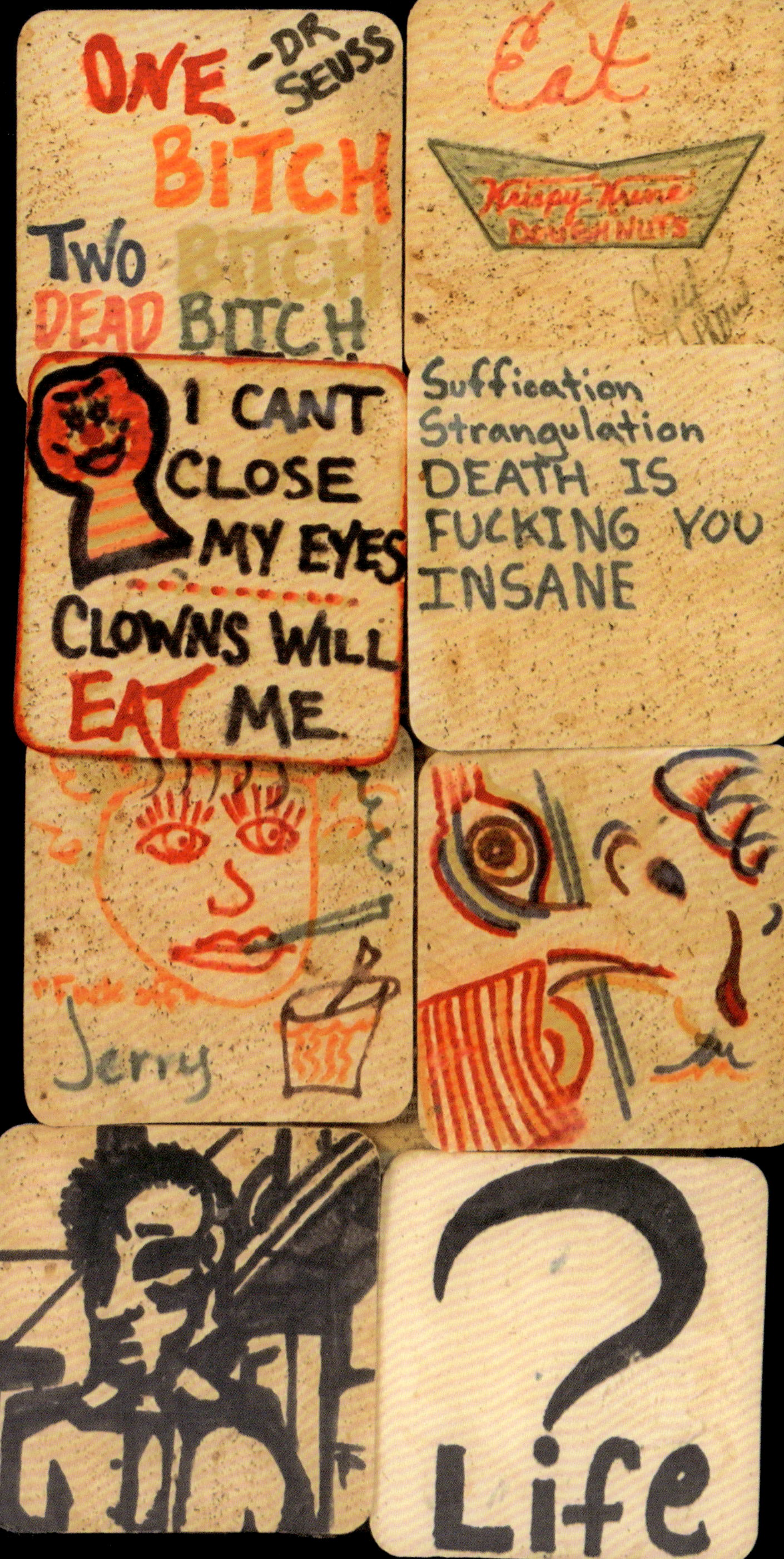
ONE BITCH
-DR SEUSS
TWO BITCH
DEAD BITCH
Eat
Krispy Kreme
DOUGHNUTS
I CANT CLOSE MY EYES
CLOWNS WILL EAT ME
Suffication
Strangulation
DEATH IS FUCKING YOU INSANE
Jerry
Life

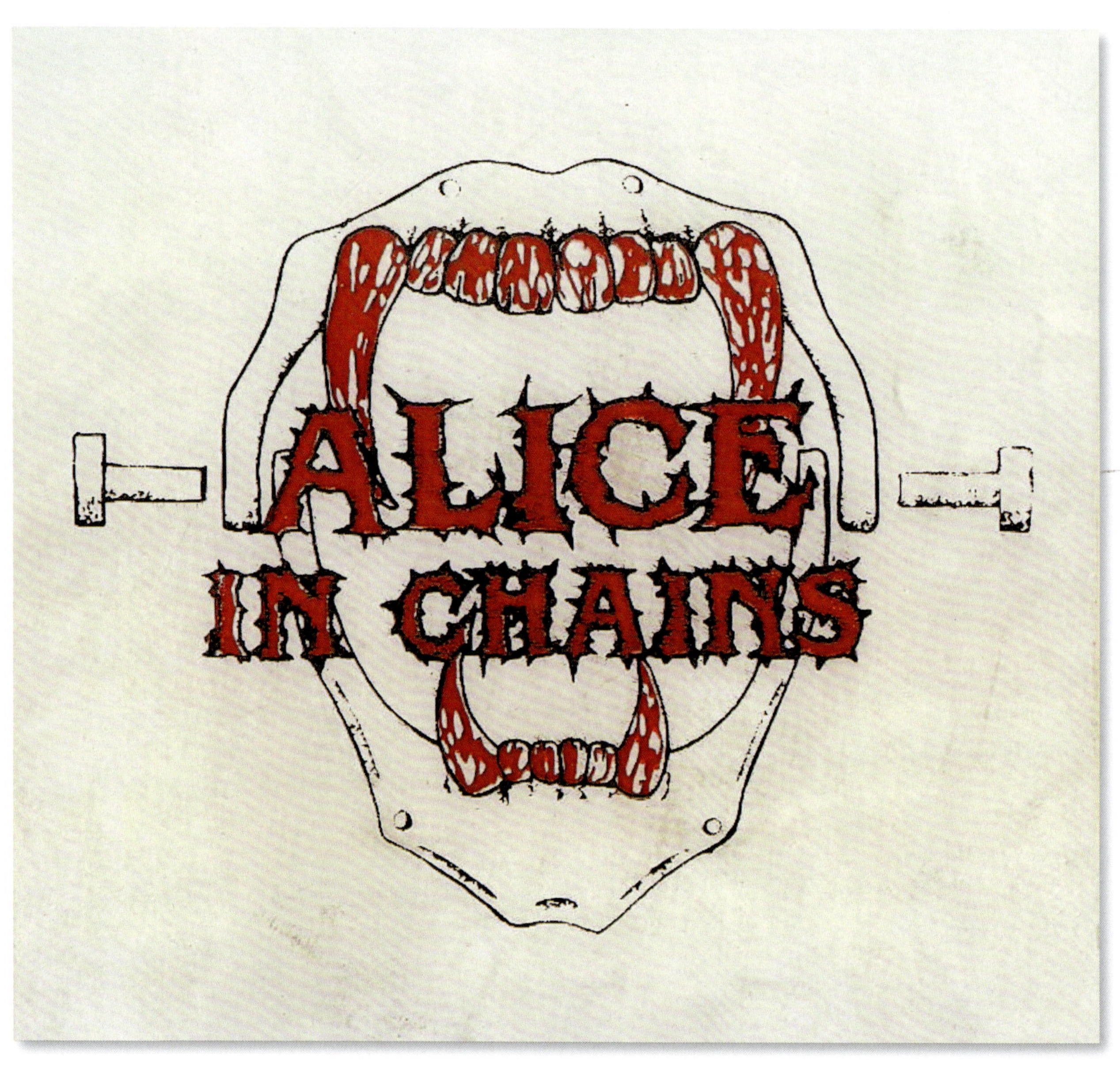
ALICE
IN CHAINS

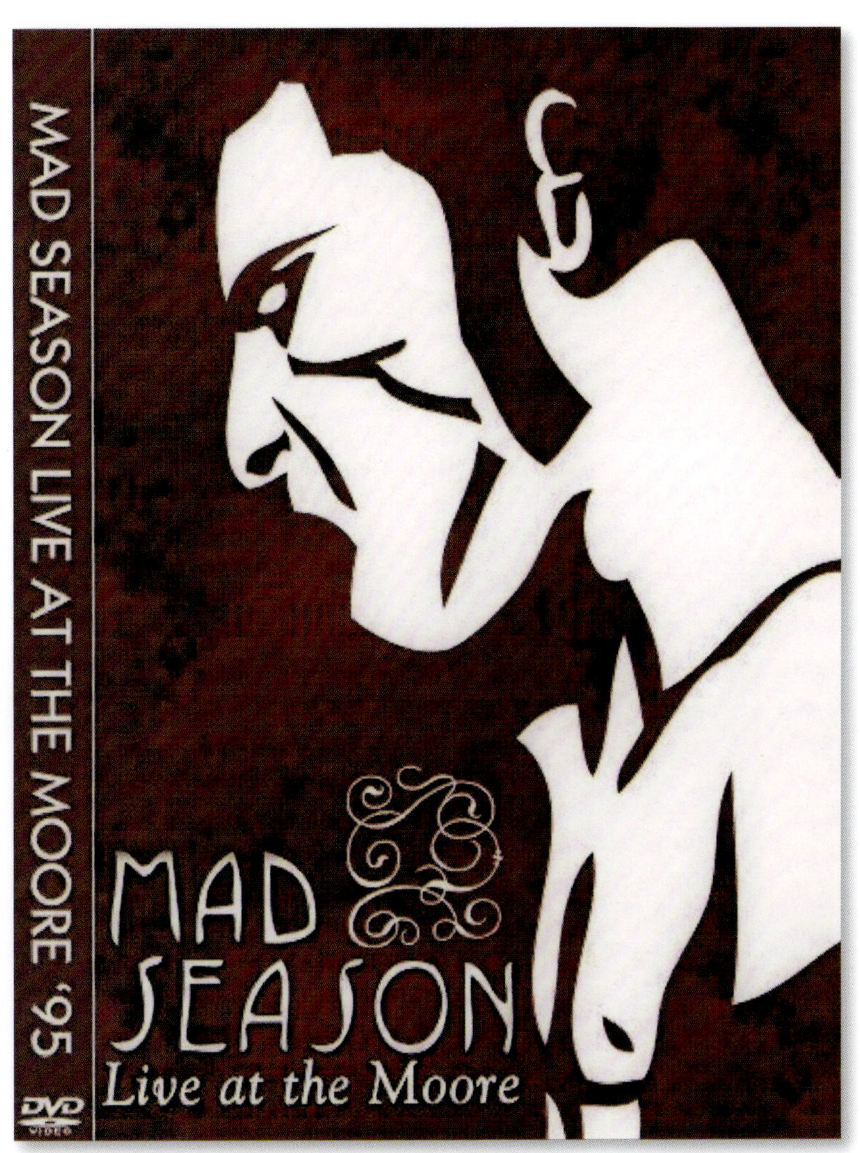

Self-portrait #6. One of only a handful of live performances by Mad Season.

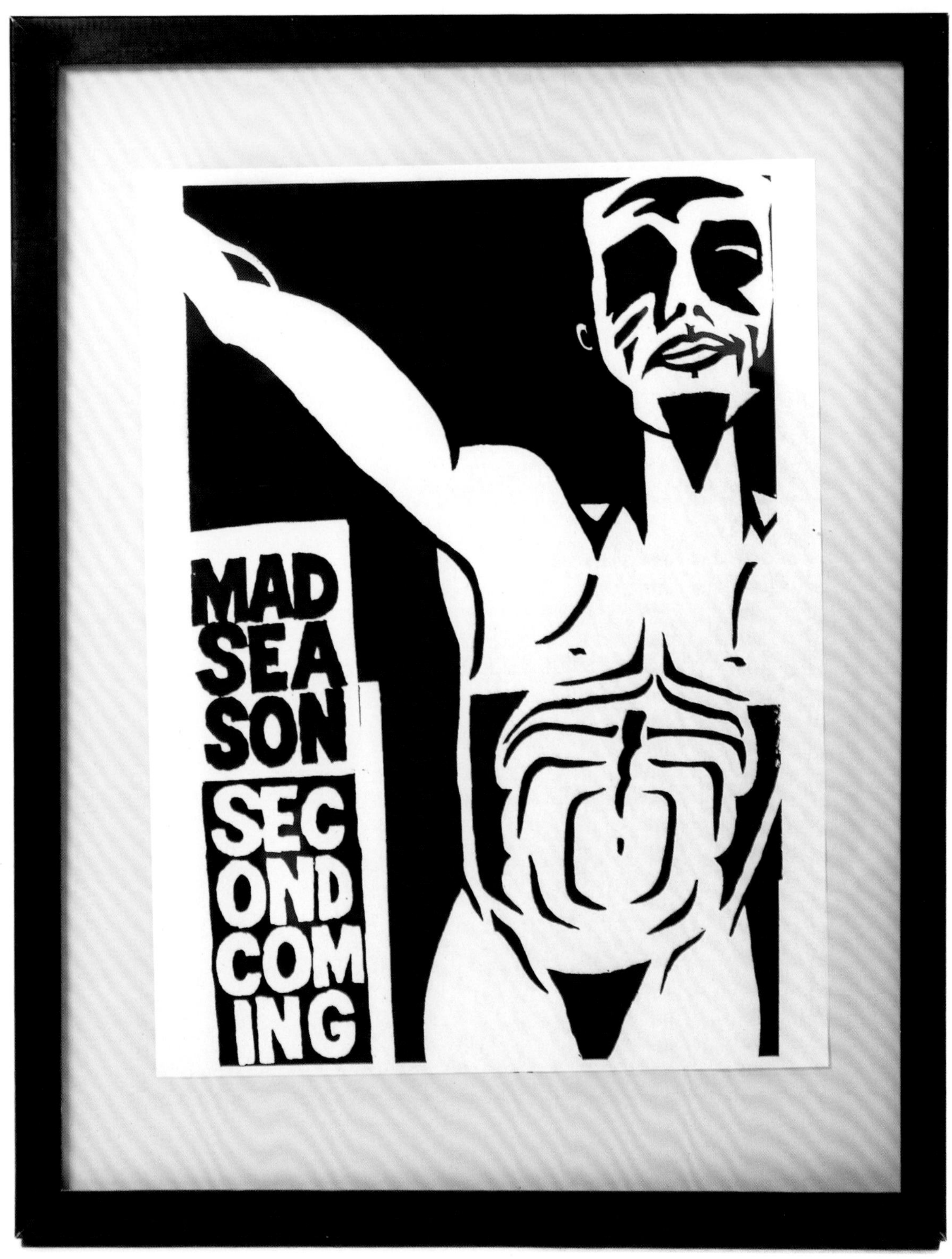

Self-portrait #7.

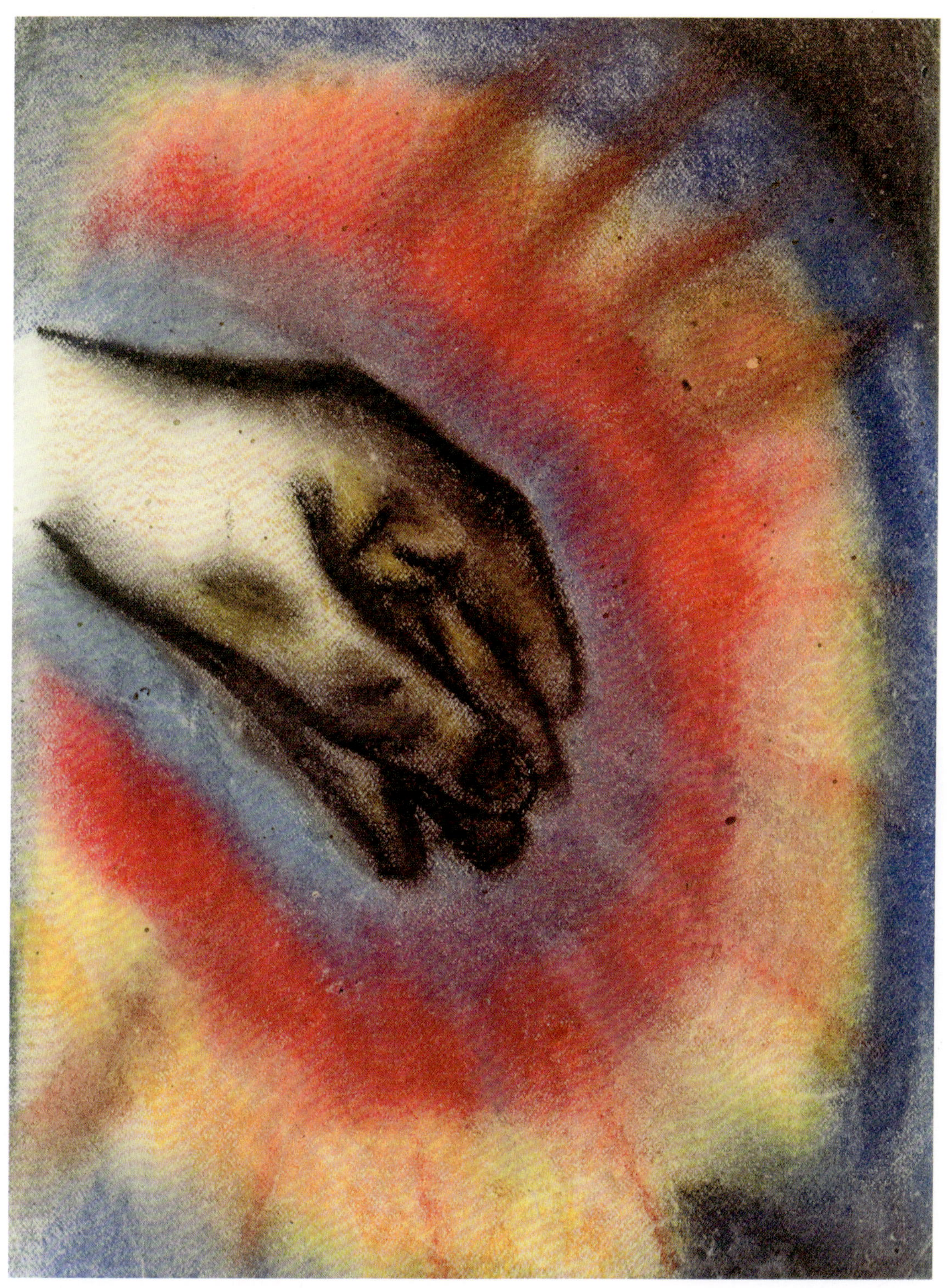

Layne had a fever when he was about 5 or 6. He saw a hand coming down toward him from the ceiling. That vision may have inspired this drawing.

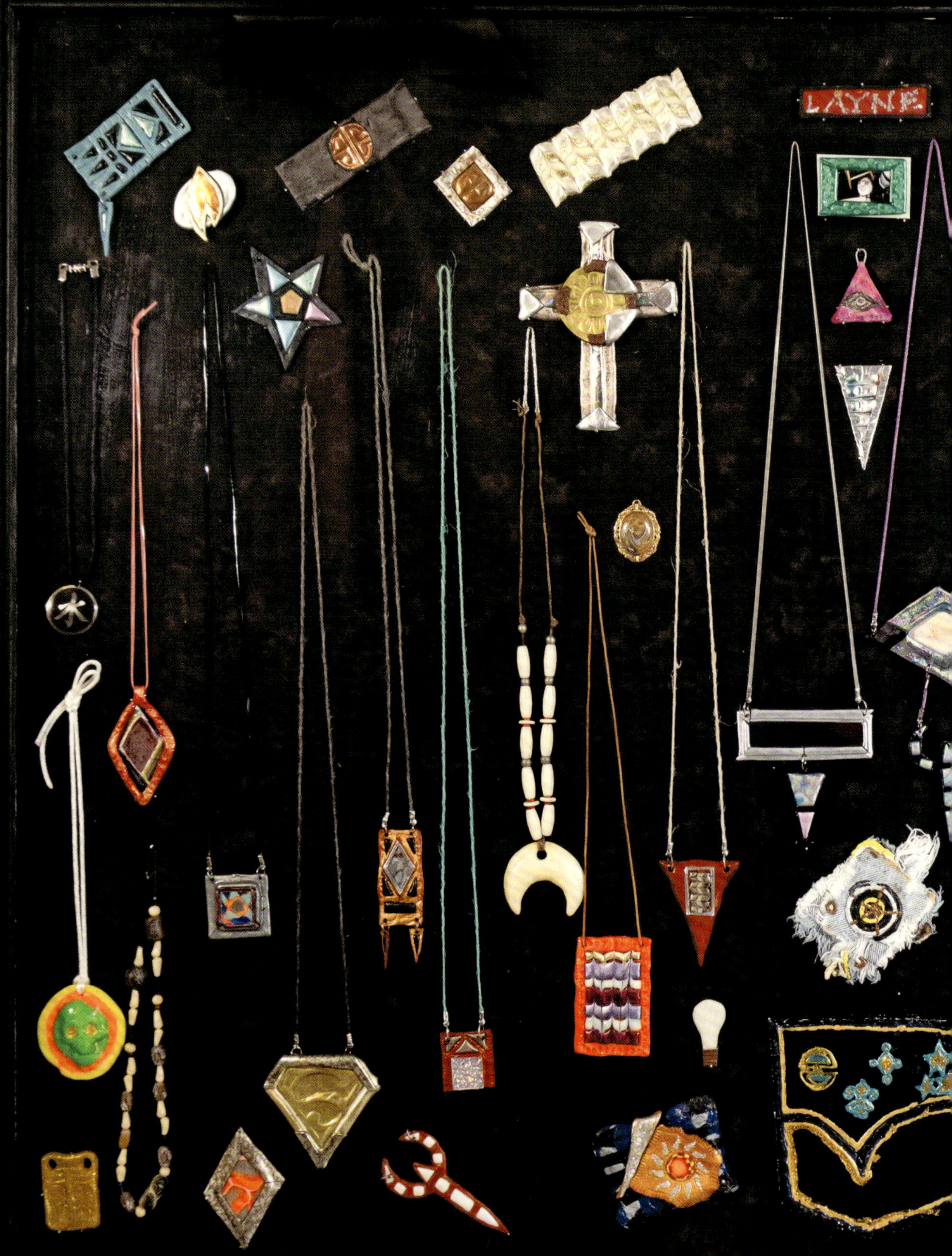
LAYNE

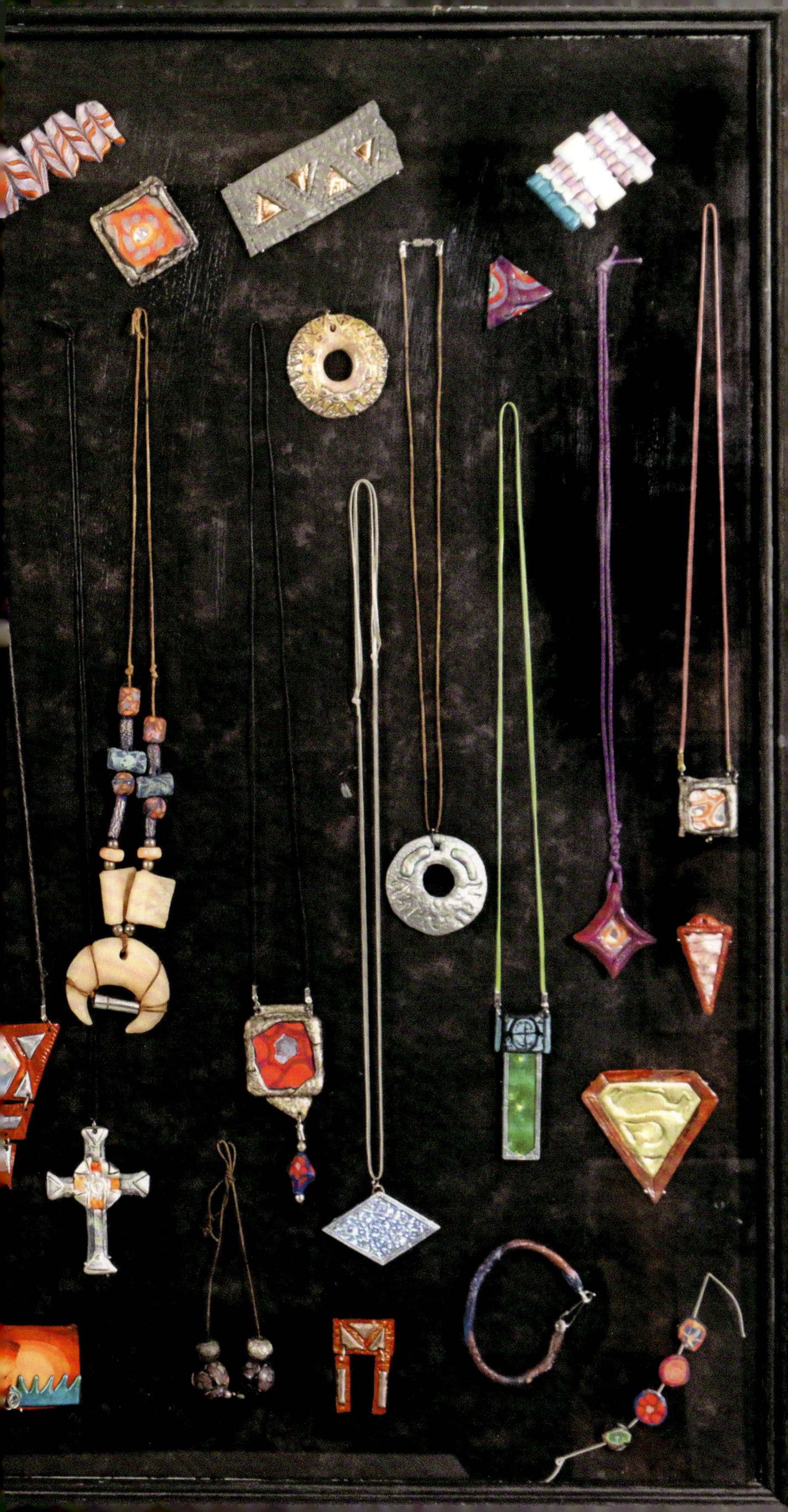

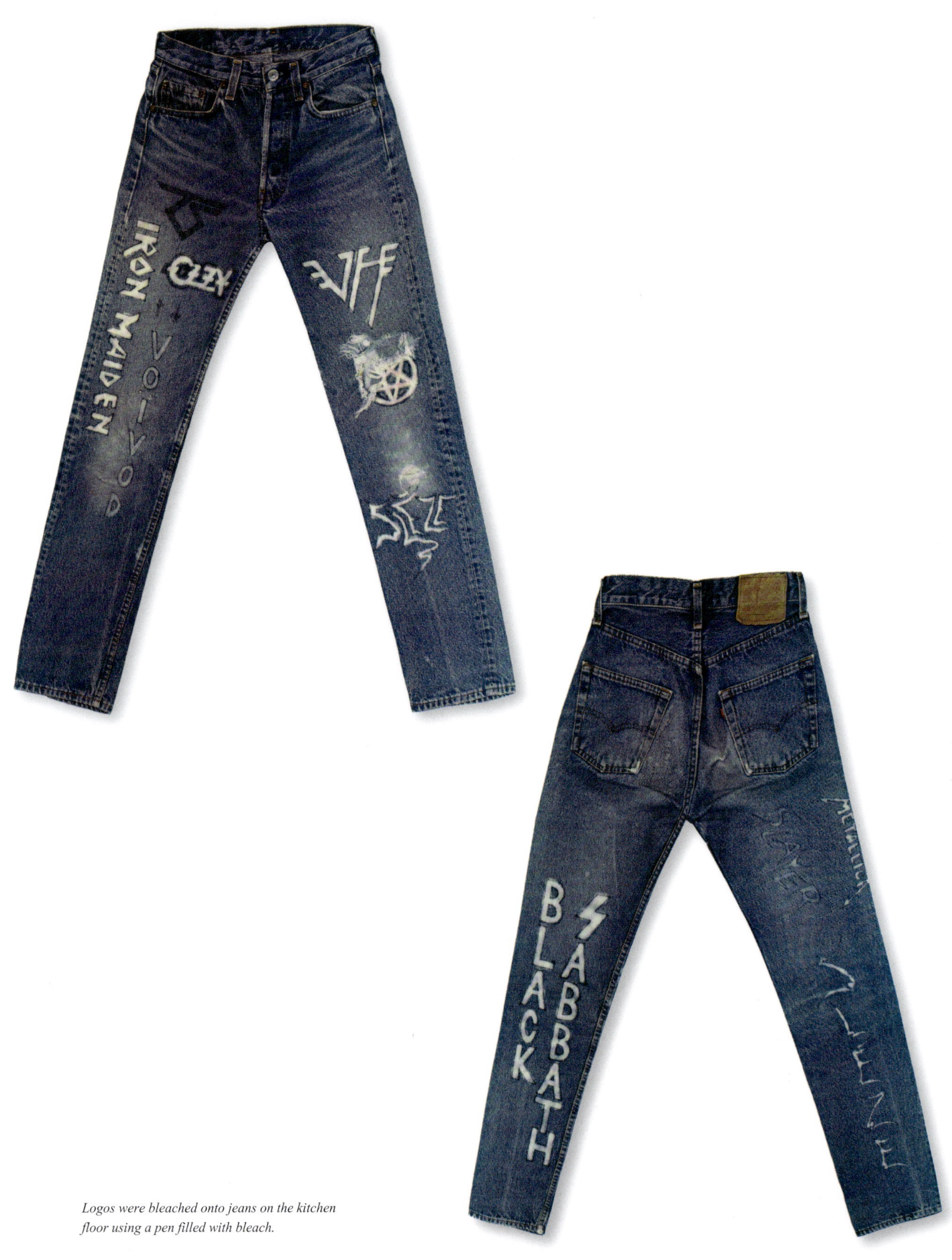

Logos were bleached onto jeans on the kitchen floor using a pen filled with bleach.

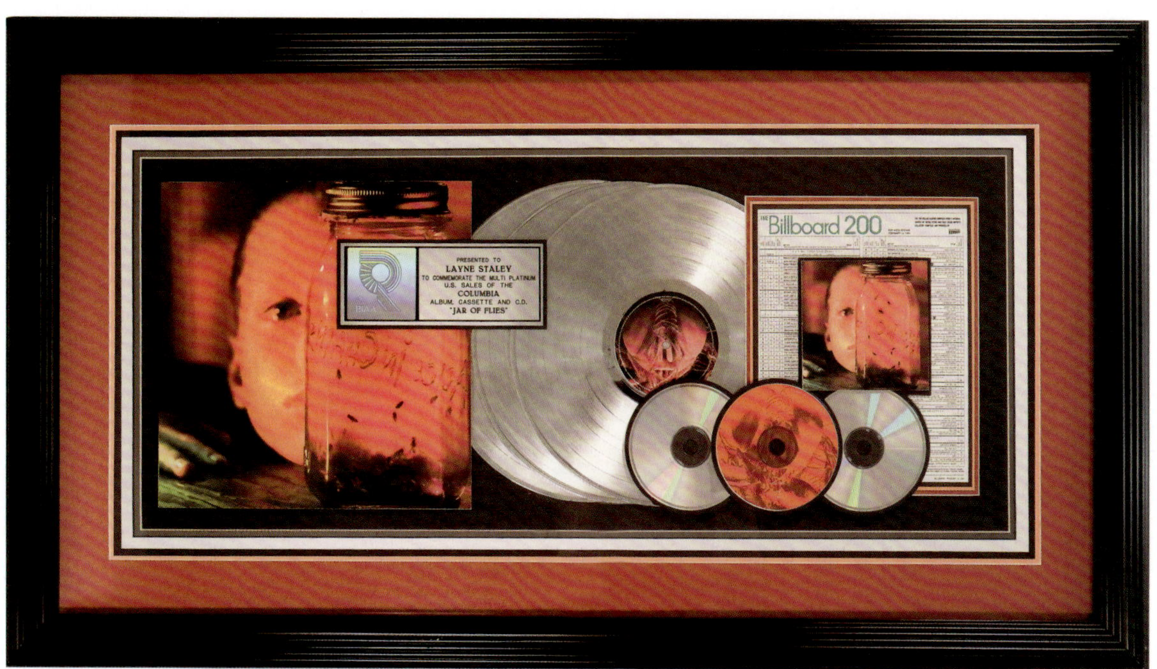

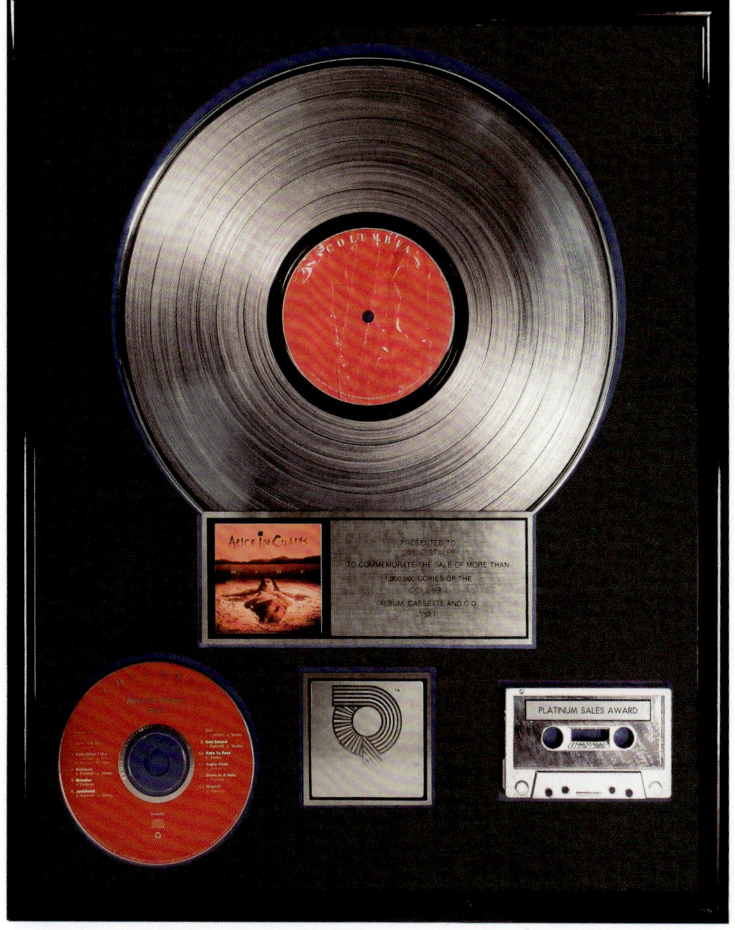

above: Jar of Flies *EP, cassette, and CD—multiplatinum sales.*

left: Dirt *album, cassette, and CD commemorating 1 million copies sold. Since Layne passed,* Dirt *has been certified 5x Platinum.*

WORKING WITH LAYNE STALEY

I've been blessed in my life, in that I have had the great fortune of working with some of the greatest singers of my generation. Sometimes it was in the studio, sometimes it was live onstage, and sometimes it was a combination of both, but in every case the singer's talent changed my musical soul forever. People like Mark Lanegan (Screaming Trees), Michael Stipe (R.E.M.), Chris Cornell (Soundgarden), and Patti Smith (punk icon) are some of the singers I've had the privilege of playing with. But one of those singers stands out with an intensity and clarity above all, and that was Layne Staley. His vocal abilities and his command of lyrical poetry stands out with the greatest singers of all time, and even though we only toured and recorded together for a few short years between 1992 and 1995, the memory of that time is burned into my memory like a fiery fever dream.

I want to put this story in context against the backdrop of the burgeoning Seattle music scene in the late 1980s and early 1990s. As countless history books have already written, it was a unique time in American music history, which has not been replicated in the 40 years since. Many incredible bands came out of that music scene, far more than I can possibly name here, but the ones I knew personally were Mudhoney, TAD, Soundgarden, Screaming Trees, Nirvana, Pearl Jam, and of course Layne's incredible band, Alice in Chains.

Alice, as they were known in the one-word vernacular, had what I would say was the best combination of authentic heaviness, combined with a superb melodic sensibility that allowed them to cross over into the mainstream, while at the same time sounding completely original. This is not an easy thing for any band to accomplish, and it's especially interesting to consider that some of their best and heaviest music was acoustic, something that few bands have attempted and even fewer succeeded at. Alice did both.

You have to remember that every band in Seattle at that time was using volume and heaviness as an aspect of their sound, but Alice had the ability to take one of Jerry Cantrell's virtuosic riffs and turn it into something groovy and catchy at the same time. Their songs were hypnotic and mesmerizing in the true sense of the word, and the musical foundation made by Sean Kinney, Mike Starr, and Mike Inez, combined with the soaring vocals of Layne and Jerry, singing solo and in harmony with each other, made them one of the most original and successful bands of that era.

It was Layne's voice, however, that gave the Alice sound an extra dose of shamanic magic. His searing, resonant tenor made Alice stand out above the rest. We all heard that imminent potential when their debut album, *Facelift* (1990) came out, along with their first hit song, "Man in the Box." But it was their second album, *Dirt* (1992), where I think they achieved a masterpiece in songcraft, in any genre, grunge, rock, or otherwise. It's one of the best albums made over the last 50 years.

I hadn't seen Alice play a live show in Seattle, even though they had been kicking around the music scene for a few years up to that point. I was on tour with my first band, the protogrunge band Skin Yard, and then I joined Screaming Trees in 1991, so in the years between 1990 and 1995, I wasn't in Seattle very much at all. I think the first time I saw Alice was when I saw the movie *Singles*, where Alice had a cameo in the film. It wasn't until the Screaming Trees and Alice were put on tour together in 1992 that I finally saw them perform live on stage for the first time. It was our first gig together, on November 13th, 1992, in Fort Lauderdale, Florida, the first of several dozen shows that we would play together all over the United States, Canada, and Europe, taking us well into 1993.

During the course of the tour, Layne and I became pretty good friends, with occasional outings to walk around in the cities of Europe, always with my bandmate Mark Lanegan. Layne and I talked about the work we had both done prior to becoming touring rock musicians, and it turned out that both of us had been construction workers, framing houses, and doing the hard, honest labor of young men. I've always thought that housebuilding is the best work ethic, foundation for everything a musician does, because making albums is very much like building houses—it's layer upon layer of careful meticulous work.

At the individual shows, when we would write up our guest lists every night, Layne would reserve his personal list for the kids standing outside the venue who couldn't afford to buy a ticket. He felt like those kids were the real fans, the ones who showed up to see a show with nothing but hope that they might find a ticket. Because hope is all a kid has when economic opportunity has passed you by.

Now, it is true that our world tour was a great success for both bands. The *Dirt* album went platinum and then double platinum in rapid succession, and our tour was one of the most talked about during those storied 1990s years. Alice become a huge international band, and the Screaming Trees had a smaller, but equally important rise in our own global profile. But what I remember most distinctly about that tour and the individual shows, which I watched every night from the side of the stage, was the power of Layne's voice. It was so powerful and just astoundingly loud, to the degree that I could hear his natural, acoustic volume over the immense amplified volume of the band on stage, including Jerry's stack of guitar amps. I remember seeing Layne's rib cage compress whenever he was delivering a particularly powerful lyric or scream (also because he was usually shirtless at these shows) and when he screamed, it was the most beautiful, melodic scream I had ever heard. Not a scream like any capable rock singer can do, but more like a deep, primordial howl that pierced your heart but not your eardrums. It was the most magnificent howl I have ever heard, and to this day I've never heard anyone come close to it.

The other side of the story is that the tour was the most debauched adventure I have ever experienced, as every form of decadence that can be experienced on a rock tour was present, at every show, for months on end. It's not something that I think was good for any of us, and certain addictions became quite a bit worse as a result, but I also suppose that rock-and-roll madness contains a certain kind of experience. Or as William Blake once wrote, "The road of excess leads to the palace of wisdom."

There was one incident in Sweden, where the audience was particularly rowdy, because these shows varied in size, depending on the city we were playing. This show had at least 2,000 people in the standing-room-only audience, but there was a skinhead Nazi who was in the pit in front of the stage, punching women in the back of their heads. We saw it from the side of the stage, and before security could intervene Layne pulled the guy onto the stage and then slap-punched him to make an example in front of the roaring audience. The Nazi went down hard, the crowd was ecstatic, and Alice finished their set triumphantly.

The next day, Layne was arrested by the Swedish police for assault, which seemed ridiculous considering that the Nazi was the one who started the violence. I think Layne might have had to pay some kind of fine or restitution, but after that show, we all realized that even though Layne was not necessarily the biggest or burliest guy on the tour (that would have been me, Mark Lanegan, and Alice's security guard, John Sampson), but Layne was certainly fearless when it came to stopping violence—with violence. After the story broke in the international music news, there were no more fights to be seen at our shows.

After the tour concluded in the spring of 1993, we all went different directions to do our own headlining tours around the world, but Alice had clearly ascended to the throne of the best heavy rock band in the world. By the end 1993, Alice, Nirvana, and Pearl Jam were equally the best live bands in the world—and they all came from Seattle.

It was in 1994, when the Screaming Trees were on hiatus in Seattle to write our next album, when I got a call from Pearl Jam guitarist Mike McCready. He wanted to start a new band—a side project really, which would feature me on drums, Mike on guitar, a bassist he had met in a Minnesota rehab clinic named John Baker Saunders, and for the singer Mike wanted to get Layne Staley. Now, all of us were already playing with incredible singers at that time—I was working with Mark Lanegan in Screaming Trees, and Mike was working with Eddie Vedder in Pearl Jam. But it was Layne's voice that made us all desire something different, something that was transcendent and shamanic, and perhaps even slightly dangerous.

alternate verses to the song, side by side. They followed the same approach for my other song, "I'm Above," and that song became the title track for the album.

One of the main things that stood out to me during these recording sessions was the way in which Layne approached his vocals. He preferred to do them late at night, and since I was more of a morning person, I wouldn't always stick around to watch him do his vocals. However, the handful of times that I did stay were pretty incredible to behold. Layne seemed to have his vocals already worked out in his mind, and he would record them in a single take, with just a few fixes or punch-ins here and there. Then he would proceed to do three or four backing vocals with harmonies, which were also preformed in his mind. It was incredible to observe and hear, he was just like a machine laying it down perfectly. And remember, this was in 1994 where we were recording on 2-inch magnetic tape, so digital Auto-Tune was not even available. Back in the 1990s, you actually had to sing in tune because if you didn't, everyone could hear it. Or as we used to say back then, "The tape doesn't lie."

Lyrically however, it was clear that Layne was processing some real traumas in his life. He and Mike and I were exactly the same age at the time, 27 years old. That's still pretty young, but it is old enough to have lived some real-life experiences and have some stories to tell. I felt like Layne was singing for all of us, for our entire generation—his lyrics are still so timeless, 30 years later.

Layne also held closely a copy of Kahlil Gibran's classic *The Prophet*, which he always had next to his lyric journal. He referenced *The Prophet* frequently for inspiration, occasionally using its metaphors for his lyrics. Like the phrase from one of the poems in the book, Layne likened us musicians to "burning arrows that arc across the darkening skies." I always remember and love that one, because in some of my own dark times, I remembered Layne's voice speaking those very words.

Mad Season only played a handful of shows when our album came out in March 1995, all of those in Seattle, and we never had the chance to tour because of our day-job bands that got busy again. Mad Season was short-lived, but it was a fireball of intense creativity, and the handful of shows we did play in Seattle, the energy we brought to the stage was even more ferocious than our studio album. In fact, I've never played in a band before, or since, that had that kind of explosive stage power.

The first rehearsal with the four of us was like putting lightning in a bottle—or more like throwing a Molotov cocktail. The songs came together so quickly, with each guy bringing in a riff, or a chord progression, or a rhythm that inspired truly original songwriting. The electric vibe that Mad Season instantly had was pure magic from day one, it was like the heaviest yet most melodic blues band that ever existed. That's how it felt being in Mad Season, and it was all we could think about. What would the next rehearsal be like, and what would the next batch of songs sound like? We were trying out new ideas at every rehearsal, with new approaches to songwriting as we jammed out the emotional-spiritual feel we were generating.

This is something that needs to be specifically addressed, which is the spiritual nature of Mad Season, and specifically Layne's incredible lyrics. Because Mad Season is the only album where Layne wrote 100% of the lyrics, it was a personal testament that he wanted to make on his own. With Alice, he shared those responsibilities with Jerry, and their songs were equally magnificent, but with Mad Season, Layne wanted to try something different, and he wanted our band to express a particular sound that could support his own lyrical vision.

We all wrote the songs together, that's why Mad Season was so interlocked musically, but each of us brought in the basic ideas that became the starting point for the songs. For example, Baker brought in the main riff for "Wake Up," and Mike had written the music for "River of Deceit" in that Minnesota rehab facility with Baker. Layne had the riff for "I Don't Know Anything," and I wrote the music for "I'm Above" and "Long Gone Day." Other songs came together from our collective jams, or perhaps a simple riff that someone presented, and then we all expanded on it. It was all so organic and natural, it was like the greatest musical love affair that I have ever had.

When I wrote the music for "Long Gone Day," it was an unusual song that started with my upright bass riff, and then I added a marimba and some Latin percussion. Mike added an acoustic guitar and shortly after that, Layne arrived at the studio. I said to Layne, "Look, I have this basic track for a song, and it's pretty different from everything we've been doing. It's totally acoustic, so you might not like it, but I'd like to play it for you." He nodded and said, "Of course," and engineer-producer Brett Eliason rolled the 2-inch tape. As the music played, I saw Layne start to smile and nod his head, and about halfway through the song he said, "I fucking love it!" That's when he suggested we bring in my Screaming Trees bandmate Mark Lanegan to sing on it with Layne. The next night, the two singers proceeded to sit at the mixing console, each with a microphone in their hand, as they sang

The last time I saw Layne in person was when I went over to visit him at a house he was renting near Queen Anne Hill in north Seattle. It was 1996 and my visit was for nothing in particular—I just stopped by to say hello. We ended up playing a video game together, just me and Layne in his large, empty house. I remember he had a gigantic platter of candy sitting on his coffee table, and we just nibbled on the candy as we played the video game together. It was some kind of game where we wandered through a labyrinthian house, looking for various treasures. Again, it was a perfect metaphor for the musical path we had chosen—music as a way to find treasures. To this day, I have never played another video game, because I want to remember the one I played with Layne.

This year, and even the very month that I am writing this, happens to be the 30-year anniversary of the release of the Mad Season album, which has continued to sell continuously all over the world. The songs "Wake Up," "River of Deceit," "I Don't Know Anything," and "Long Gone Day" are now considered to be classic rock songs that have held up over the passage of time. That's a big thing for a musician when their songs are considered classics, and I hope that the next generation of musicians and songwriters will build on those ideas. That's the job of each successive generation of musicians, to build on the ideas of the previous.

I have always felt deeply honored to have worked with such immense talents as Layne, Mike, Baker, and Mark, and when I reflect on that time, the only word that immediately comes to mind is "magical."

When Layne finally passed away in April 2002 at the age of 34, I wrote a long letter to his family describing much of what I have written here. They were so moved by that letter that it became the eulogy for his funeral.

There's not much more that I can say about Layne's greatness, but the very last I added to his eulogy was a death poem from a 15th-century Zen master. I always felt like this described Layne's musical-spiritual power best:

> My sword leans against the sky
>
> With its polished blade I'll behead
>
> The Buddha and all of his saints
>
> Let the lightning strike where it will
>
> *—Shumpo Soki, Zen master [died January 14, 1496]*

—Barrett Martin

LAYNE STALEY:
A FRIEND, AN ICON, AND AN IRREPLACEABLE VOICE

The first time I met Layne Staley was at the Music Bank in Seattle. It was the late '80s, and my band, Dali's Opera—named after Salvador Dalí—was rehearsing in a space next to Alice in Chains. Back then, the Seattle music scene was a wild, buzzing hive of creative energy, a melting pot of sounds that would soon change rock music forever. Layne stood out immediately. His presence was magnetic, his voice otherworldly. I remember hearing that voice bleed through the walls and thinking, What the hell is that? It was raw, soulful, and unlike anything else. Walking past their space and seeing this skinny, dreadlocked kid with the voice of a giant was truly shocking. That was the moment I realized Layne Staley wasn't just another singer—he was something special.

Layne's influence on me was profound, and I know I'm not alone in that. His vocal delivery was a mix of power, vulnerability, and an almost eerie beauty. It had this haunting quality, a kind of wounded intensity that cut deep. He could wail like a banshee one moment and then sink into a whisper that made you lean in closer the next. His voice didn't just sound good—it made you feel something. That's what great singers do, and Layne was one of the greatest.

It wasn't just his voice; it was the way he and Jerry Cantrell blended together that made Alice in Chains so unique. Their harmonies were dark and hypnotic, weaving together like the voices of two ghosts calling from another world. It was something no other band had, and even today, you can hear echoes of Layne in so many late '90s and early 2000s rock singers. Bands like Staind, Godsmack, and even Breaking Benjamin clearly took notes from him, consciously or not. That kind of impact isn't something you can fake—it's the mark of someone who changed the landscape of music.

Beyond his influence on music, Layne was just a genuinely kind, funny, and artistic soul. One memory that sticks out is a night at his apartment with my buddy Jonny, Aaron, and Mike McCready from Pearl Jam. Mad Season had just released their album, *Above*, and Layne had all the artwork he had created for the record laid out in front of him. His artistic side often got overshadowed by his music, but Layne was a deeply creative person in every sense. The artwork was mesmerizing—dark, surreal, and deeply personal, much like his music.

He casually told me to take a couple of pieces for myself, signing them as he handed them over. I was stunned, honored, and incredibly grateful. Then Mike McCready, watching the whole thing, blurted out, "What the hell? You made me pay for mine!" Without missing a beat, Layne grinned and shot back, "Yeah, you're not a singer." That was Layne—sharp, quick-witted, and always ready with a joke. But underneath the humor was a generosity and warmth that made him impossible not to love.

The Seattle music scene was a family back then, and Layne was a huge part of it. He embodied everything that made the era so special—raw talent, authenticity, and an unshakable sense of artistic integrity. There was no ego with Layne. He wasn't trying to be a rock star; he was just trying to express himself in the purest way possible. That's why his music still resonates today.

Losing him left a void that can't be filled. I miss him every day. His voice, his energy, his laugh—they're all irreplaceable. But I feel lucky to have known him, to have shared music and memories with him. And every time I hear his voice—whether it's "Man in the Box," "Nutshell," or "River of Deceit"—I'm reminded of the incredible human being behind those songs. Layne Staley was more than a singer. He was a force, a friend, and an artist whose legacy will never fade.

—Kevin Martin

This is Dave Mustaine and I am giving you a story. When Layne and I went with the band to go skydiving in Europe, we had been out on tour together. My publicist at the time, Val Janes, who I think worked with Alice in Chains, had been cruising around with me and she played a promotional cassette, it may have been a CD by then but it was long ago so it may very well have been a cassette, of "Man in the Box." I thought that was pretty good, but I had said, "I don't know how rock radio is going to react to somebody saying 'Shit.'" As I suspected, it was beeped for a while, but Mother Nature does things the way she does and so does the Father. We had mentioned having Alice in Chains come out on tour with us for the Clash of the Titans Tour because I liked them so much. They were on tour for a little while when the single "Would?" hit and they left the tour and went on to greatness.

During those times on tour though, we had been traveling together, and we were up in Scotland of all places, the top of Great Britain, and as you can imagine, the winds that came across at the top of that island were incredible, cold, biting, and it was very windy. Everything that you don't want to skydive in. However, for the day we wanted to go, we had a break in the weather. I can't remember who all went, I think former bassist Mike Starr went . . . I believe it was all four of us. I remember heading to the jump site and everyone was noticeably nervous and anxious for this thing to happen. I don't know how many of the guys would have passed up on jumping if someone else blinked first, but I think everyone was kind of stuck in the commitment to go skydiving with me, so we went through the training part, which is pretty short in the UK. In the United States, they make you train for a while. I did an accelerated free fall, which is when a person jumps by themselves with their own, individual parachute, whereas the guys had done tandem, which is where they have a jumpmaster who's got a gigantic parachute and a harness that a passenger can hook to the front of it. The two of them jump out of the plane together, deploy the chute, and hopefully arrive in one piece happily ever after.

We had done all the training, the moment was upon us, we were starting to get into the plane and that is when it started to become clear when no one wanted to be the first one to get into the plane. So I jumped in the plane first, then that was it and everyone else jumped in. It was probably 15 short minutes before we had gotten up to altitude, which was equivalent in meters to 13,000 feet, which is a little higher than what we jump out of in the United States. You see, the United States altitude we jump at is 12,500 feet and you deploy your chute at 4,500 feet. Naturally, they didn't have any devices that the Americans use for safety, such as an automatic altitude device, which you wear on your harness and if for any reason you hit the wing or the tail or anything on the way down and you're unable to deploy your chute if you're jumping alone like I did, this device will blow off a pilot chute and that will open up and pull out my main chute, which hopefully will deploy and deliver whoever had to use the AAD device safely to the ground. Although, they'll be hitting the ground hard because if they're unconscious, they're coming in at about 10 to 20 miles per hour depending on the wind and all that stuff. So once we got in the air, I don't remember the order we jumped out in, but when we got on the ground, the boys had become men. And it was one of the funnest times in my life with another band. We usually do stupid stuff like go-karting or bowling, or dumb stuff like that, but this was a magnificent opportunity to get close to the guys. I would do it again if I could, but I promised my wife I wouldn't be jumping anymore after Justis was born.

—Dave Mustaine

Layne Staley was not a man you could judge by appearances, and you were a fool if you saw him first without knowing him or tried to.

He was kind of a lanky dude—6 ft 1 in and weighing in at around 150 lbs—but in truth, Layne was actually a huge giant, his size and uplifting spirit residing in that towering heart and soul, and most loudly in his music. I recall Jerry (Cantrell) telling me how he had been repeatedly floored by the strength, power, and ginormous presence in Layne's voice—certainly a hell of a lot more than 150 lbs' worth, more like some behemoth Paul Bunyan.

I first met him at the Club With No Name on Highland in Hollywood circa 1991. Alice in Chains was a newer band around town, fresh from Seattle, and he was excited to meet me because I was in the band Suicidal Tendencies! He said, "Hey Robert, you have to meet my girlfriend—she loves you guys. In fact, she says Suicidal are better than my band, Alice in Chains!" I was like, "Whaaat??" and we had a good laugh!

Yeah, his positivity and relentless quest to have fun and stay festive stood out to me when I first met him. He was a warm and witty guy for sure back then.

There was absolutely no ego with Layne—just genuine love and respect.

In 1993, Suicidal toured Australia with Alice in Chains. They had huge success with their album *Dirt*, which was everyone's favorite album at the time, and supporting them was big fun as that sense of humor flowed from Layne through the band. It was summer camp at its finest—never a dull moment. Layne would have these insane late-night fire-breathing contests at the hotel bar (Bacardi 151 was the fuel) with Rocky George (Suicidal's guitarist)—this little dude taking Big Rocky to his fire-breathing limits! Poor Rocky ended up with blistered lips and singed hair—all in good fun, of course—but looking at his face the day after these events, I'd say he took a slight beating! I spent that tour trying to be responsible and maintain my "on-tour Aussie surf and gym workout regimen," yet despite these fire contests and other nocturnal shenanigans, the first person I'd see at 9:00 a.m. every morning was Layne Staley, by the pool basking in the sun with a huge smile, a glass of OJ, and a polite, "Roberto." I'm like, This motherfucker's superhuman! Not just in his voice, but in his stamina, edge, and attitude.

My favorite individuals have always been folks who are grounded and humble yet still maintain that hoodrat warrior quality and passion-driven creativity that gushes from the heart. They walk the earth with wisdom while still battling their demons. It would become clear that Layne was a wounded warrior with an angel spirit that would pour through his voice and songwriting to lift us all.

As we know, life isn't easy. Layne sadly knew that sharper than most, yet he constantly shared that magic spirit. And as I listen to that music he so beautifully helped make, and think about that Paul Bunyan–sized spirit and soul, it's impossible not to imagine Layne watching us all with his infectious smile, content in the knowledge that his beautiful, fire-breathing energy continues to infuse us all.

—Robert Trujillo

With Layne, it wasn't just the lyrics he sang, it was the way he delivered it.

I still remember the first time I heard his voice. It was concert footage of him singing "Love, Hate, Love" on some late-night MTV show. A guttural imperfect but perfect voice. I recorded it on VHS and watched it hundreds of times. I then realized the impact of an artist truly singing from a "real place," a lived experience of a broken man. I was all in at that moment.

A couple of years later I had a similar experience when I saw him singing "Junkhead." He was singing the quiet parts out loud with such a forceful grace. A perfect delivery. Something that was so raw, yet so beautiful because it instantly made me feel connected to him and the band on a deep level.

I'm forever grateful for those moments he shared with us. Layne and his work with AiC will forever be iconic to me and to this world.

—Scooter Ward

I have two distinct memories about my favorite band, Alice in Chains: the first time I heard them and the time they changed my life.

The first time I heard them was obviously "Man in the Box." Already, there was a shift happening in music in general, but AiC was the first time I heard all the elements that really resonated with me: darkness, metal, rock, and amazing lyrics. And it all circled and swarmed around Layne Staley's voice. From that moment on, he was one of my biggest influences and favorite singers.

The day they changed my life was the day I heard "Would?"

I was sitting on my couch, the movie *Singles* hadn't even come out yet, and the video premiered on MTV. The bass rumbled from my Zenith and I was never the same. The sheer power that Layne sang with was unreal, especially the outro as the modulation descended into a pseudo-Phrygian scale of chords that allowed Mr. Staley to pour every inch of his soul and pain into every note he chose. It was in that moment that I realized I could write about anything I wanted: addiction, depression, obsession, anguish . . . I didn't need to look to the clichés that I'd been bombarded with for years. I was free.

I can say with all honesty:

No Layne, no me.

I wouldn't have been brave enough to explore the things I have.

So, Mr. Staley, sincerely . . .

Thank you.

—Corey Taylor

Layne Staley...Man. That name alone really draws me back to those early '90s memories when the music scene was not only exploding again but really overrunning the older metal scene that we all called "hair metal." And thank God for that! Every band at that moment couldn't help but look like a group of ugly women with bad skin, even worse makeup, and torn fishnets. I'm so happy I was into punk rock during that movement.

I actually remember hearing about Nirvana first and the havoc they were wreaking on the music scene. But the more I started hearing other bands from this new "grunge" genre, the more I personally started loving this fresh new sound from the Pearl Jams and the Soundgardens of this era. It was powerful! And as a matter of fact, if it weren't for people like Eddie Vedder bringing back that deeper Elvis-style voice, I would've never had a chance at converting over to a singer.

But then I heard Alice in Chains, and for me, it was mesmerizing from the very start. An old friend/guitarist had turned me on to the *Live Facelift* concert recording that was released right around the time of their first album. I remember just sitting there in my sister's living room, completely hypnotized by Layne's vocals. His tone is really what resonated with me the most. But his lyrics and his melody choices were just so insanely delicious! It was dark but bluesy. And his runs were brilliant.

I can honestly say that he, for sure, was the second time lightning had struck me in the music world and left such a permanent imprint on my brain, reinforcing my mission to one day become a "rock star" instead of just a musician. Joe Perry was the first one to strike me that way. And weirdly enough, I had only been a drummer up until this point. But when 1995 rolled around and I decided to transition myself from drummer to front man, you can bet your ass that Layne fucking Staley was at the front of my thoughts—with his powerfully beautiful vocals and cool, mysterious stage presence—inspiring me to form Godsmack and giving me some of the tools I was looking for to be successful at a whole new level in music.

I'm sure you could ask many bands, and you would get many different opinions on "what defines the sound of a band." But if you ask me, it's hands down the singer. Of course, the instruments, players, melodies, and vibes that the music sets as a foundation for the whole song are critical, but it will never be complete until the vocals go down. A song is not a song until the vocals go down. And those vocals will also define the strength of the song. And they will certainly identify the sound of your band. You can replace a drummer or a guitar player, and they can literally replicate the music for the fans to still enjoy—but once you replace the singer, the entire sound of the band changes. Imagine Aerosmith without Steven Tyler? Layne Staley is irreplaceable.

The end.

—Sully Erna

Alright, let me tell you about the early days of shooting Alice in Chains, especially Layne. The very first time was for *Rolling Stone*, and I always remember the date: September 11th, 1991. Even with the magazine being a bit fussy about the sunglasses in the photos, I knew right away there was something special about them. Thankfully, they let me shoot them again just a few weeks later, back in their element in Seattle. That second shoot, up at the recording studios, that's where we really captured them. Those photos became pretty iconic, and I still feel a great sense of pride looking back at them.

Meeting them for the first time, down in Orange County, you could tell they were working hard, touring like crazy. But even with that tour weariness, there was a cool vibe about them. And Layne, even though he was a bit quieter, often hanging back with his shades, there was an undeniable presence about him. He had this intensity, even when he wasn't saying much. But the band as a whole, they were good guys, really good. Down-to-earth, you know? No rock-star BS like some of those other bands. Just genuine Seattle guys.

That second shoot in Seattle, at the studio, I got to spend a bit more time around them. They were focused on their music, but there was a real camaraderie there. And even though Layne was introverted, like Kurt, when he did engage, there was a real intelligence and thoughtfulness to him. You could see the depth in his eyes.

And then there was that *RIP* Magazine party on October 6th, 1991. Man, that was an incredible night. The Palladium in Hollywood was buzzing. Soundgarden, Pearl Jam, Alice in Chains—and Spinal Tap headlining! The energy in that room was electric. And at the end of the night, Alice came out and played some Temple of the Dog songs. That was just something else, a real moment. You could feel the connection between those bands, that Seattle sound.

Looking back at those early days, you could see the talent, the raw power of Alice in Chains, and the unique charisma of Layne. Even in those early photos, there's a vulnerability and an artistry that shines through. It was clear they were on their way to something big, and it was a privilege to capture a little piece of that journey. Those were good times, capturing the beginning of something truly special.

—Chris Cuffaro,
Photographer

Layne was the light of darkness. He was the only angelic man I have ever known. His light was brighter than his dark. But in the end the darkness took my friend and brother. Layne and I had a deep timeless bond. A well-known astrologer I highly regard said Layne and I have shared many lifetimes together. You can see this deep connection in the plethora of images we created together and in his amazing eyes. I love Layne's eyes; you can see his amazing soul in them. I'm forever grateful for those moments I had with him and with the band Alice in Chains. We created some of my favorite images together. Of all the bands I had the pleasure in working with and their amazing singers, and of all the bands I have listened to, no one touches Layne! With Layne there was something more because Layne was something more. It's as if he came from a different star, a star they haven't found yet. That haunting beautiful voice that would drop you to your knees, then take you places you didn't know existed. So much hope, so much pain, so much love. He shared it all! He was a true shooting star here among us, a messenger for our hearts and for our souls. A messenger through song that penetrated us deeper than any other singer ever will.

Layne had such a beautiful sweet soul and it reflected out into the world. However, on stage he was lightning and thunder. I loved capturing him live onstage, he was his own, his energy untouchable as he exploded onstage with depth and power. You couldn't take your eyes off of him or your camera! But my favorite moments with him were those moments where we would just hang out and talk of music, photography, spirituality, and of course women! There isn't a day that goes by that I don't think of him and the moments that live in me forever. The world lost a rock star. But I lost my dear friend and brother. I lost those amazing brother hugs that I still feel in my body! There will never be a light on this earth as bright as yours!!

—Paul Hernandez, Photographer

I met Layne around 1985 when he was 18 and I was 16. Though we went to different high schools, we shared the same circle of friends. At the time, my best friend was dating someone well-known in the local scene, and through them, my world expanded into the orbit of the older crowd and music community. I found myself spending more and more time at various houses and hangouts where musicians and creatives gathered.

Back then, I didn't yet know much about the local bands—I was still finding my way. For context, this would have been around Layne's *Sleze* days. Those were good times. Everyone seemed to know each other, connected by music, creativity, and a strong sense of community.

I was taking a photography class in high school and carried my camera everywhere. As Layne and I got to know each other, we quickly discovered our shared love for the arts—he talked about his music and writing, and I shared my passion for photography. Eventually, as one of his early bands was evolving into what would become Alice in Chains, he said:

"Oh! You're doing photography—I want you to take photos for our band."

That's how I started photographing Layne and our friendship developed.

At the time, we all spent a lot of time at the Music Bank, a rehearsal space under the Ballard Bridge that became a second home for many musicians. I can still picture the old rickety railroad tracks we had to cross to get there, my little orange '76 Hondamatic bouncing through the potholes like it had no business making it through. The Music Bank was more than a rehearsal space—it was a hub, a creative haven, and a memory vault. Oh, the stories from that place still flood back.

I began taking photos of rehearsals, and eventually Layne asked me to shoot promotional images for the band and to start coming to their shows as their guest photographer. At the time, they were going by *Alice 'N Chains* and were starting to build a strong local following.

In early 1987, we scheduled a promo shoot in an empty rehearsal room at the Music Bank—Layne loved the look of the cracked cement walls. I distinctly remember setting it up with lighting with Layne and Nick. The idea was entirely Layne's, and he was buzzing with excitement. We had lighting, makeup, a crimper, and plenty of hairspray—it was everything you'd expect from the late '80s. Though I wasn't a professional photographer, Layne treated the shoot as if it were the real deal. He believed in what we were doing, and that belief meant the world to me.

He then gave me a pass for their *Accidents Will Happen Tour 87* summer tour that year, where I served as their band photographer—front and back of house. I never charged for any of it, because what I gained was worth far more than money. Layne pushed me out of my comfort zone, encouraged me, and gave me space to grow creatively. That was his gift—he saw people's potential and nurtured it.

We were just kids, figuring it out as we went—but we were creating photographic art together.

I moved to Denver, Colorado, a few years before Layne passed, and the news hit me hard. I don't think I've ever truly said goodbye. He was an incredibly special soul, a brilliant and funny creative with a heart of gold. Even after achieving fame, he never stopped being that same grounded guy. We eventually lost touch as life took us in different directions, but in those formative years, he gave so much of himself.

His belief in me helped shape my artistic journey. That was his superpower—he inspired confidence and lifted up those around him by creating with them.

Layne was generous, profoundly kind, talented, and irreplaceable. It breaks my heart that he's gone. But I'm forever grateful to have known him and to have been part of his world and creative journey.

—Carolyn Cawrse,
Photographer

The first time I met Layne Staley wasn't really a formal introduction—just a quick handshake before Alice in Chains took the stage to open for Mother Love Bone at the Central Tavern. It was 1989, and I had already spent a couple of years photographing Mother Love Bone, so my introduction to Layne was simply as the photographer.

To be honest, I wasn't much of a rock fan at the time—punk had always been more my thing. But the moment Layne started singing, everything changed. In person, he was quiet, almost reserved, and his voice didn't seem to match the guy I'd met just moments earlier.

Photographing him wasn't like shooting a typical front man. He wasn't flashy or overly animated, which made capturing his presence more of a challenge. But the images I did get told a deeper story—the microphone cord wrapped tightly around his arm, his head bowed, eyes closed. That cord, to me, seemed like more than just stage equipment; it looked like a security blanket, something familiar, something to hold on to. There was a palpable tension—a silent, soulful battle playing out in real time.

A part of me never wanted to get too close to him offstage. I recognized the demons he carried, maybe because I was familiar with my own. And every time I photographed him, I had to tap in to those same shadows within myself, just to do him justice.

—Lance Mercer, Photographer

Layne and I became friends not long after I moved to Seattle, and what stood out right away—beyond that unmistakable voice—was his incredibly dry, almost sneaky sense of humor. He had this way of dropping a perfectly timed, deadpan comment that would catch you off guard and leave you laughing hours later. He could be quiet and introspective, but when he let you in, he was sharp, funny, and deeply thoughtful. There was a warmth to him that didn't always come through onstage, but if you were lucky enough to know him offstage, you saw it—layered beneath the darkness was a genuinely nice guy who could find the absurdity in just about anything.

One night at the Off Ramp, Layne and I were standing in the back by the sound booth, half shouting over the noise. I made some comment about the bathroom being a health hazard, and without missing a beat, he deadpanned, "That's where Seattle's next wave of bands is being cultured." He said it so seriously I almost believed him for a second before we both cracked up. That was Layne—his humor was bone-dry, perfectly timed, and just a little bit twisted.

—Alison Braun, Photographer

FAN ART

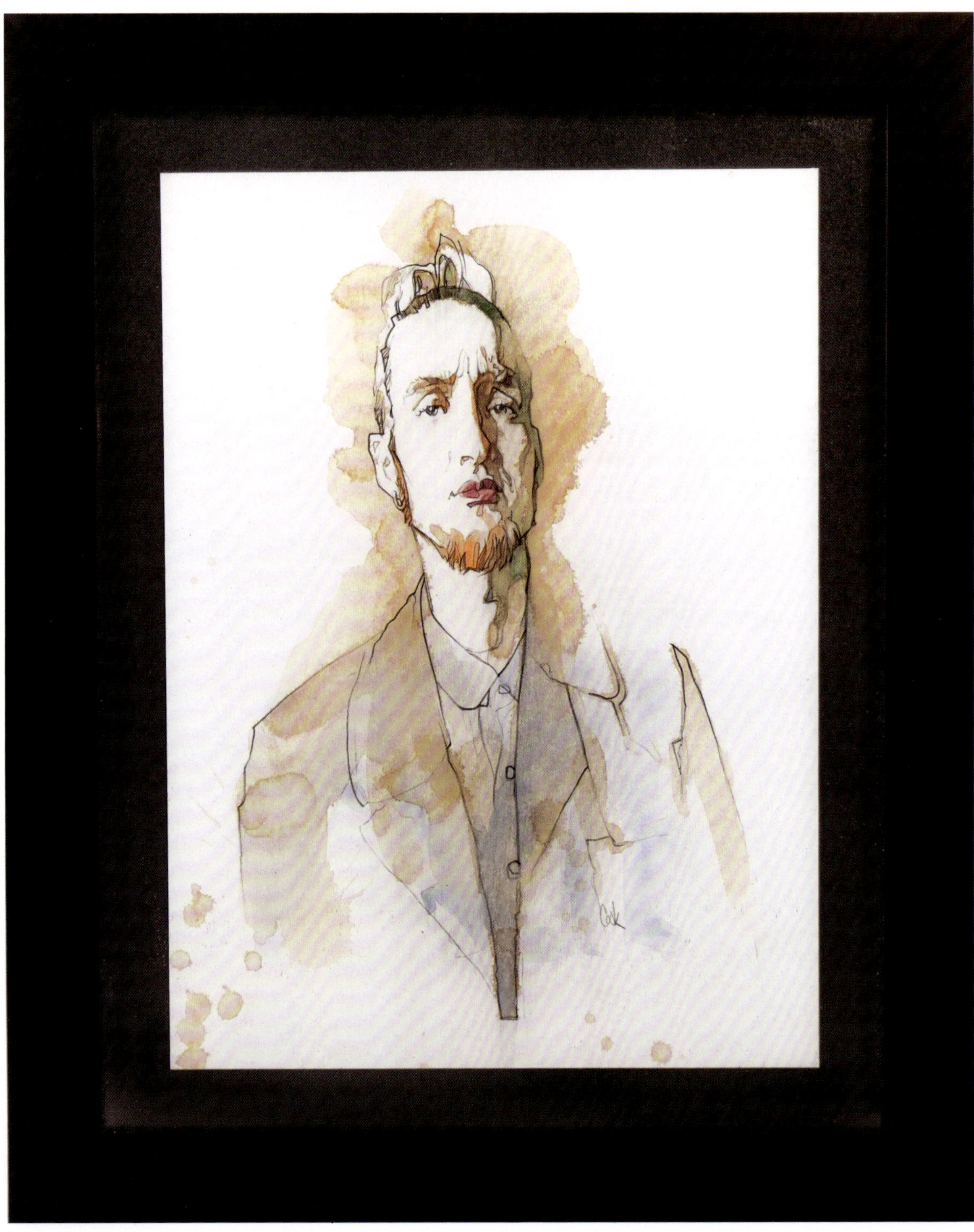

Created by Bud Cook.

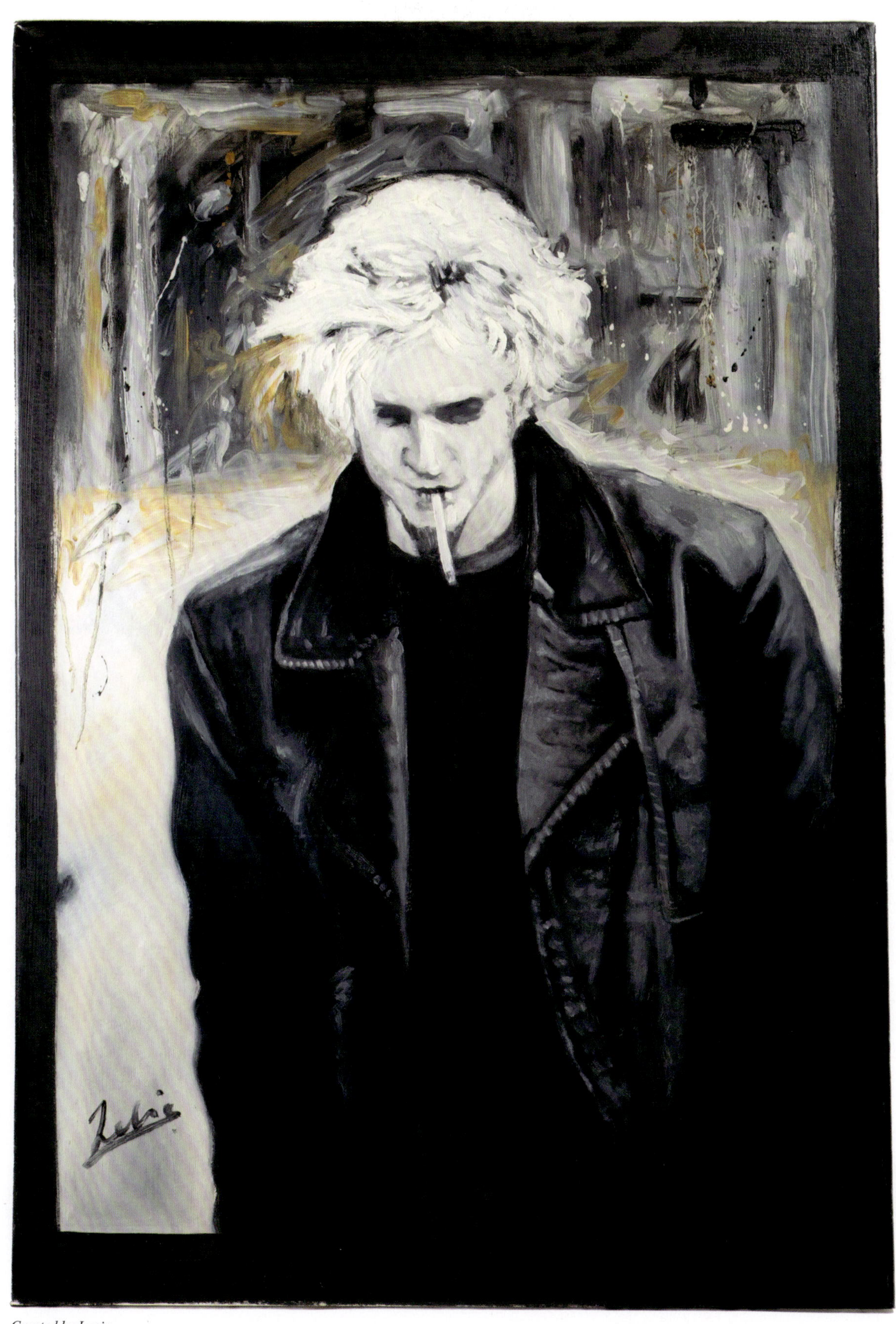

Created by Lucio.

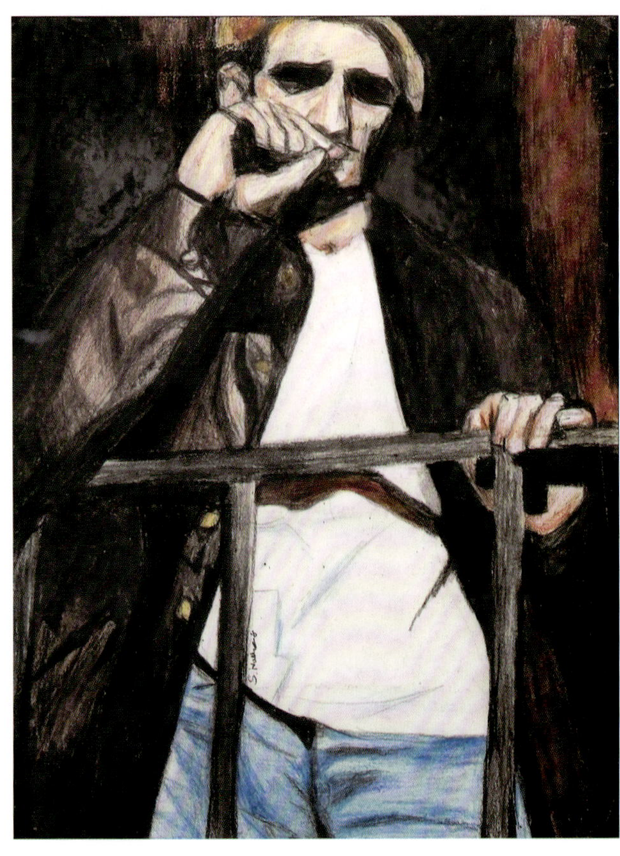

Created by Sarah Hanks Denmon.

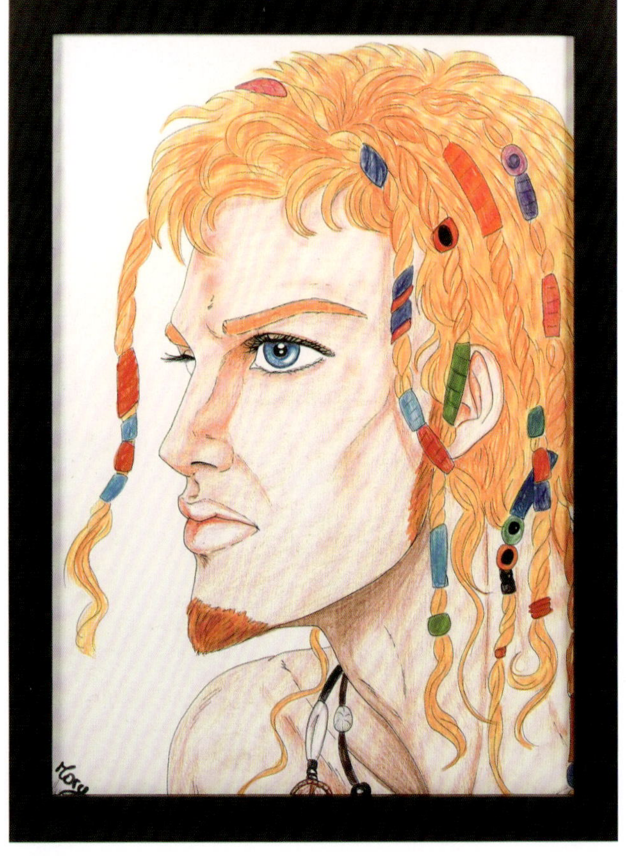

Created by "Mory" Morena Oro.

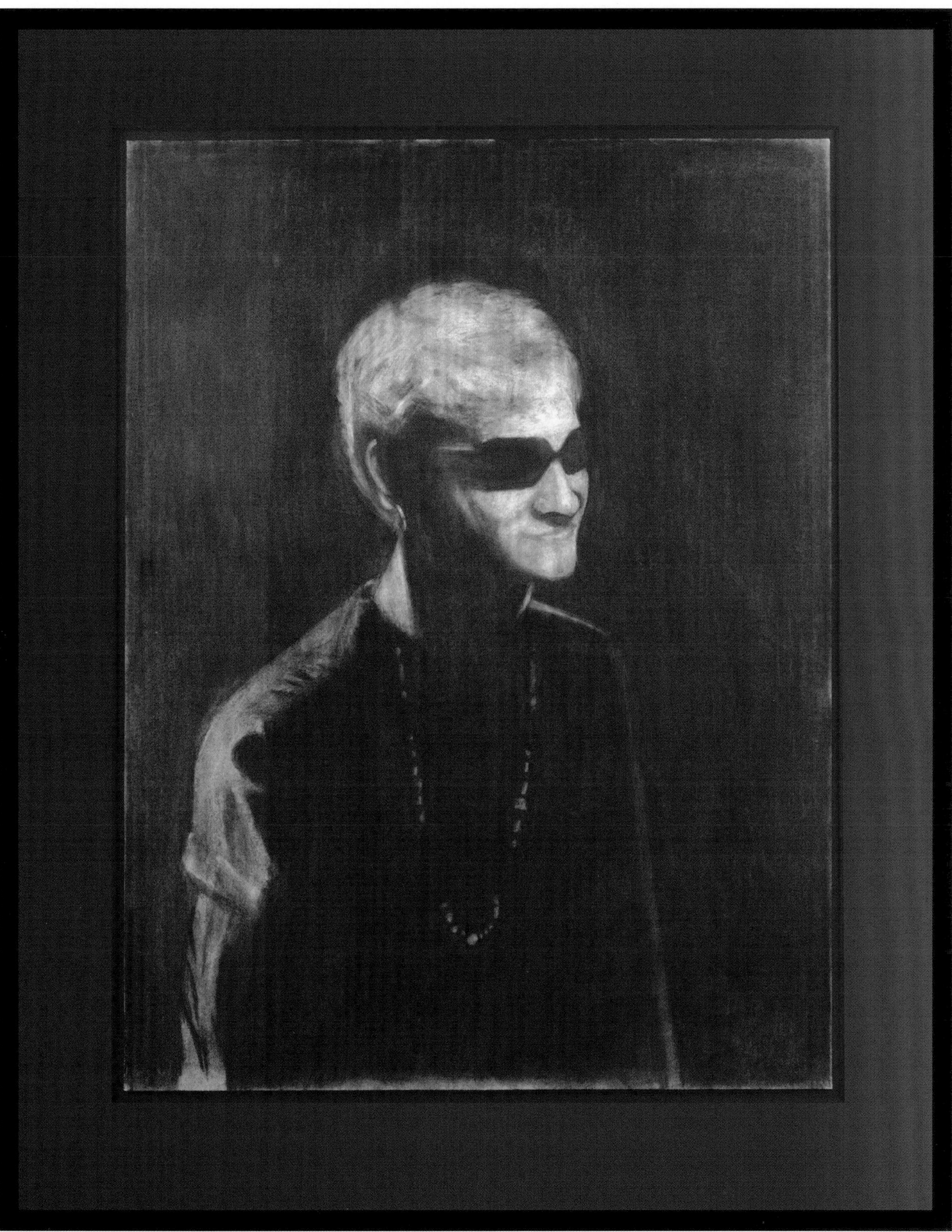

Created by Kori Kim.

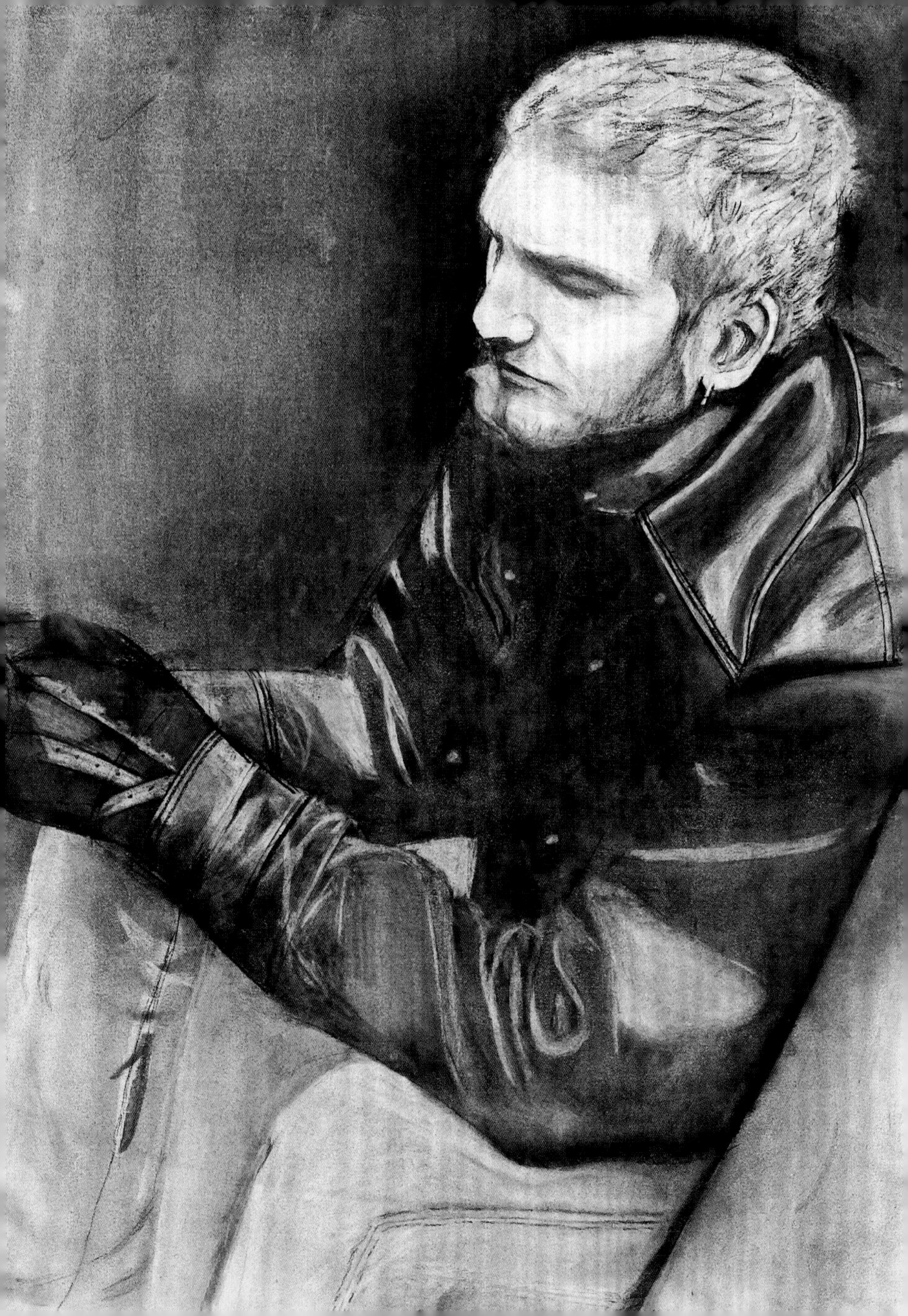

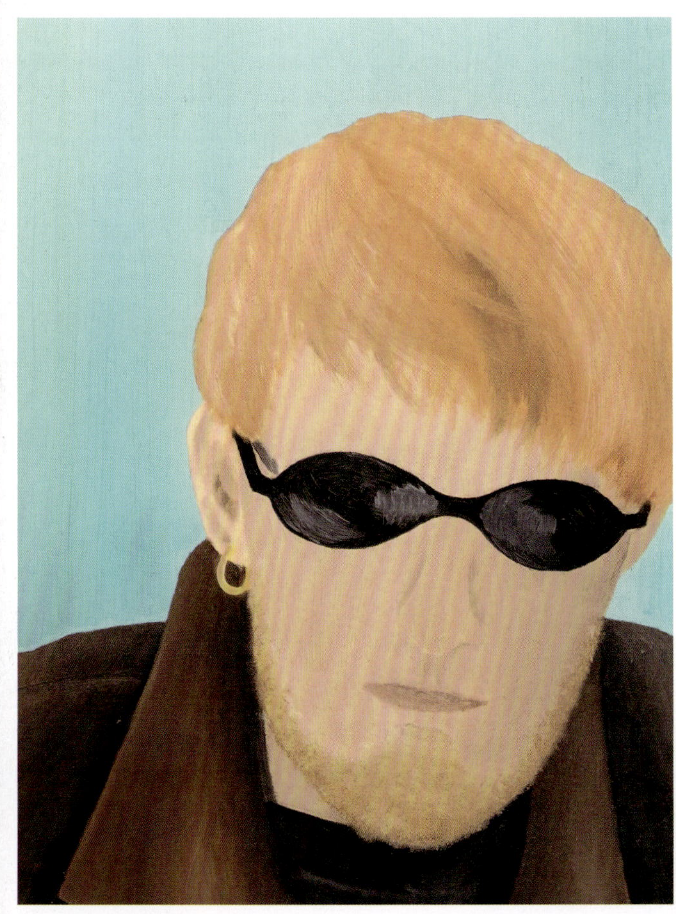
Created by Rei Naga.

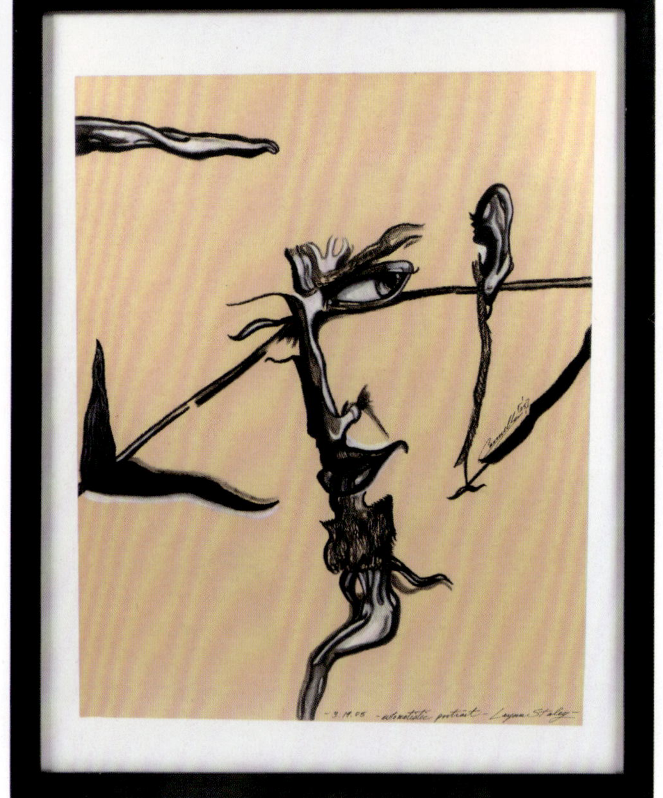
Created by Paul Cannella.

Created by Kori Kim.

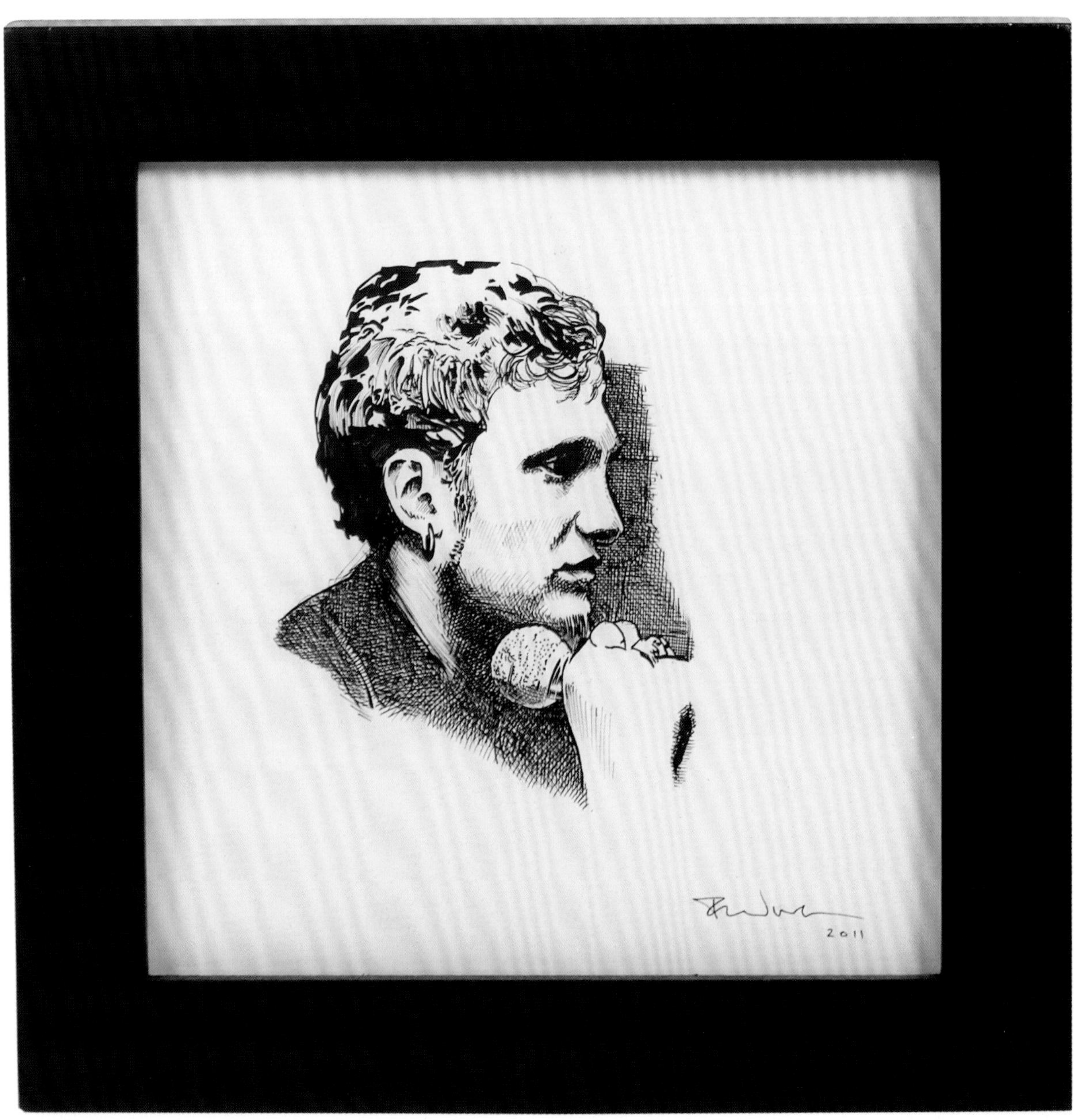

Artist unknown.

Created by Avery Villalobos.

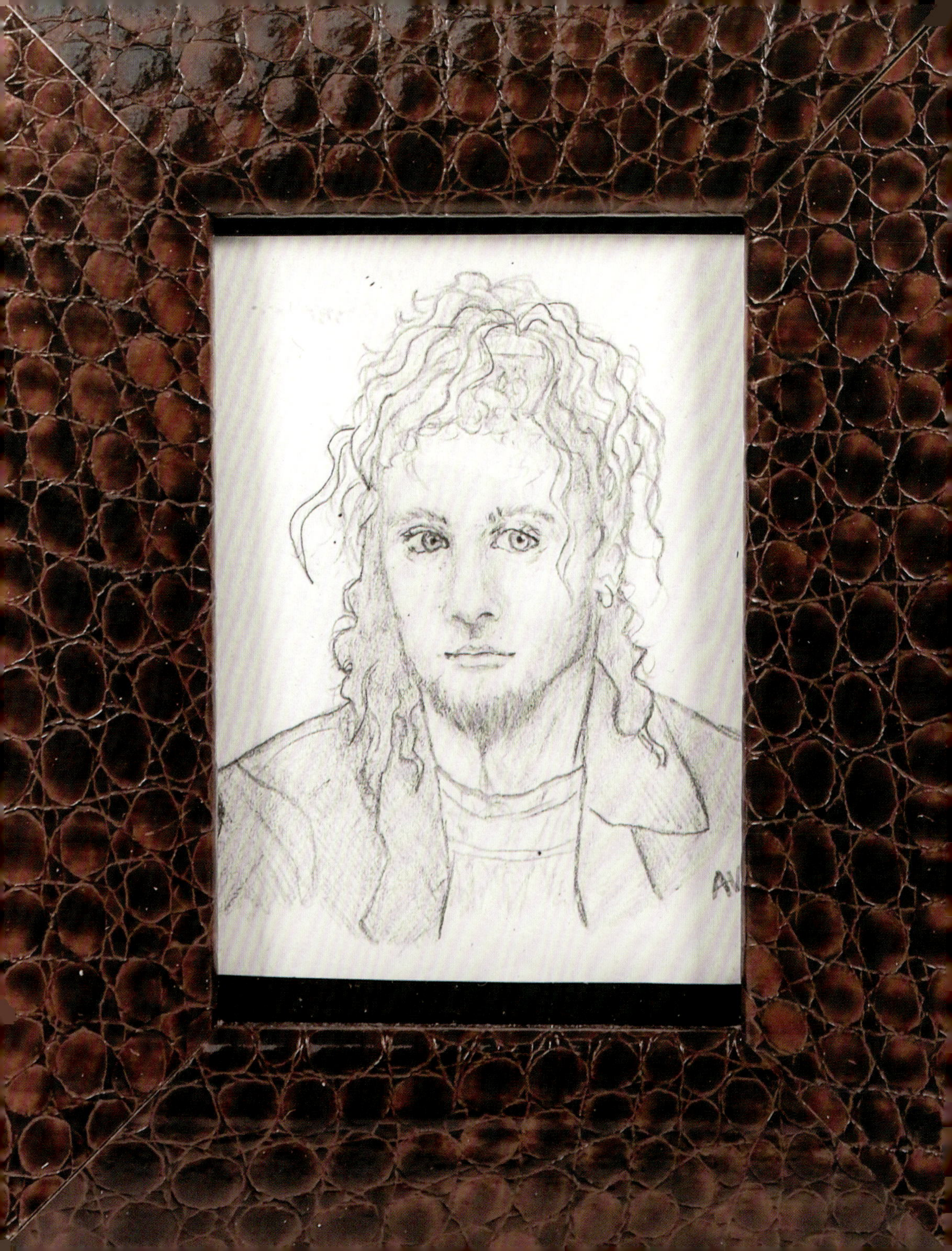

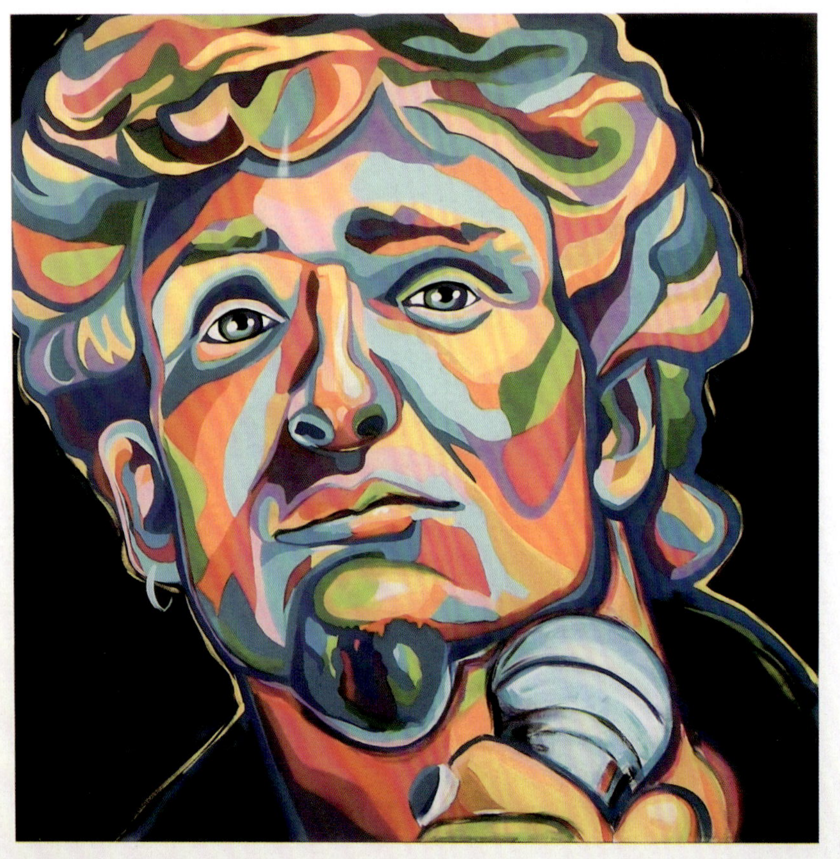

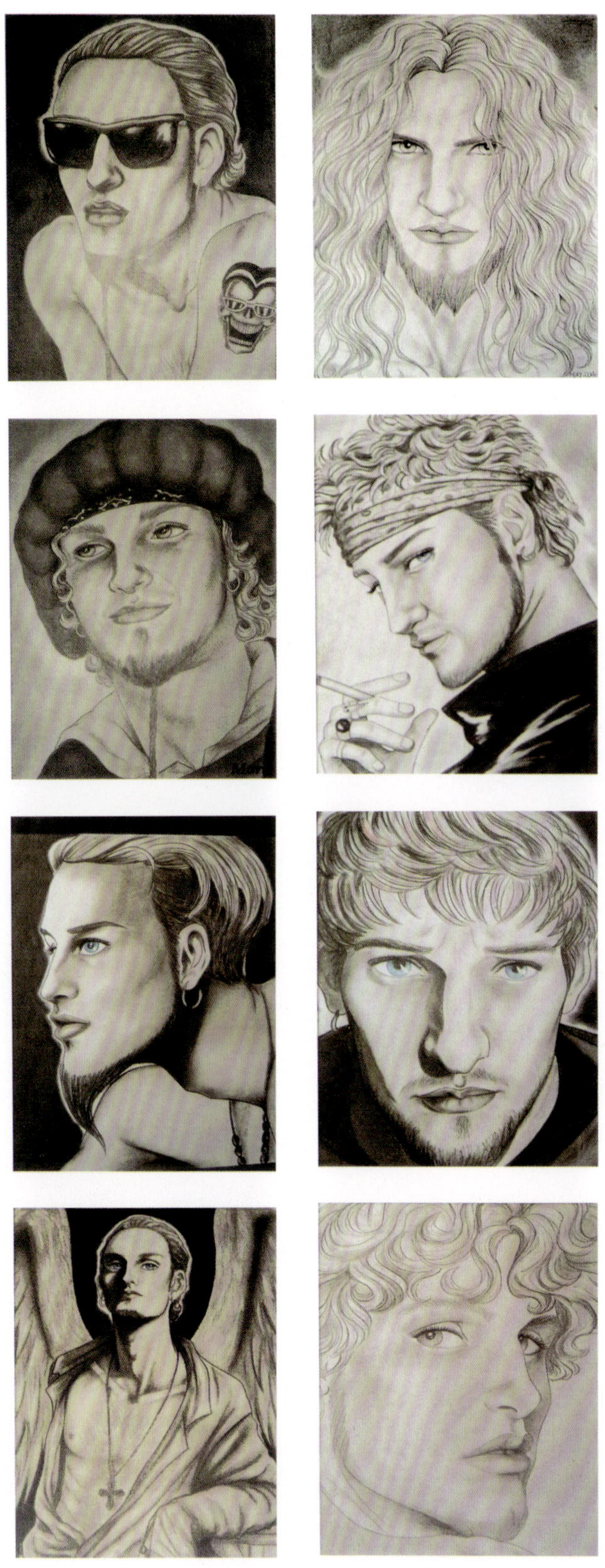

opposite: Artist unknown. above: Created by "Mory" Morena Oro.

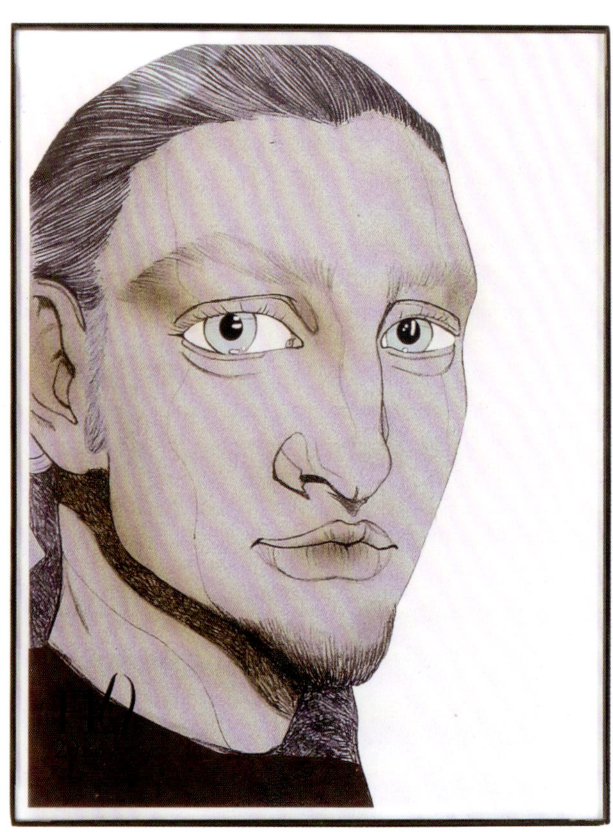

Created by Florence Paquotte.

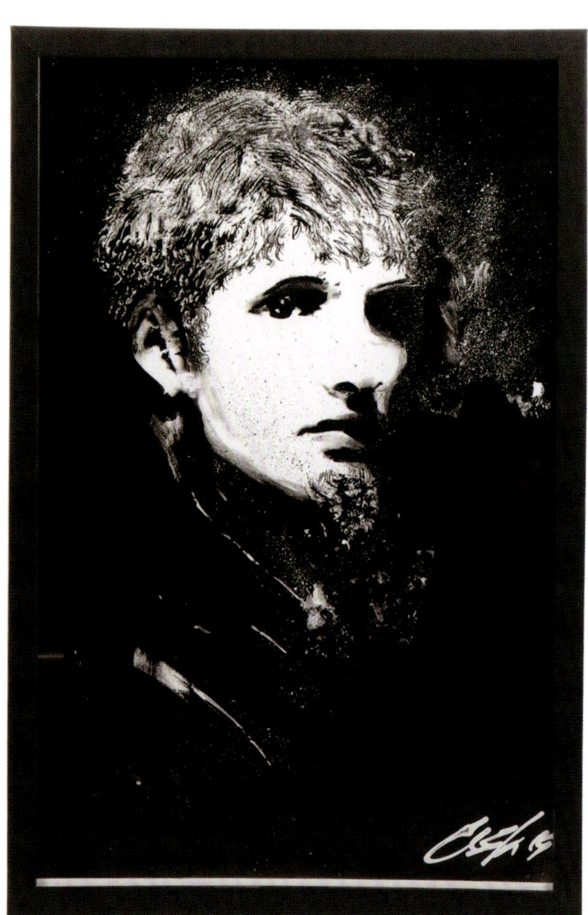

Created by Charles.

Artist unknown.

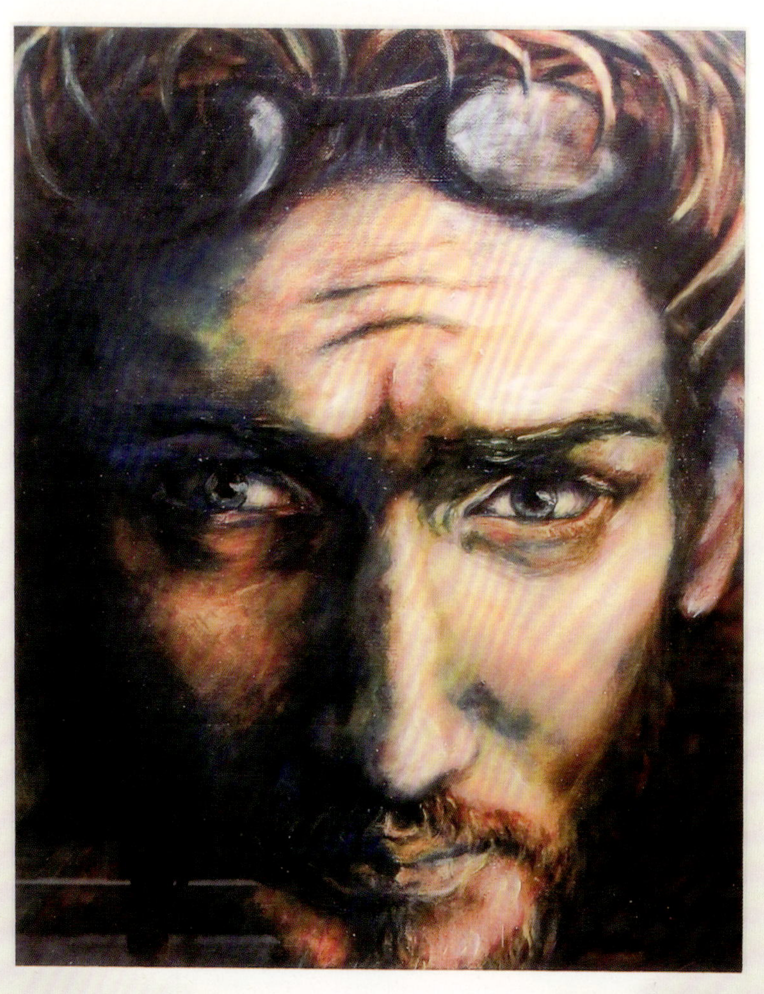

PART FOUR: FUTURE

LAYNE STALEY MEMORIAL FUND AND THERAPEUTIC HEALTH SERVICES

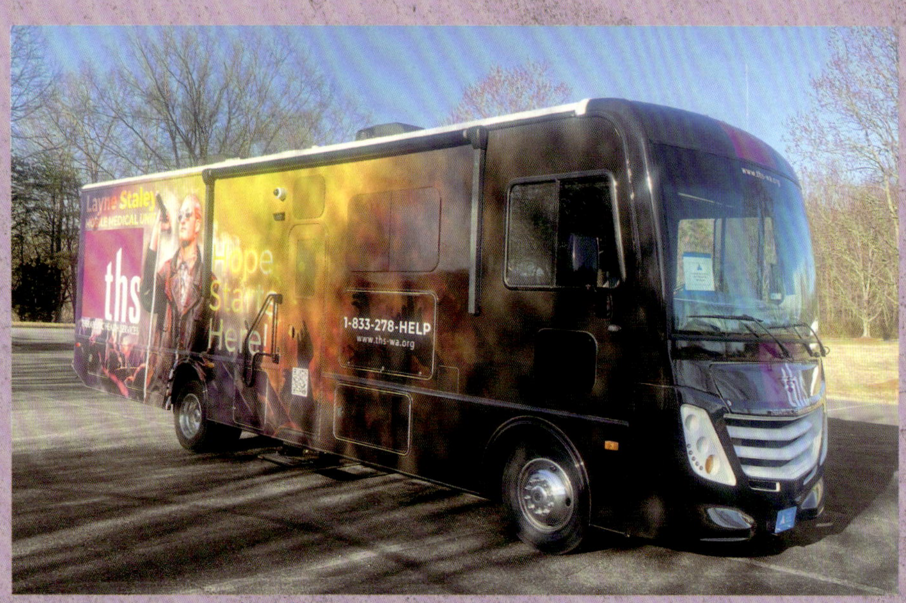

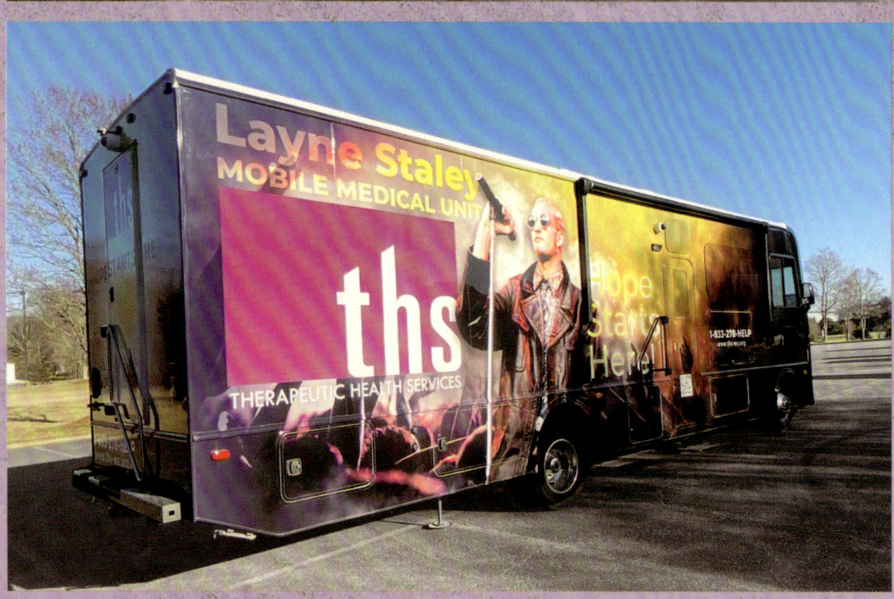

LAYNE STALEY MEMORIAL FUND

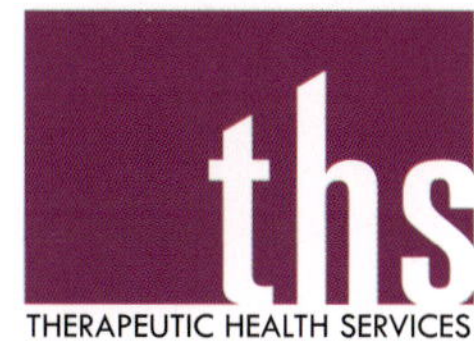

Shortly after Layne's death in 2002, his parents, Nancy McCallum and Phil Staley, began receiving donations from fans all over the world.

Nancy and Phil worked with Therapeutic Health Services, one of the Pacific Northwest's largest providers of medication-assisted treatment for opioid addiction, to create the Layne Staley Memorial Fund.

Nancy sees Layne's fund as a way of "partnering with Layne on the next step in his work. He was very honest with people about the effects of drug use, urging them not to follow in his footsteps. Those were the messages in his songs, endearing him to his fans."

Donations made to the fund support treatment, counseling, and support for those struggling with addiction to opioids. Over the years thousands of dollars have been contributed by faithful fans who resonate with Layne's words and music.

Most recently, funds from the Layne Staley Memorial Fund have been used to partially underwrite the purchase of Therapeutic Health Services' first mobile medication unit. Wrapped in glorious images of Layne singing to adoring fans, the new custom-built vehicle lowers barriers to treatment by taking medication to the people who need it most. The vehicle will focus on residents living in tiny home villages throughout the greater Seattle area. Meeting people where they are at with medication and counseling support helps men and women overcome the dual challenges of addiction and homelessness.

Layne's legacy lives on through the fund and the vital support the mobile medication unit provides to some of the most vulnerable residents in our community.

Donations can be made by visiting: https://ths-wa.org/support/layne-staley-memorial-fund/. For more information about Therapeutic Health Services, visit https://ths-wa.org/.

At Therapeutic Health Services, our vision is to improve quality of life for all, our mission is to foster healing and recovery. We do this by helping to rehabilitate individuals and heal families affected by alcohol dependence, drug dependence, or mental illness. For over 50 years we have helped individuals and families lead healthy and productive lives. We offer the most effective evidence-based, culturally appropriate behavioral health treatment in an outpatient setting. Our strengths-based, trauma-informed treatment includes one-on-one and group counseling sessions, life skills groups, vocational groups, case management, and relapse prevention groups. Our experienced, compassionate, and professional staff includes licensed chemical dependency and mental health professionals, case managers, nurses, ARNPs, physicians, and psychiatrists. Providing programs and services individualized to the unique goals and capabilities of the individual allows us to help our patients achieve positive outcomes. Our primary care team helps our substance use and mental health patients to manage their overall physical health as well as commonly occurring chronic conditions. In an average year, our 9 service locations in King and Snohomish Counties serve approximately 4,500 adults and nearly 750 youth and young adults in our community. Therapeutic Health Services is the largest nonprofit provider of medication-assisted treatment for opioid addiction in Washington State. We specialize in treating high-risk, low-income, ethnic minority, multisystem-involved, and "harder to serve" adults and youth.

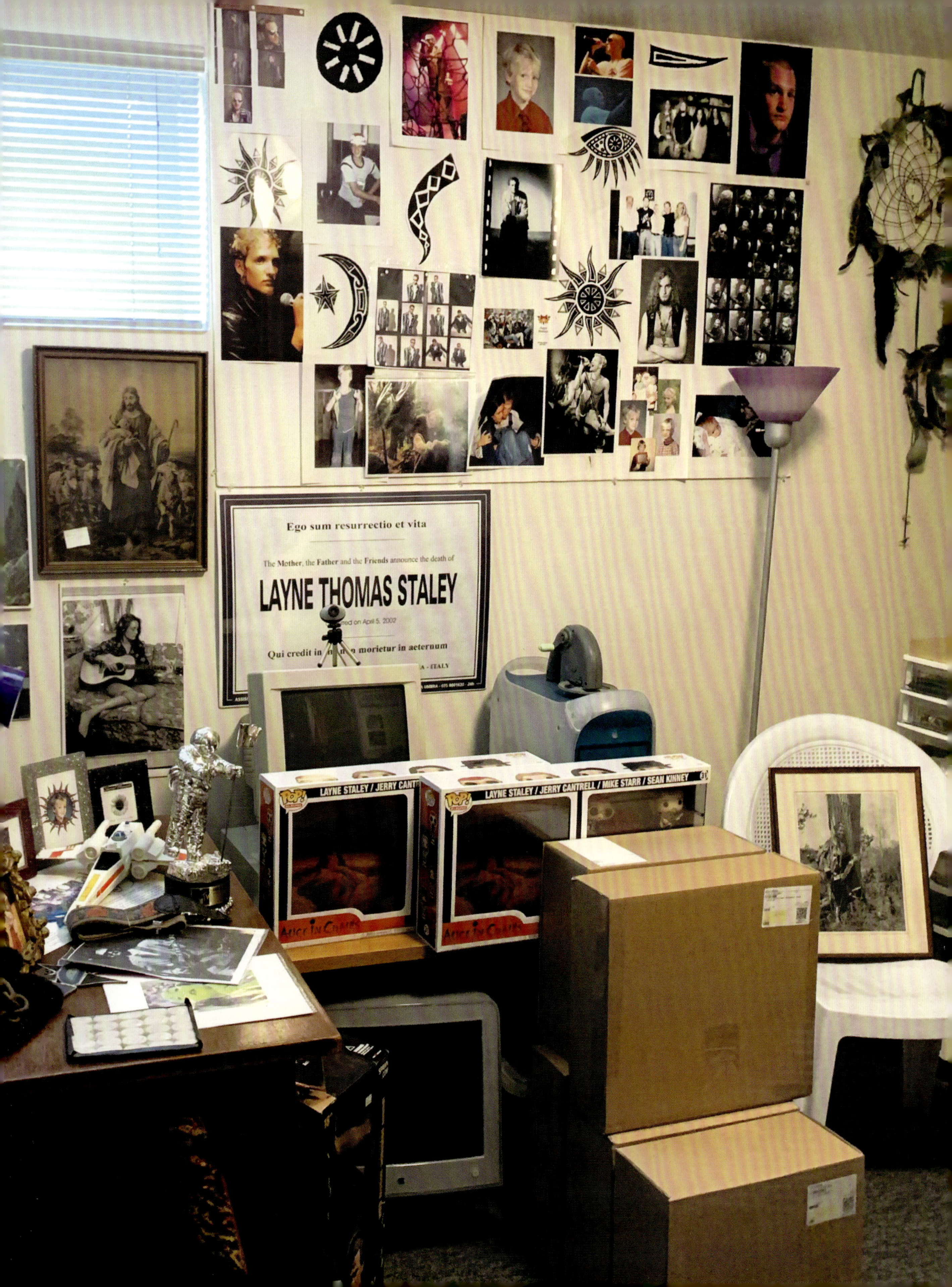
Ego sum resurrectio et vita
The Mother, the Father and the Friends announce the death of
LAYNE THOMAS STALEY
LAYNE STALEY / JERRY CANTRELL / MIKE STARR / SEAN KINNEY
POP!

ACKNOWLEDGMENTS FROM NANCY MCCALLUM

Thank you, Phil Staley, for allowing me unhindered access to all that remains of Layne's words and art. Without our collaboration, this work would have been impossible. Without Jim Elmer's humor and dedication to me and our family, ours would have been a very different story. Our children and grandchildren have kept me "in the world of the living" with their day-to-day ups and downs, celebrations, communication, and example of love and hard work.

In addition to family and close friends, the "wind beneath my wings" has been correspondence (in the form of emails, letters, and gifts) from Layne's worldwide friends and fans for these past 23 years. "Thank you," also, to those who added their written contributions.

There are those who steered me through the unpredictable legal and accounting waters. I'd have thrown my hands up from the beginning. Whew! To James at Primary Wave and Edward at Insight Editions/ Weldon Owen go my deep gratitude for encouraging me on, when the path to completion was dark.

As my anchor, I just wouldn't have made it through these past few years, without "my darling Ed." Thank you, Honey. You're my treasure.

weldon**owen**

an imprint of Insight Editions
P.O. Box 3088
San Rafael, CA 94912
www.weldonowen.com

CEO Raoul Goff
SVP Group Publisher Jeff McLaughlin
VP Publisher Roger Shaw
VP Creative Chrissy Kwasnik
Executive Editor Edward Ash-Milby
Assistant Editor Kayla Belser
Managing Editor Michelle Hope
VP Manufacturing Alix Nicholaeff
Senior Production Manager Joshua Smith
Strategic Production Planner Lina s Palma-Temena

Weldon Owen would also like to thank Bob Cooper, Zack Bolotin, and Carolyn Cawrse.

ISBN: 979-8-88674-320-3
Manufactured in China by Insight Editions
10 9 8 7 6 5 4

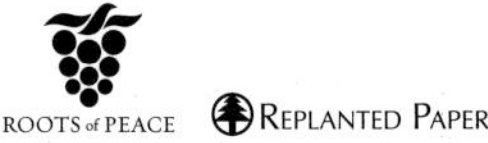

Insight Editions, in association with Roots of Peace, will plant two trees for each tree used in the manufacturing of this book. Roots of Peace is an internationally renowned humanitarian organization dedicated to eradicating land mines worldwide and converting war-torn lands into productive farms and wildlife habitats. Roots of Peace will plant two million fruit and nut trees in Afghanistan and provide farmers there with the skills and support necessary for sustainable land use.